BATTLE HYMN™

FAREWELL TO THE FIRST GOLDEN AGE

B. CLAY MOORE
BY & JEREMY HAUN

AN IMAGE COMIC

Image Comics, Inc.

Erik Larsen - Publisher
Todd McFarlane - President
Marc Silvestri - CEO
Jim Valentino - Vice-President

Eric Stephenson - Executive Director
Jim Demonakos - PR & Marketing Coordinator
Mia MacHatton - Accounts Manager
Laurenn McCubbin - Art Director
Allen Hui - Production Artist
Joe Keatinge - Traffic Manager
Jonathan Chan - Production Assistant
Drew Gill - Production Assistant
Traci Hui - Administrative Assistant

www.imagecomics.com

BATTLE HYMN VOL. 1: FAREWELL TO THE FIRST GOLDEN AGE. 2006. Published by Image Comics, Inc., Office of publication: 1942 University Avenue, Suite 305, Berkeley, California 94704.

ritten by: B. Clay Moore

rawn by: Jeremy Haun

hapter One Inked by: Ande Parks

olored by: Dave Bryant

ettered by: Greg Thompson

riginal series covers by:
    Jeremy Haun & Brian Frey (issues 1-3)
    Jeremy Haun & Dave Bryant (issue 4)
    Tony Moore (issue 5)

ogo Design by: Brian Frey

rade Production and Design by: Jeremy Haun

Clay would like to dedicate this book
to his friend Troy Griffin, and to all
the men and women who find
themselves too far from home in the
name of duty.

Jeremy would like to dedicate this
book to his son Ethan, who makes
him a happy camper.

NTRODUCTION
y Tony Moore

mart, witty, action-packed, and great to look at. All the things people ay about me also hold true for this book, which has been one of the best eads I've had in a long time. I could practically feel the cold, prying, overnment eyes over my shoulder, and hear the bullets whizzing past ny ears as I turned each page. I love a book that engulfs me, and I lways always always love a good war comic. Consequently, I loved attle Hymn more than my work-dulled brain can accurately express n words.

. Clay Moore is one of the finest writers in the industry. He's got a reat range and his work is always engaging and insightful. He has a nack for characterization that few could dream of, and when his tories are done, I feel like I've walked away from the experience with little something, like a sense of accomplishment, despite knowing I pent precious work hours reading comic books.

Jeremy's no slouch, either. His storytelling is top notch, clear and lynamic, and he's a master of really setting the mood on a page with nis excellent lighting and rendering, and what's more, he's really just getting going. He's a workhorse, to boot , so he'll be plowing ahead hrough the artistic growth at a much fairer clip than most guys lrawing comics today, and I shudder to think about the work he'll be cranking out a couple years from now.

I count both of these guys among my dearest friends, and I could gush at length about them. Each is a powder keg in his own right, but teamed up on a realistic human-level World War II story that presents things how they probably would have happened if superheroes walked the land, and these two guys are like Fat Man and Little Boy both detonated in my brain's pleasure centers.

Boy, have you just done yourself a huge favor. Congratulations on your excellent taste.

-Tony Moore
Artist: the Walking Dead, Fear Agent, the Exterminators

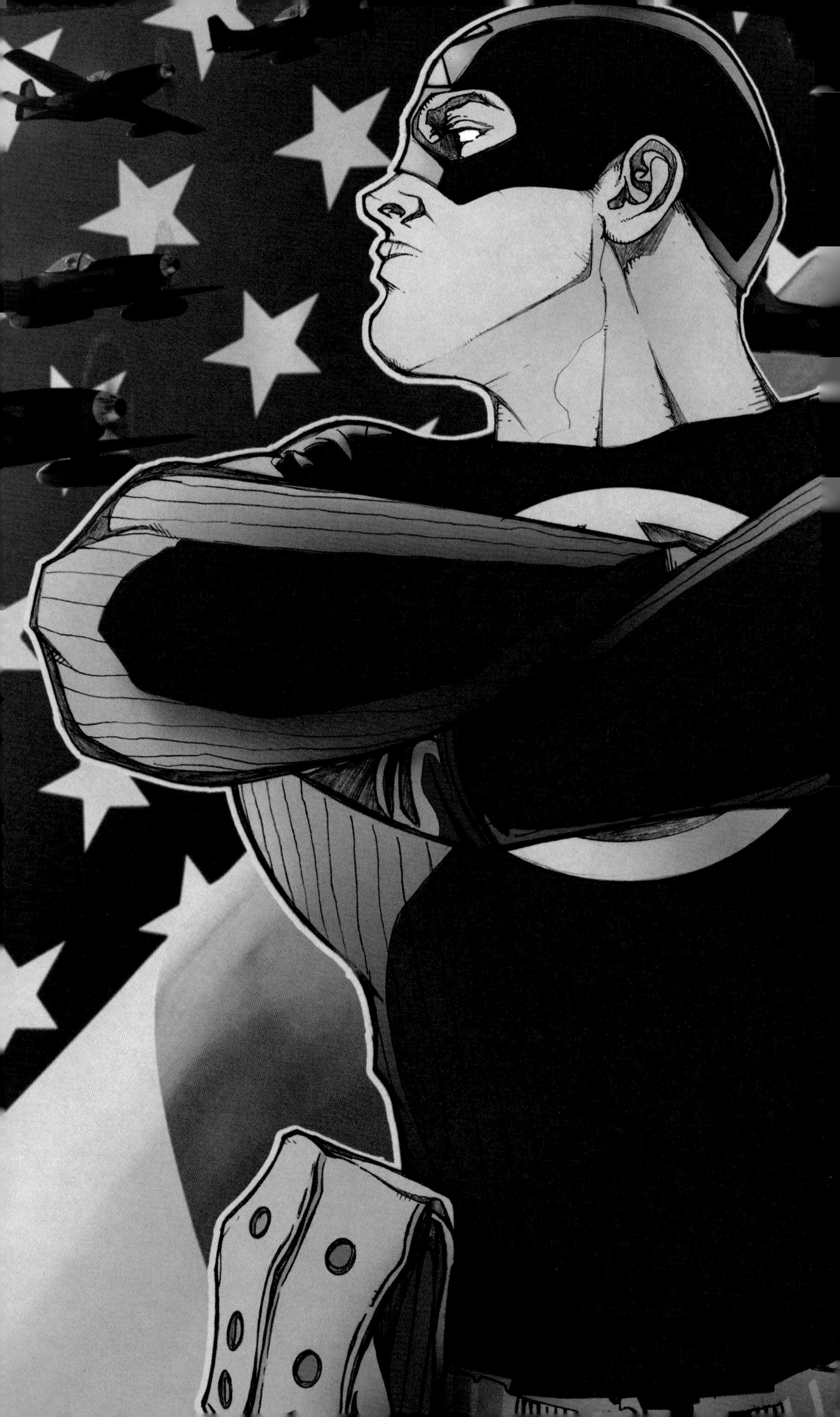

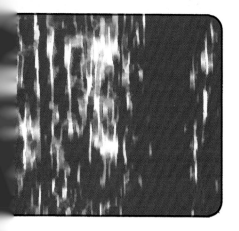

AMERICA ON PARADE
The Nation's Newswrap with Walter Petrick

IN FOGGY SAN FRANCISCO PROFESSOR ERICH CLOUD REVEALS THE EIGHTH WONDER OF THE WORLD.

STARTLED ONLOOKERS COULD HARDLY BE PREPARED FOR THIS MIRACLE OF MODERN AMERICAN INGENUITY.

YES, IT'S THE WORLD'S FIRST ATOMIC MAN. CALL IT "CLOUD'S ANDROID."

BUT THEIR NERVES ARE CALMED WHEN PROFESSOR CLOUD EXPLAINS THAT HIS NUCLEAR POWERED MAN IS IN REALITY A ROBOT, UNDER HIS COMPLETE CONTROL AT ALL TIMES.

THE IMPOSING DYNAMO TOOK YEARS TO DEVELOP AND PROFESSOR CLOUD AND HIS TEAM HOPE TO ONE DAY PRODUCE THE ROBOT IN MASS QUANTITIES, ENRICHING THE LIVES OF ALL AMERICANS.

THE COMING OF THIS ARTIFICIAL MAN MARKS THE DAWNING OF NEW AND EXCITING AGE...THE ATOMIC AGE.

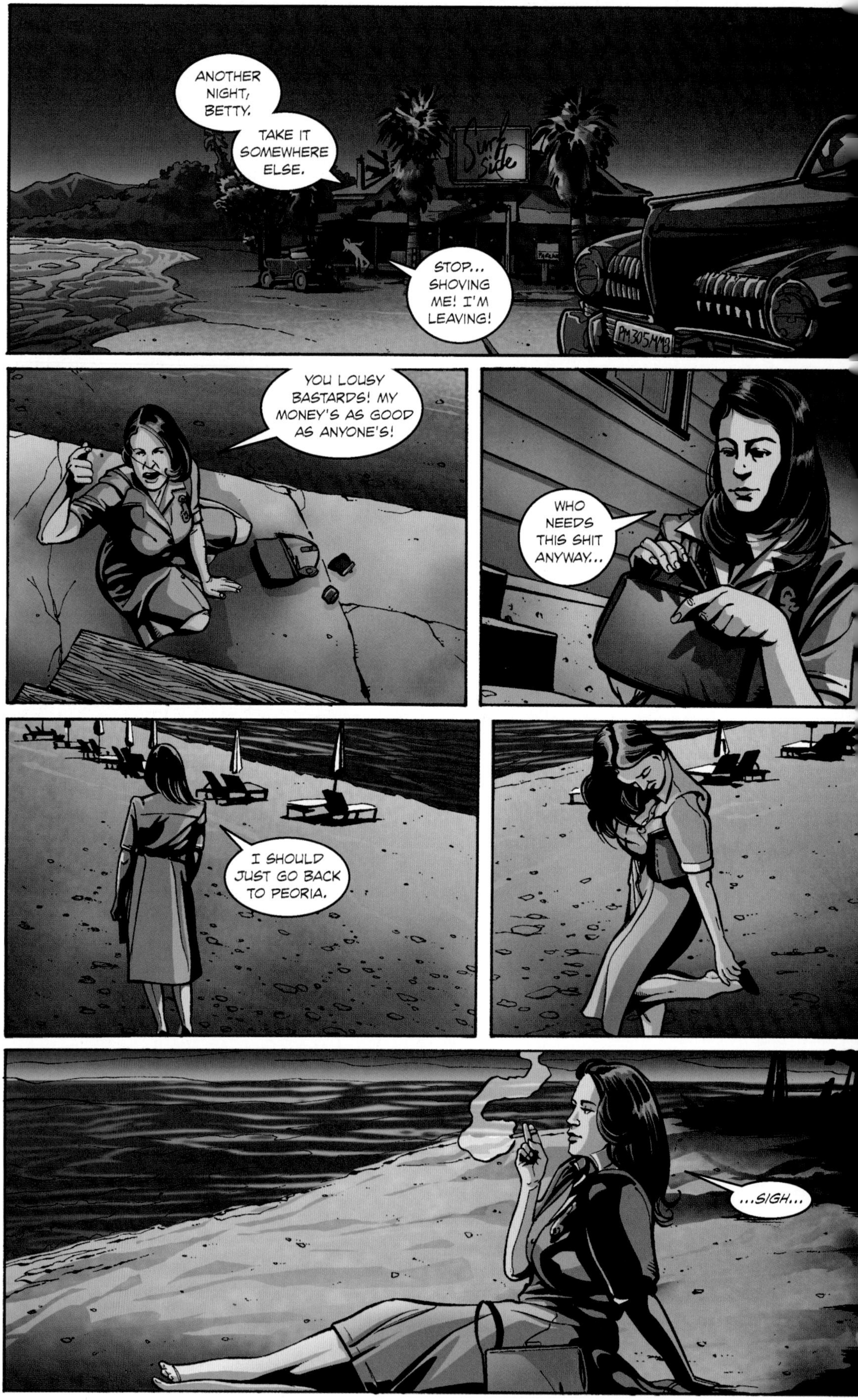
ANOTHER NIGHT, BETTY.
TAKE IT SOMEWHERE ELSE.
STOP... SHOVING ME! I'M LEAVING!
YOU LOUSY BASTARDS! MY MONEY'S AS GOOD AS ANYONE'S!
WHO NEEDS THIS SHIT ANYWAY...
I SHOULD JUST GO BACK TO PEORIA.
...SIGH...

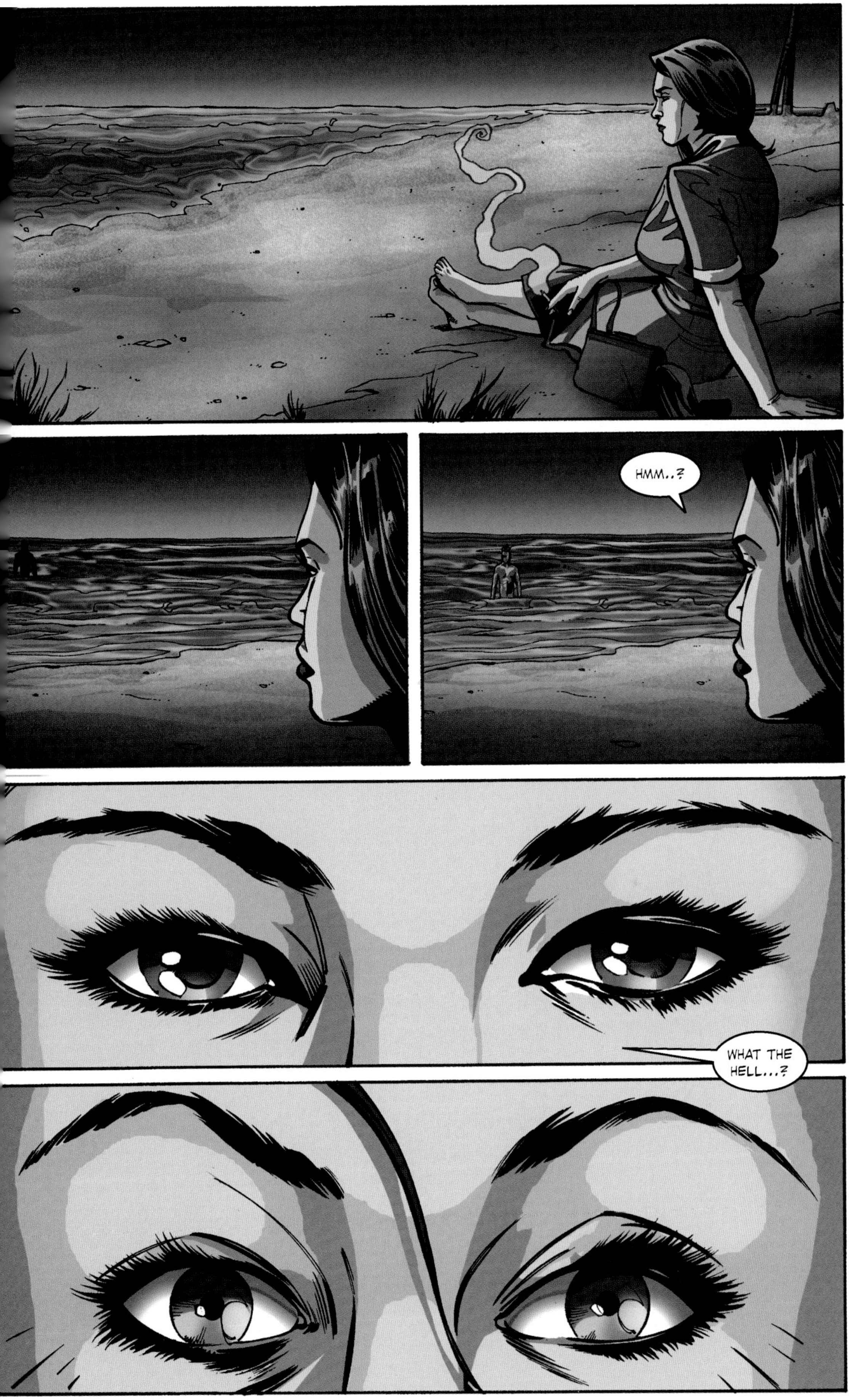
HMM..?
WHAT THE HELL...?

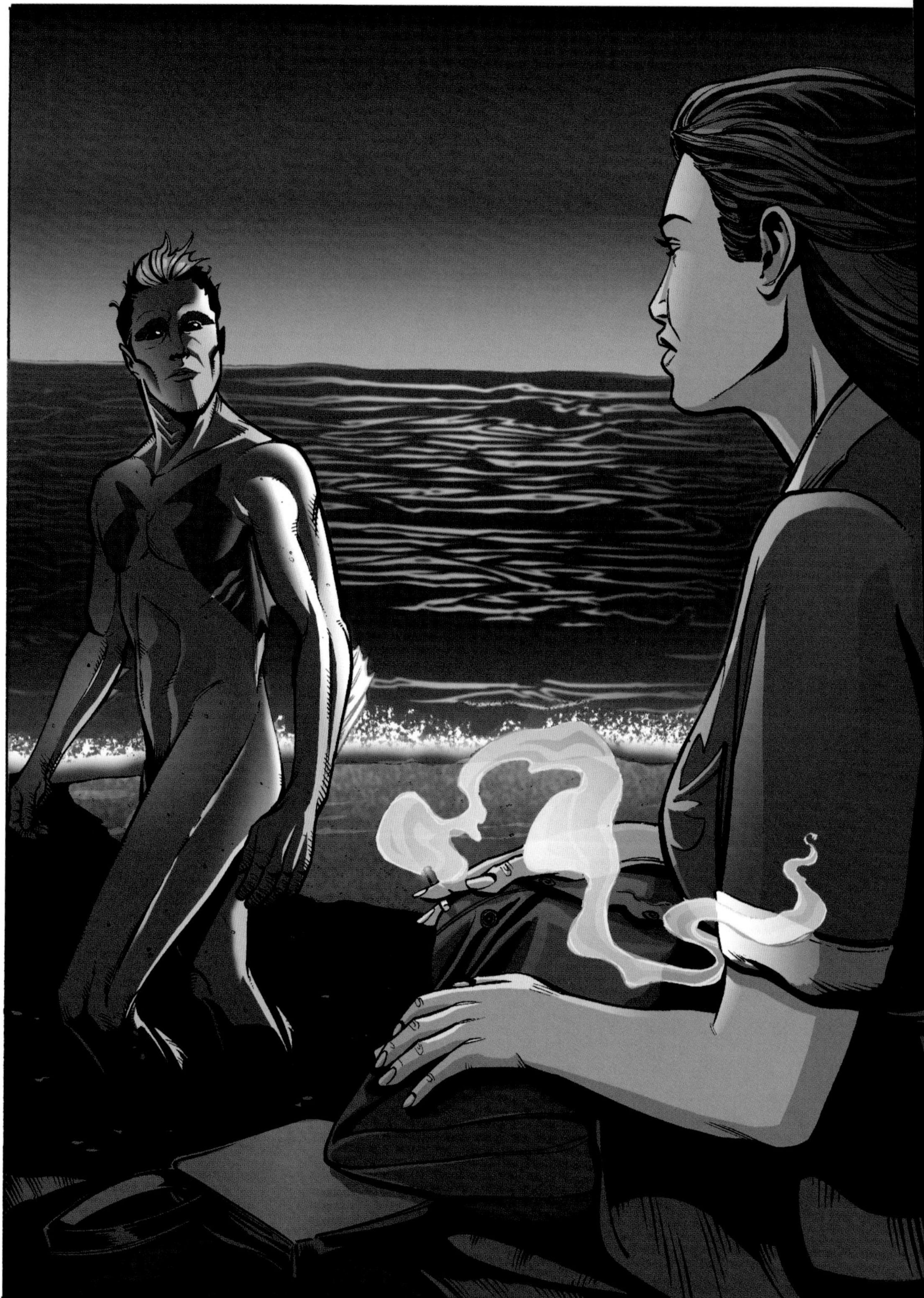

BATTLE HYMN:
Book One

"...The Awful Roar Of Its Many Waters"

Written by B. Clay Moore
Art by Jeremy Haun
Inks by Ande Parks
Colors by Dave Bryant
Letters by Greg Thompson

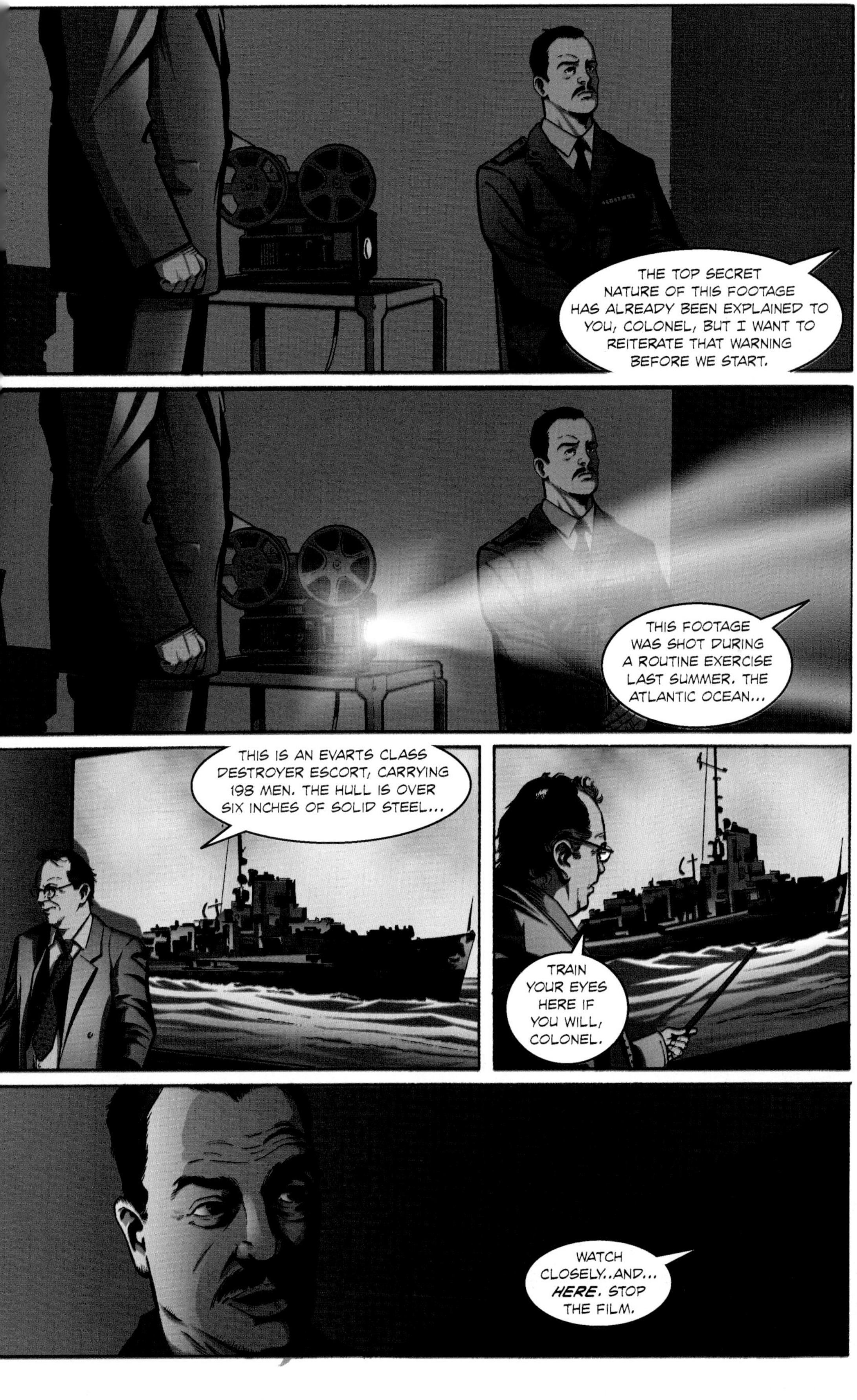
THE TOP SECRET NATURE OF THIS FOOTAGE HAS ALREADY BEEN EXPLAINED TO YOU, COLONEL, BUT I WANT TO REITERATE THAT WARNING BEFORE WE START.
THIS FOOTAGE WAS SHOT DURING A ROUTINE EXERCISE LAST SUMMER. THE ATLANTIC OCEAN...
THIS IS AN EVARTS CLASS DESTROYER ESCORT, CARRYING 198 MEN. THE HULL IS OVER SIX INCHES OF SOLID STEEL...
TRAIN YOUR EYES HERE IF YOU WILL, COLONEL.
WATCH CLOSELY..AND... ***HERE.*** STOP THE FILM.

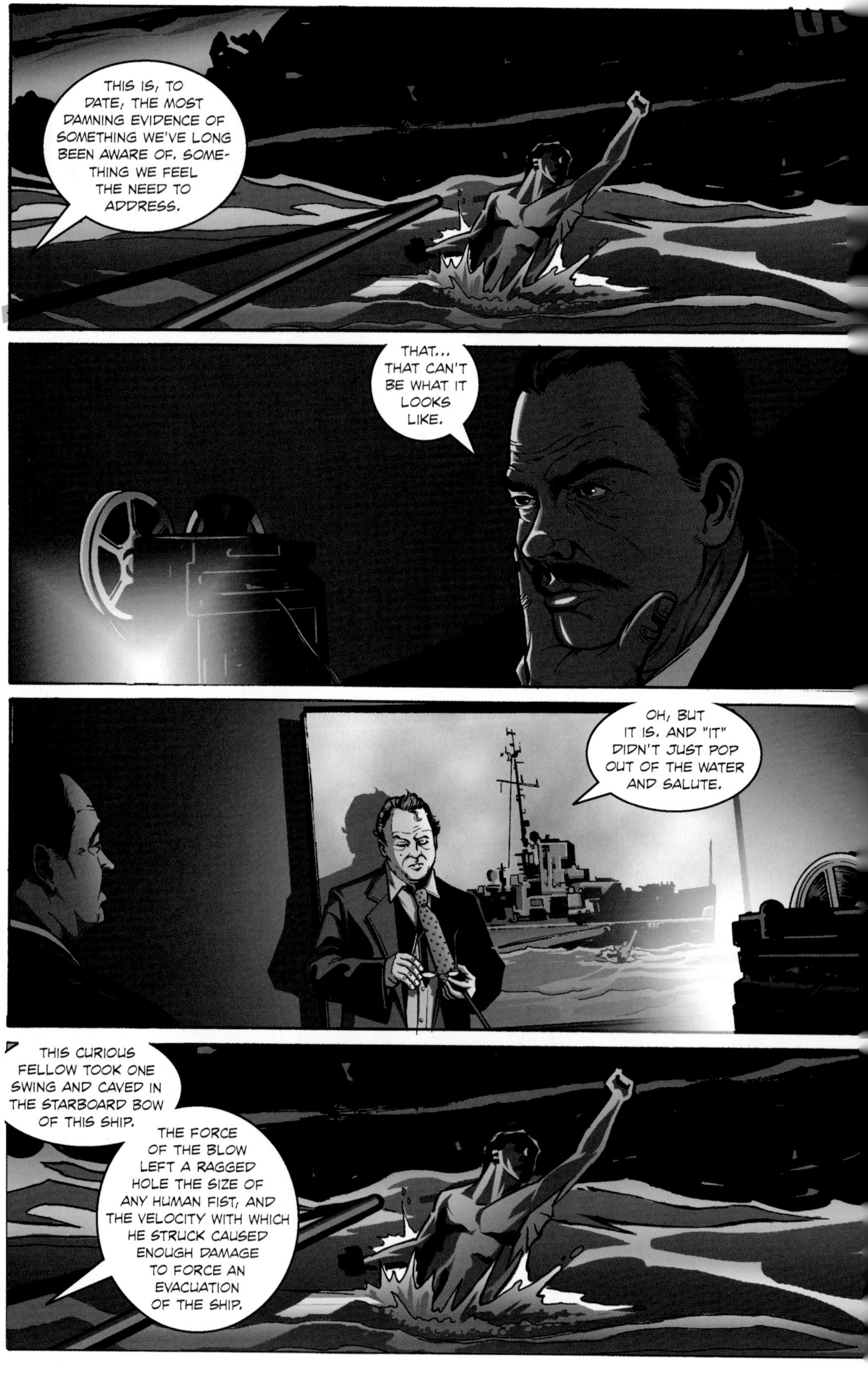
THIS IS, TO DATE, THE MOST DAMNING EVIDENCE OF SOMETHING WE'VE LONG BEEN AWARE OF. SOME-THING WE FEEL THE NEED TO ADDRESS.
THAT... THAT CAN'T BE WHAT IT LOOKS LIKE.
OH, BUT IT IS. AND "IT" DIDN'T JUST POP OUT OF THE WATER AND SALUTE.
THIS CURIOUS FELLOW TOOK ONE SWING AND CAVED IN THE STARBOARD BOW OF THIS SHIP.
THE FORCE OF THE BLOW LEFT A RAGGED HOLE THE SIZE OF ANY HUMAN FIST, AND THE VELOCITY WITH WHICH HE STRUCK CAUSED ENOUGH DAMAGE TO FORCE AN EVACUATION OF THE SHIP.

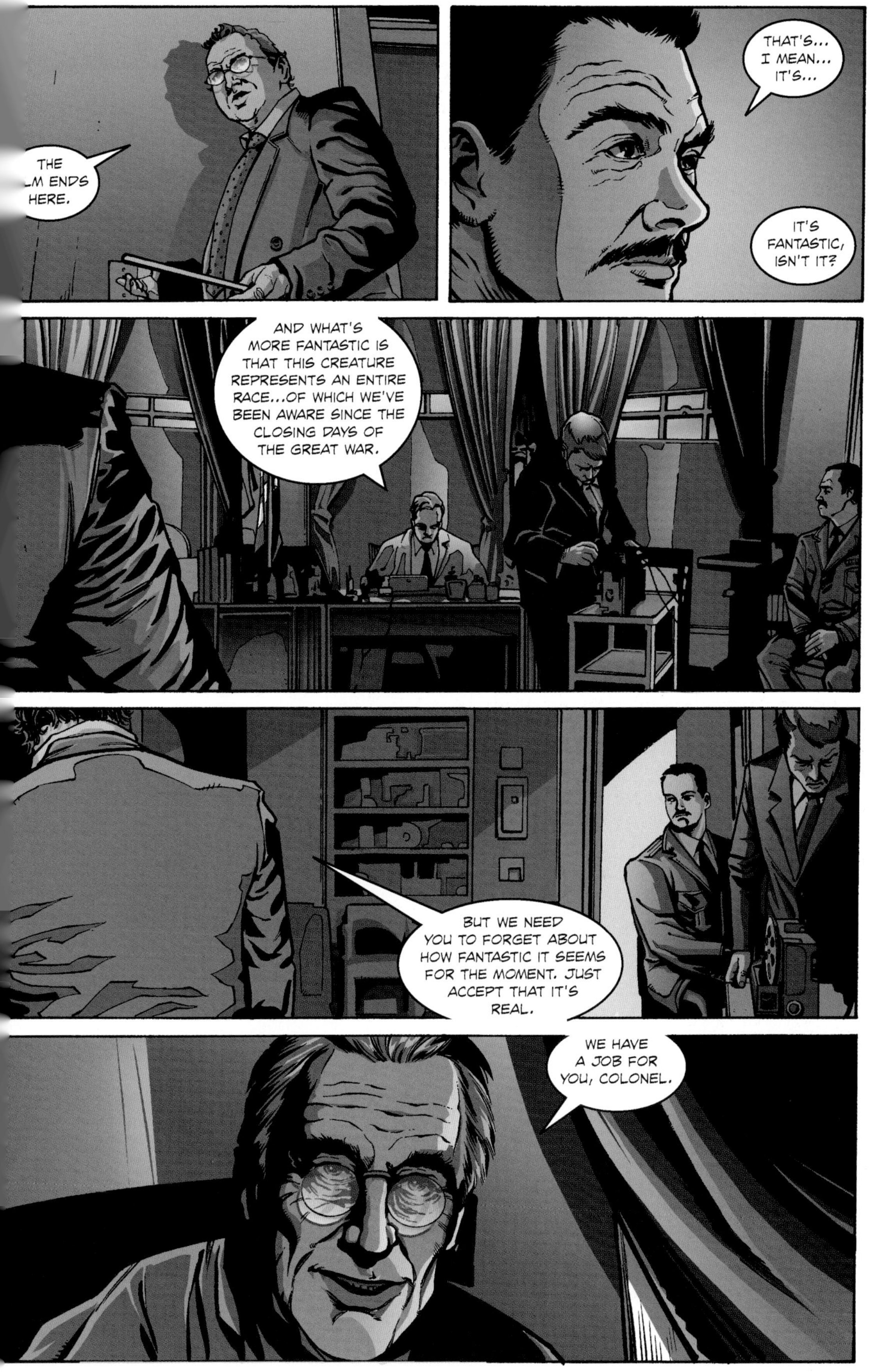
THE
LM ENDS
HERE.
THAT'S... I MEAN... IT'S...
IT'S FANTASTIC, ISN'T IT?
AND WHAT'S MORE FANTASTIC IS THAT THIS CREATURE REPRESENTS AN ENTIRE RACE...OF WHICH WE'VE BEEN AWARE SINCE THE CLOSING DAYS OF THE GREAT WAR.
BUT WE NEED YOU TO FORGET ABOUT HOW FANTASTIC IT SEEMS FOR THE MOMENT. JUST ACCEPT THAT IT'S REAL.
WE HAVE A JOB FOR YOU, COLONEL.

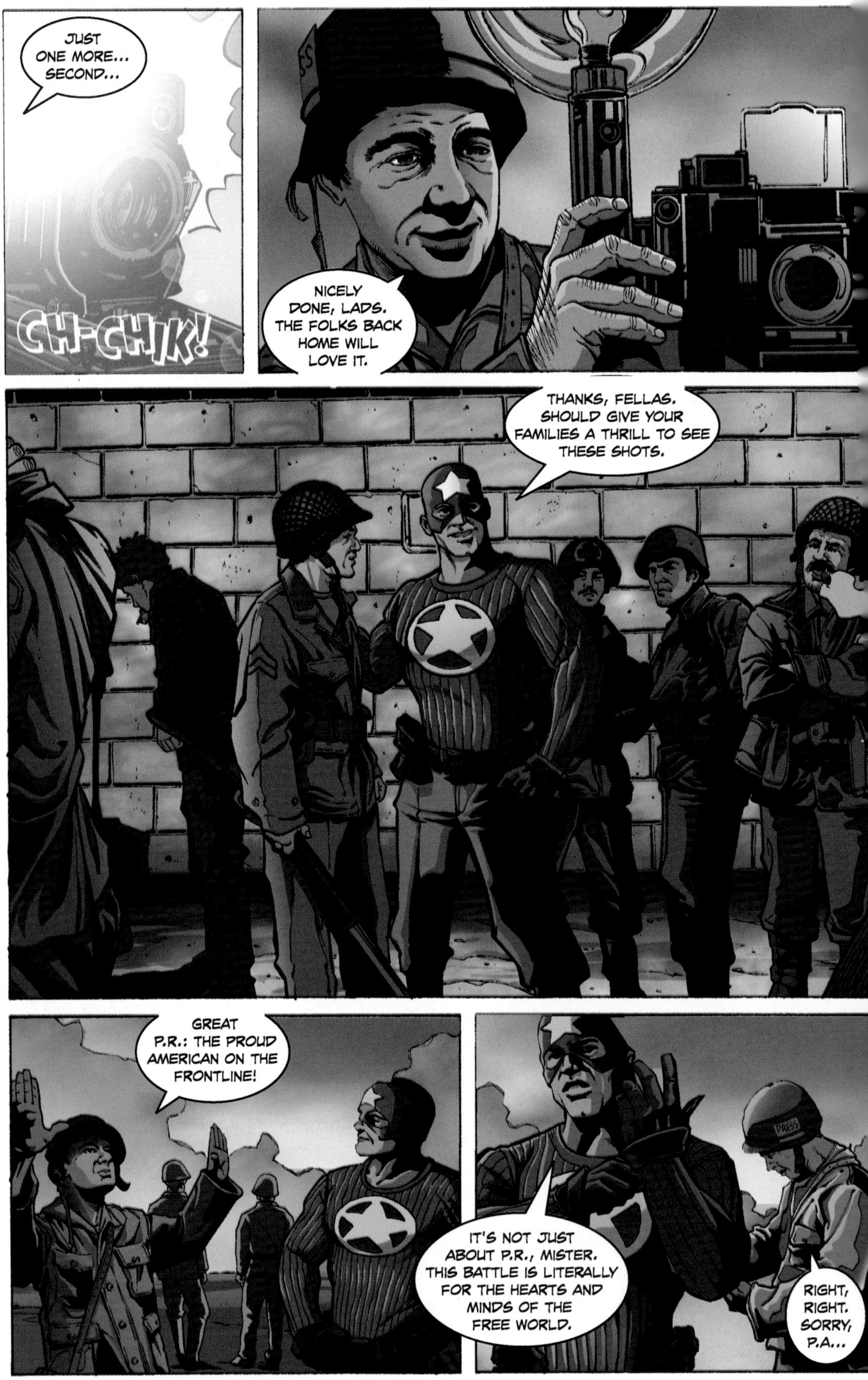
JUST ONE MORE... SECOND...
CH-CHIK!
NICELY DONE, LADS. THE FOLKS BACK HOME WILL LOVE IT.
THANKS, FELLAS. SHOULD GIVE YOUR FAMILIES A THRILL TO SEE THESE SHOTS.
GREAT P.R.: THE PROUD AMERICAN ON THE FRONTLINE!
IT'S NOT JUST ABOUT P.R., MISTER. THIS BATTLE IS LITERALLY FOR THE HEARTS AND MINDS OF THE FREE WORLD.
RIGHT, RIGHT. SORRY, P.A...

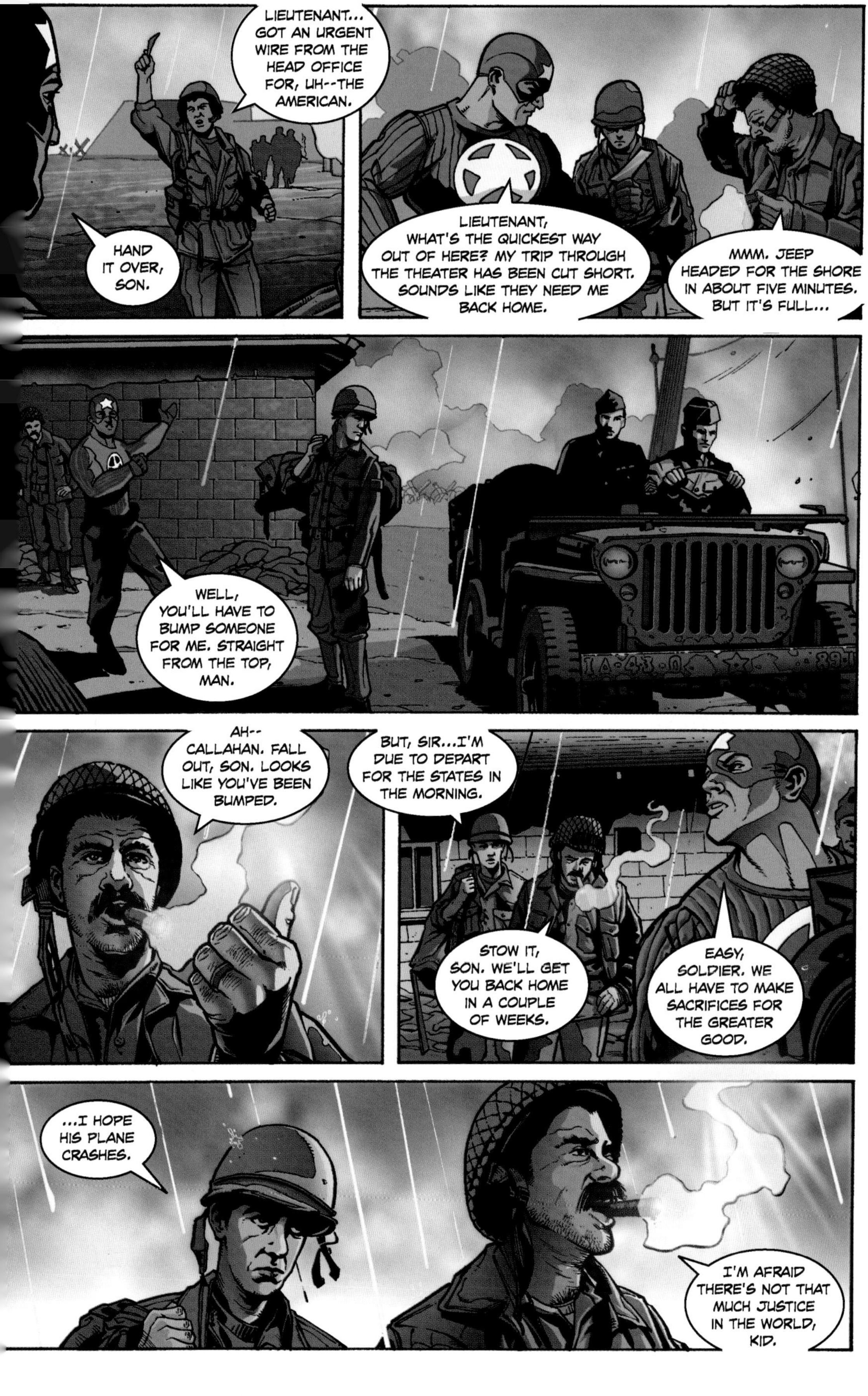
LIEUTENANT... GOT AN URGENT WIRE FROM THE HEAD OFFICE FOR, UH--THE AMERICAN.
HAND IT OVER, SON.
LIEUTENANT, WHAT'S THE QUICKEST WAY OUT OF HERE? MY TRIP THROUGH THE THEATER HAS BEEN CUT SHORT. SOUNDS LIKE THEY NEED ME BACK HOME.
MMM. JEEP HEADED FOR THE SHORE IN ABOUT FIVE MINUTES. BUT IT'S FULL...
WELL, YOU'LL HAVE TO BUMP SOMEONE FOR ME. STRAIGHT FROM THE TOP, MAN.
AH-- CALLAHAN. FALL OUT, SON. LOOKS LIKE YOU'VE BEEN BUMPED.
BUT, SIR...I'M DUE TO DEPART FOR THE STATES IN THE MORNING.
STOW IT, SON. WE'LL GET YOU BACK HOME IN A COUPLE OF WEEKS.
EASY, SOLDIER. WE ALL HAVE TO MAKE SACRIFICES FOR THE GREATER GOOD.
...I HOPE HIS PLANE CRASHES.
I'M AFRAID THERE'S NOT THAT MUCH JUSTICE IN THE WORLD, KID.

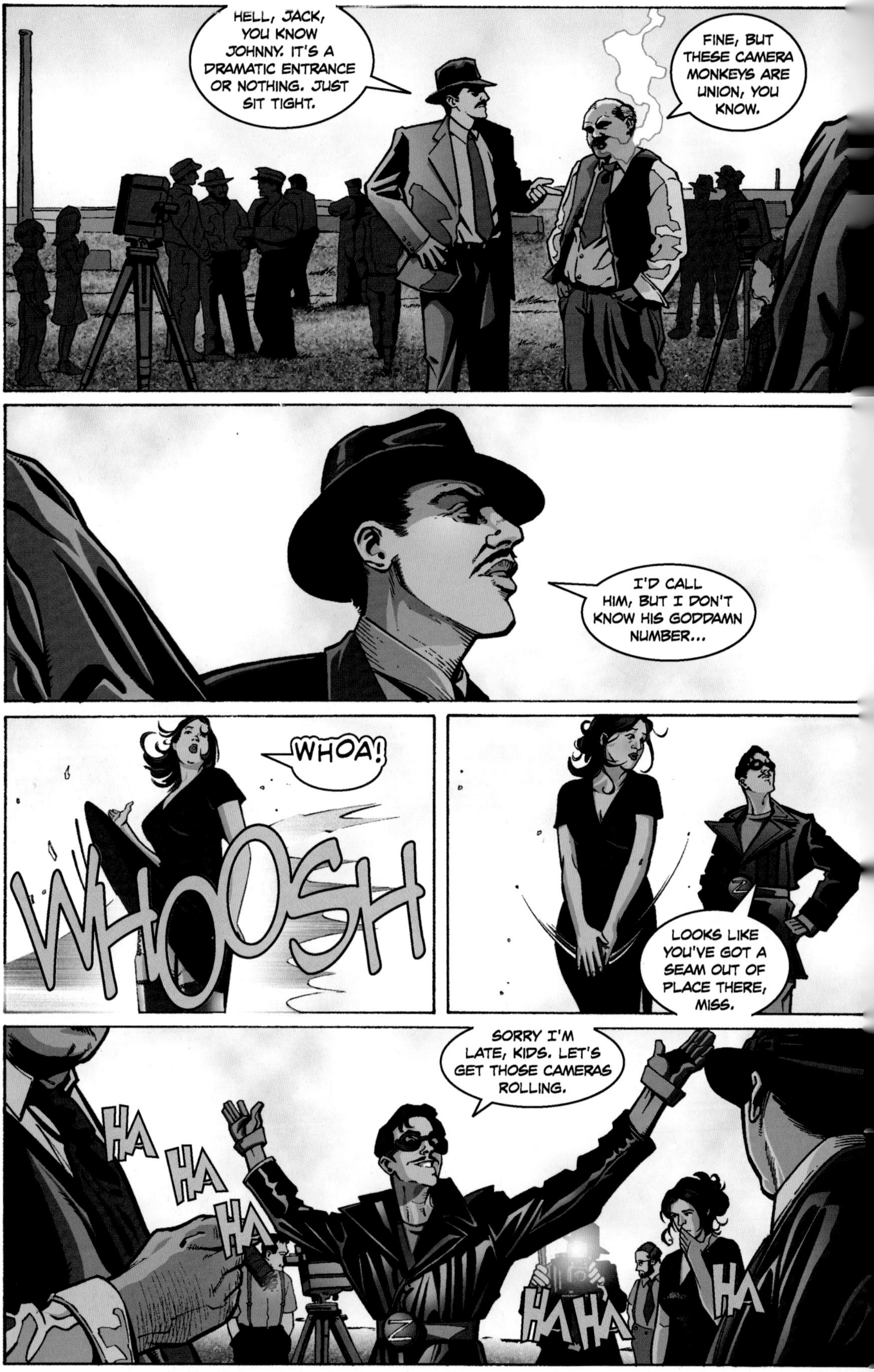
HELL, JACK, YOU KNOW JOHNNY. IT'S A DRAMATIC ENTRANCE OR NOTHING. JUST SIT TIGHT.
FINE, BUT THESE CAMERA MONKEYS ARE UNION, YOU KNOW.
I'D CALL HIM, BUT I DON'T KNOW HIS GODDAMN NUMBER...
WHOA!
WHOOSH
LOOKS LIKE YOU'VE GOT A SEAM OUT OF PLACE THERE, MISS.
SORRY I'M LATE, KIDS. LET'S GET THOSE CAMERAS ROLLING.
HA HA HA
HA HA
HA

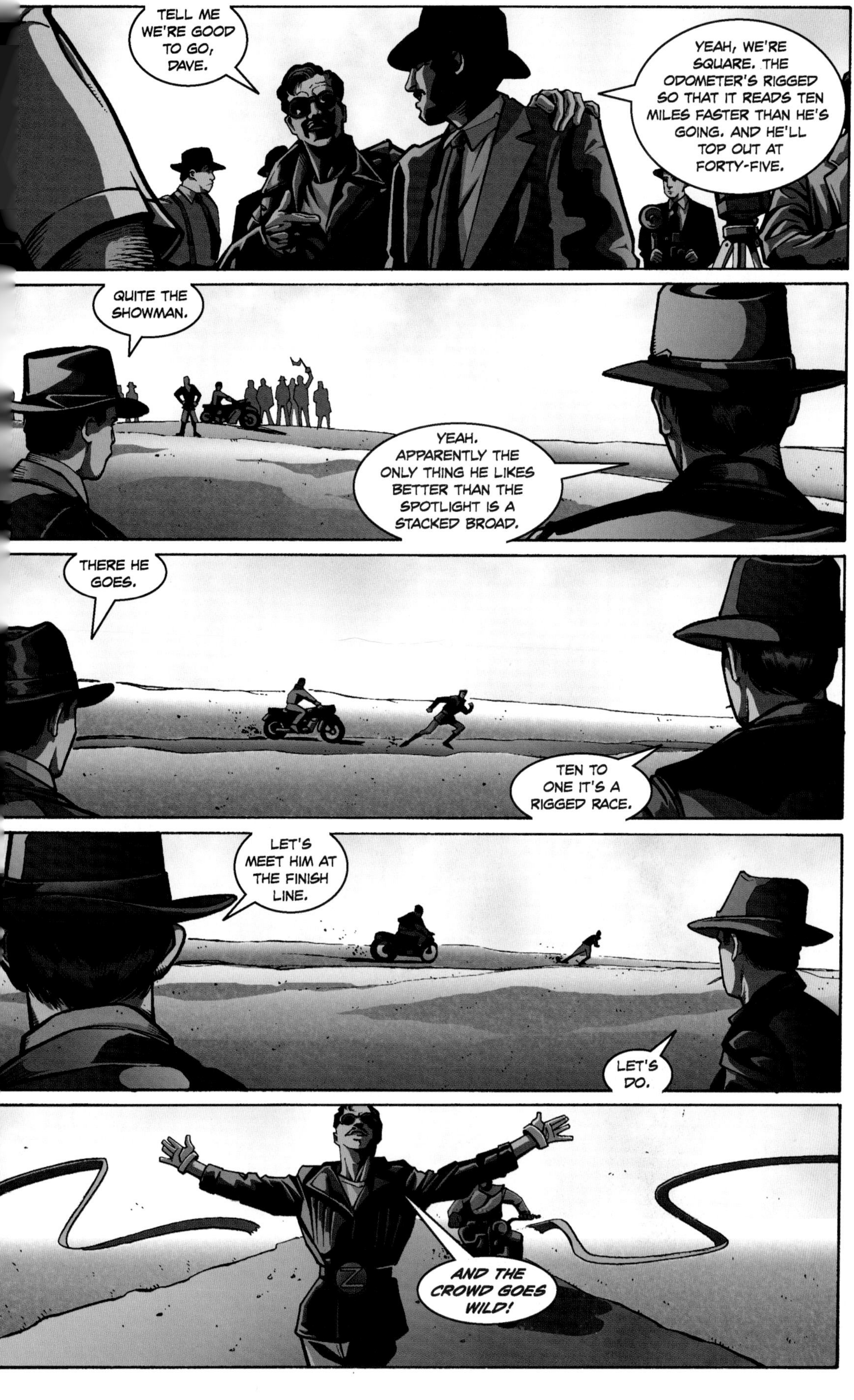
TELL ME WE'RE GOOD TO GO, DAVE.
YEAH, WE'RE SQUARE. THE ODOMETER'S RIGGED SO THAT IT READS TEN MILES FASTER THAN HE'S GOING. AND HE'LL TOP OUT AT FORTY-FIVE.
QUITE THE SHOWMAN.
YEAH. APPARENTLY THE ONLY THING HE LIKES BETTER THAN THE SPOTLIGHT IS A STACKED BROAD.
THERE HE GOES.
TEN TO ONE IT'S A RIGGED RACE.
LET'S MEET HIM AT THE FINISH LINE.
LET'S DO.
AND THE CROWD GOES WILD!

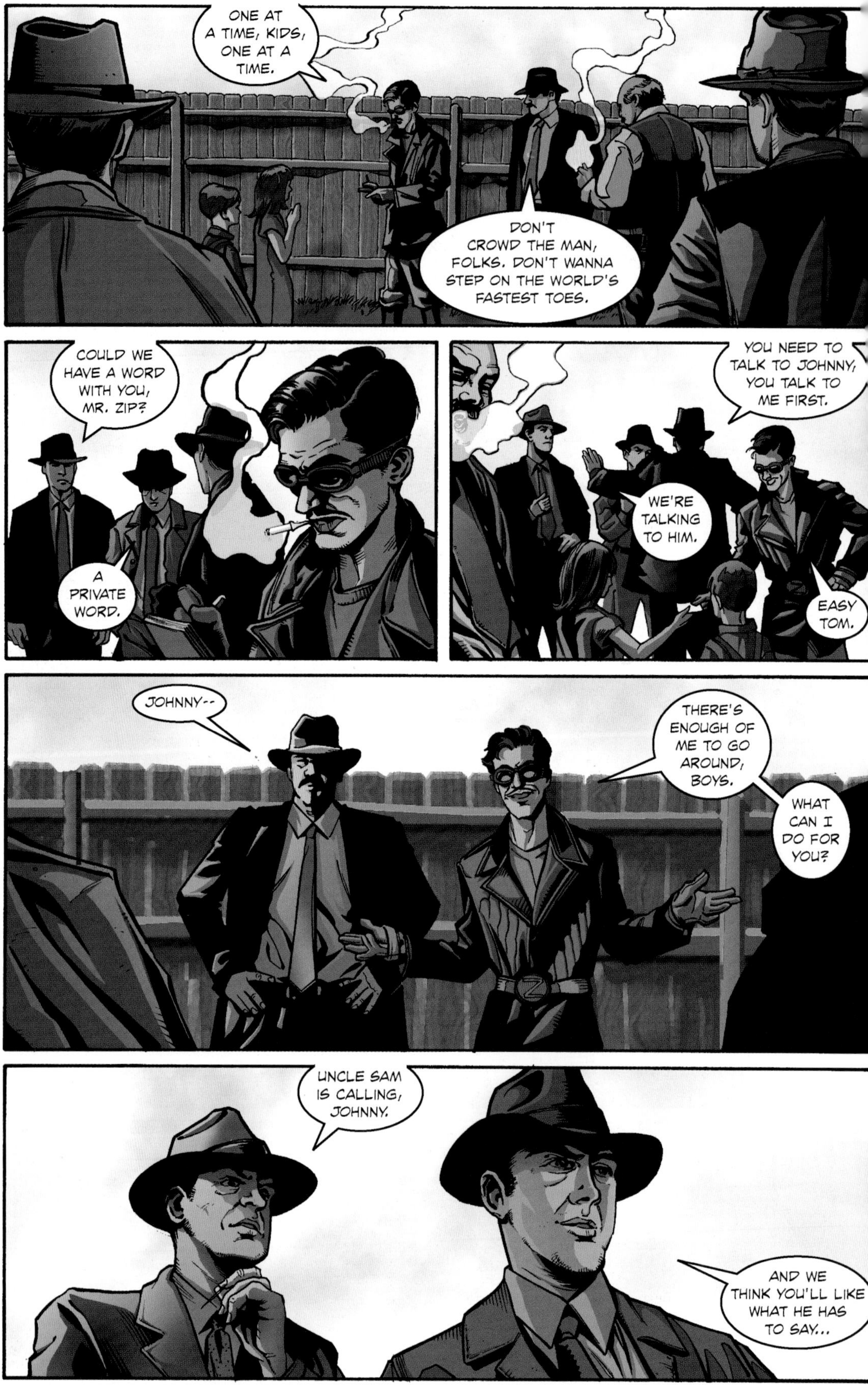
ONE AT A TIME, KIDS, ONE AT A TIME.
DON'T CROWD THE MAN, FOLKS. DON'T WANNA STEP ON THE WORLD'S FASTEST TOES.
COULD WE HAVE A WORD WITH YOU, MR. ZIP?
A PRIVATE WORD.
YOU NEED TO TALK TO JOHNNY, YOU TALK TO ME FIRST.
WE'RE TALKING TO HIM.
EASY TOM.
JOHNNY--
THERE'S ENOUGH OF ME TO GO AROUND, BOYS.
WHAT CAN I DO FOR YOU?
UNCLE SAM IS CALLING, JOHNNY.
AND WE THINK YOU'LL LIKE WHAT HE HAS TO SAY...

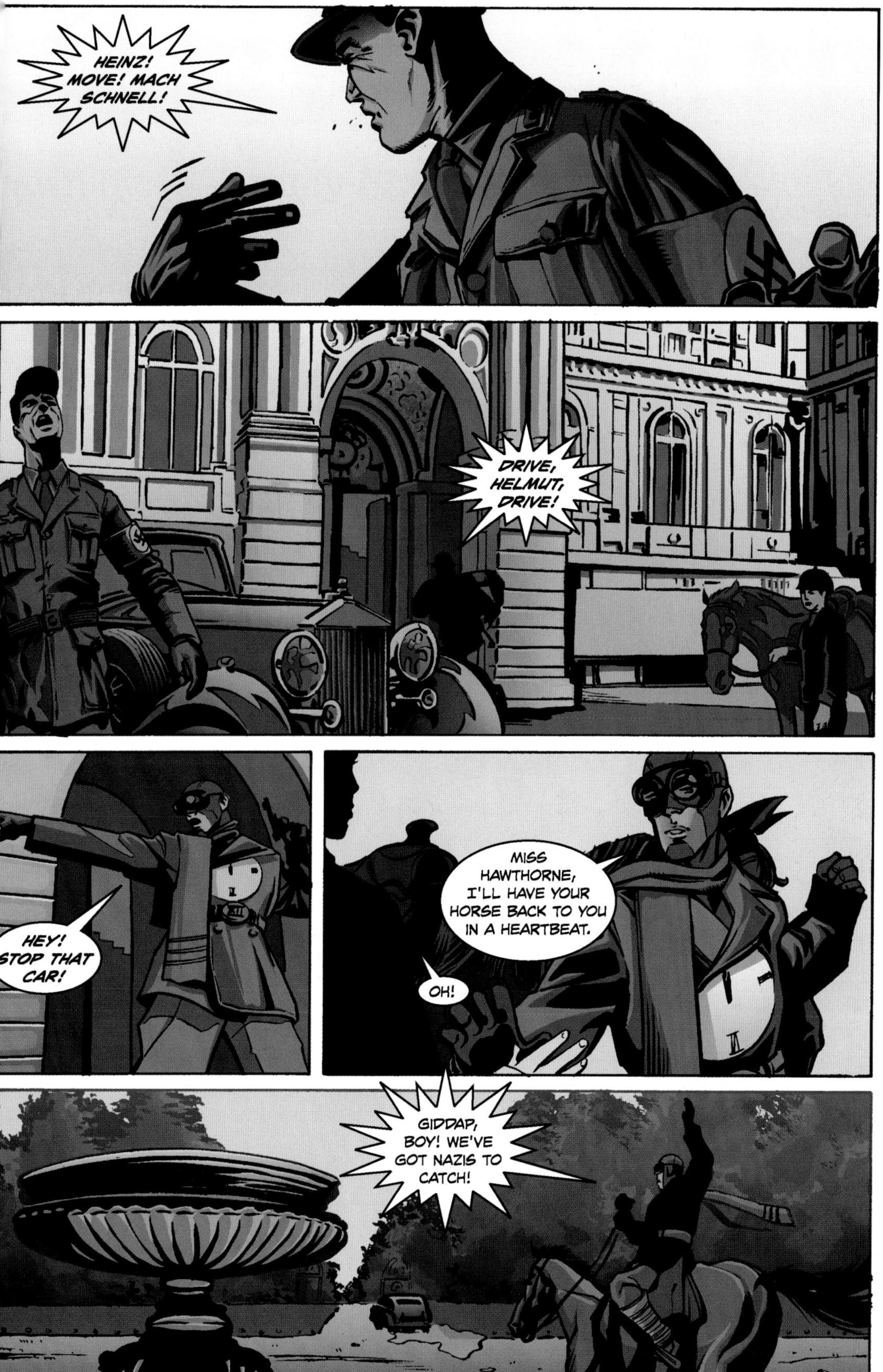
HEINZ! MOVE! MACH SCHNELL!
DRIVE, HELMUT, DRIVE!
HEY! STOP THAT CAR!
MISS HAWTHORNE, I'LL HAVE YOUR HORSE BACK TO YOU IN A HEARTBEAT.
OH!
GIDDAP, BOY! WE'VE GOT NAZIS TO CATCH!

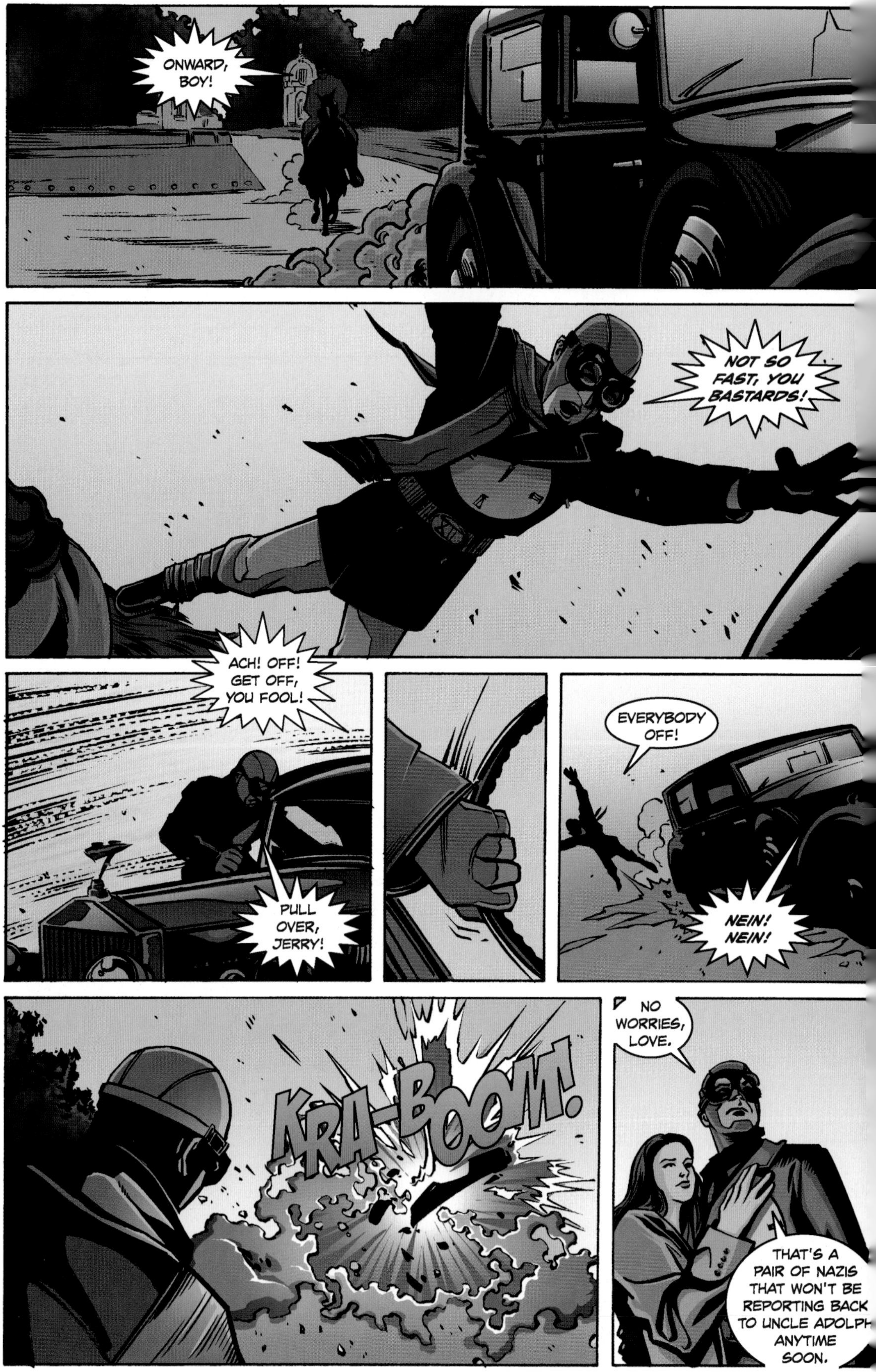
ONWARD, BOY!
NOT SO FAST, YOU BASTARDS!
ACH! OFF! GET OFF, YOU FOOL!
PULL OVER, JERRY!
EVERYBODY OFF!
NEIN! NEIN!
KRA-BOOM!
NO WORRIES, LOVE.
THAT'S A PAIR OF NAZIS THAT WON'T BE REPORTING BACK TO UNCLE ADOLPH ANYTIME SOON.

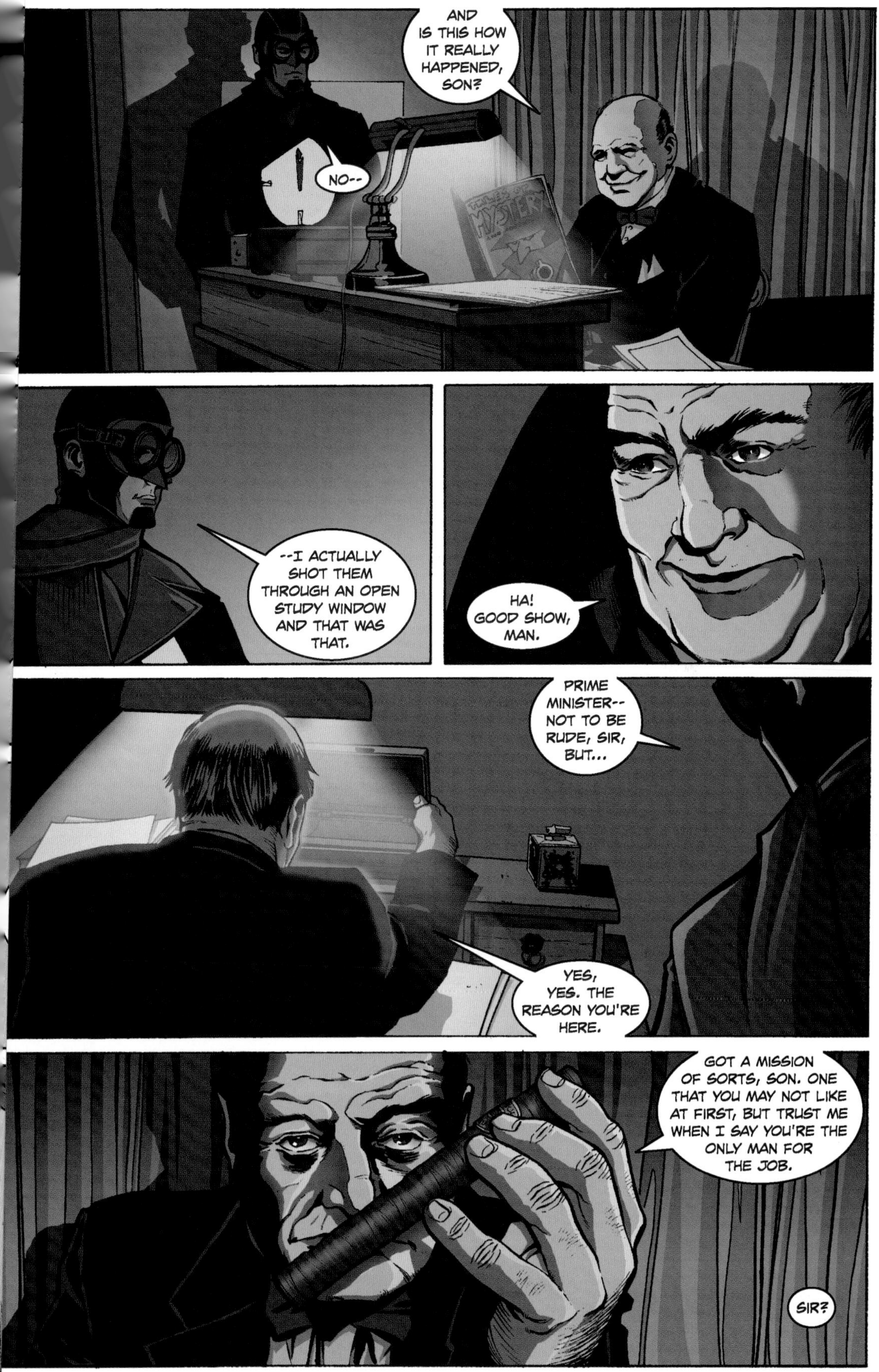
AND IS THIS HOW IT REALLY HAPPENED, SON?
NO--
--I ACTUALLY SHOT THEM THROUGH AN OPEN STUDY WINDOW AND THAT WAS THAT.
HA! GOOD SHOW, MAN.
PRIME MINISTER-- NOT TO BE RUDE, SIR, BUT...
YES, YES. THE REASON YOU'RE HERE.
GOT A MISSION OF SORTS, SON. ONE THAT YOU MAY NOT LIKE AT FIRST, BUT TRUST ME WHEN I SAY YOU'RE THE ONLY MAN FOR THE JOB.
SIR?

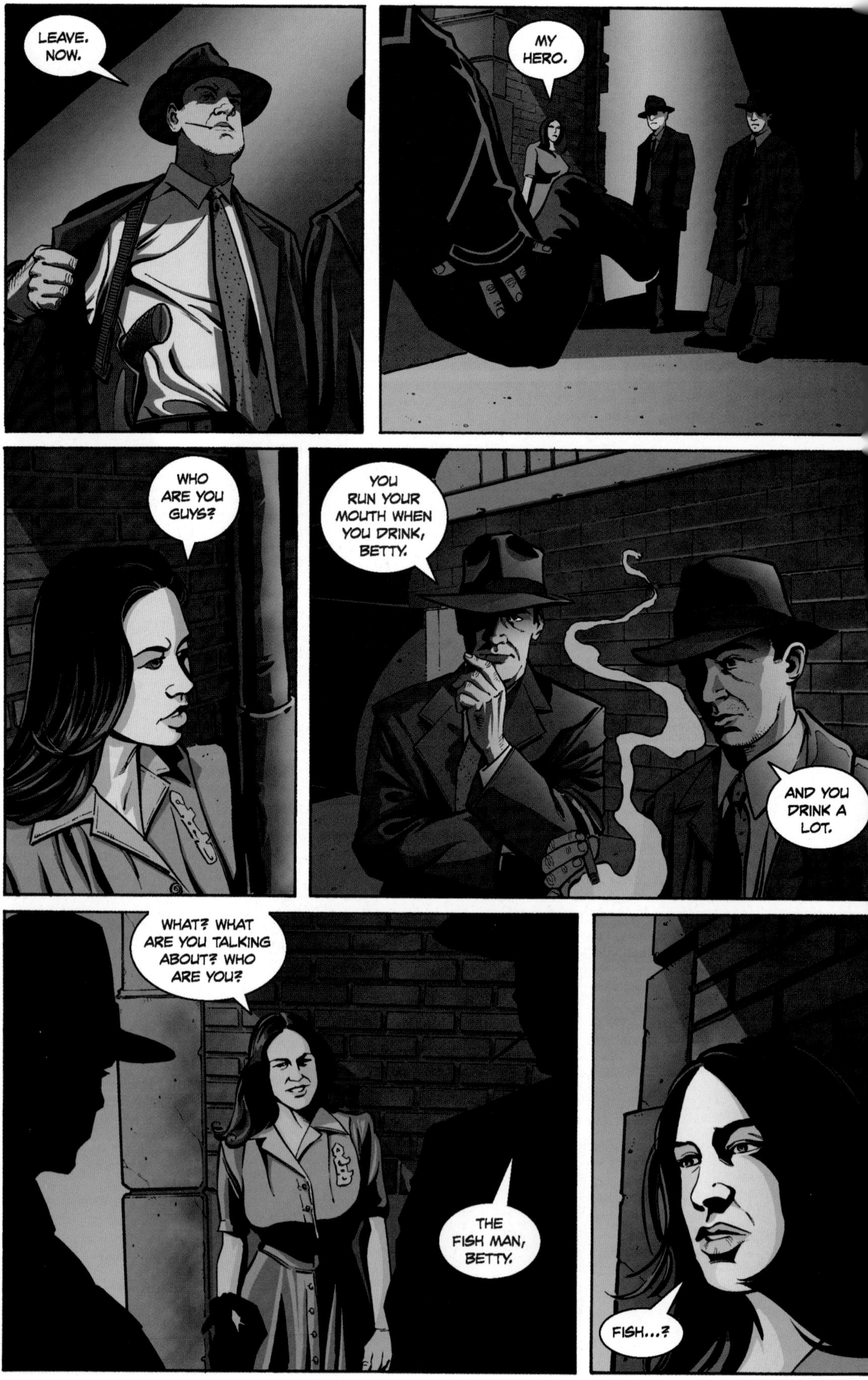
LEAVE. NOW.
MY HERO.
WHO ARE YOU GUYS?
YOU RUN YOUR MOUTH WHEN YOU DRINK, BETTY.
AND YOU DRINK A LOT.
WHAT? WHAT ARE YOU TALKING ABOUT? WHO ARE YOU?
THE FISH MAN, BETTY.
FISH...?

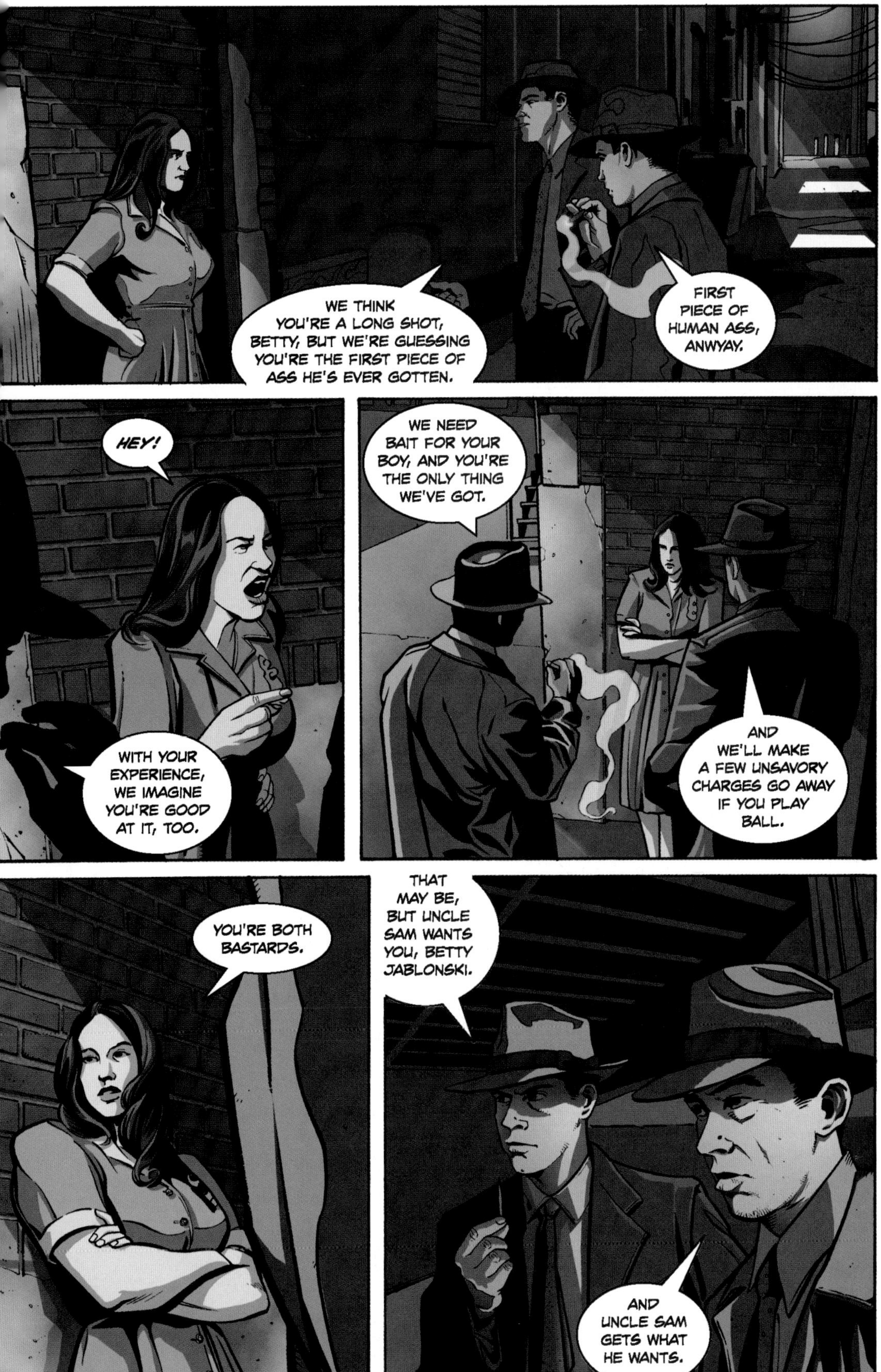
WE THINK YOU'RE A LONG SHOT, BETTY, BUT WE'RE GUESSING YOU'RE THE FIRST PIECE OF ASS HE'S EVER GOTTEN.
FIRST PIECE OF HUMAN ASS, ANWYAY.
HEY!
WITH YOUR EXPERIENCE, WE IMAGINE YOU'RE GOOD AT IT, TOO.
WE NEED BAIT FOR YOUR BOY, AND YOU'RE THE ONLY THING WE'VE GOT.
AND WE'LL MAKE A FEW UNSAVORY CHARGES GO AWAY IF YOU PLAY BALL.
YOU'RE BOTH BASTARDS.
THAT MAY BE, BUT UNCLE SAM WANTS YOU, BETTY JABLONSKI.
AND UNCLE SAM GETS WHAT HE WANTS.

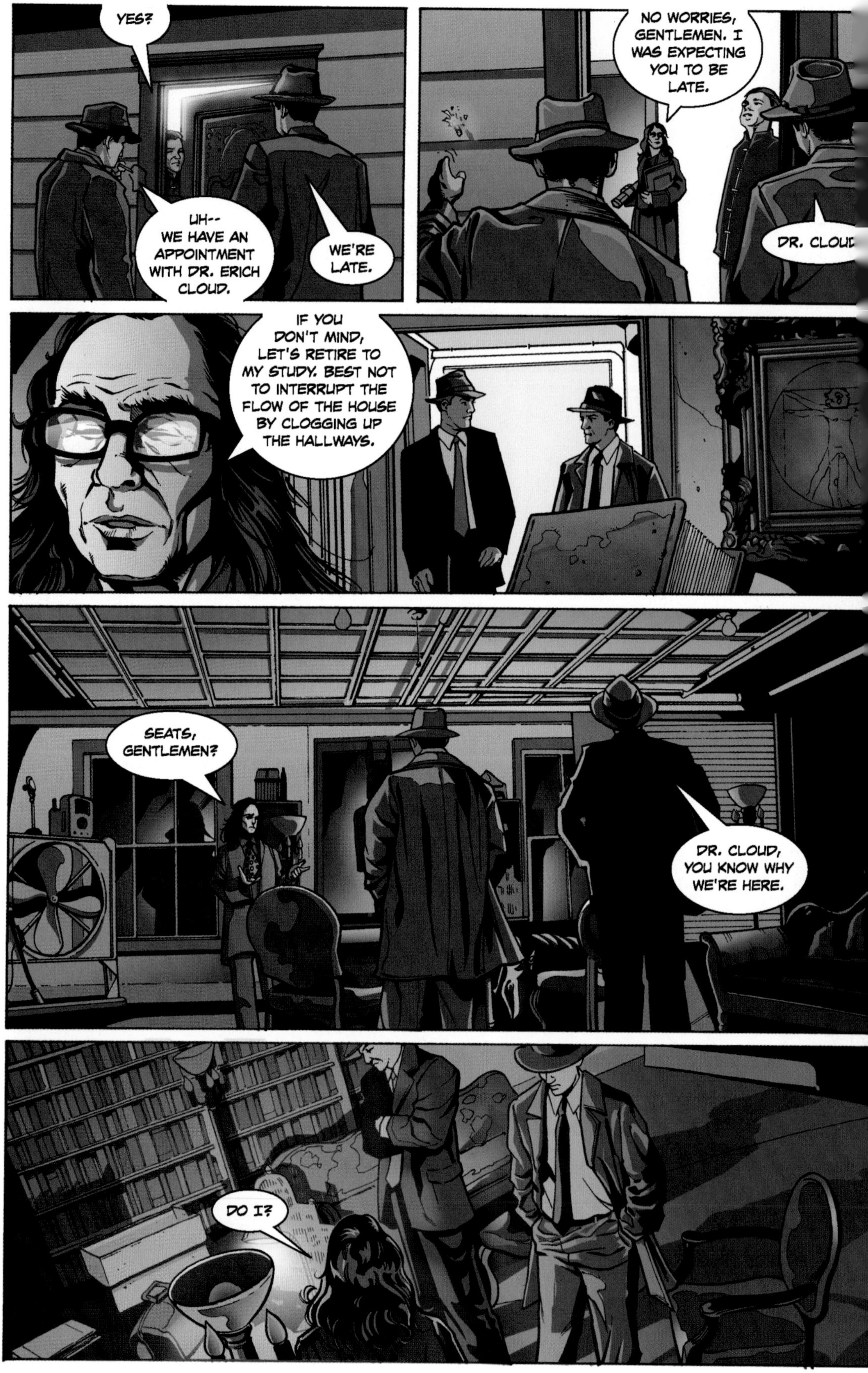
YES?
UH-- WE HAVE AN APPOINTMENT WITH DR. ERICH CLOUD.
WE'RE LATE.
NO WORRIES, GENTLEMEN. I WAS EXPECTING YOU TO BE LATE.
IF YOU DON'T MIND, LET'S RETIRE TO MY STUDY. BEST NOT TO INTERRUPT THE FLOW OF THE HOUSE BY CLOGGING UP THE HALLWAYS.
SEATS, GENTLEMEN?
DR. CLOUD, YOU KNOW WHY WE'RE HERE.
DO I?

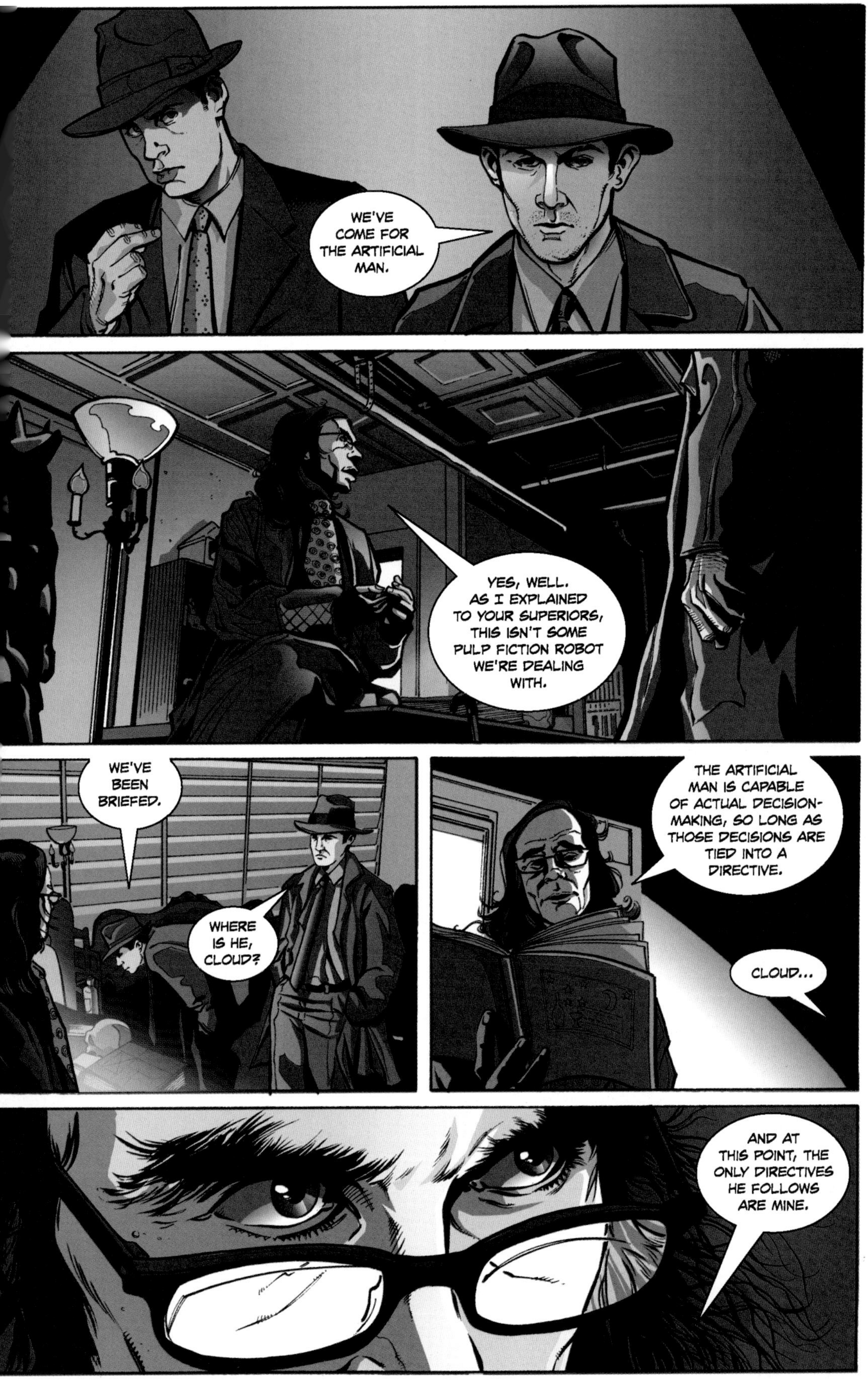
WE'VE COME FOR THE ARTIFICIAL MAN.
YES, WELL. AS I EXPLAINED TO YOUR SUPERIORS, THIS ISN'T SOME PULP FICTION ROBOT WE'RE DEALING WITH.
WE'VE BEEN BRIEFED.
WHERE IS HE, CLOUD?
THE ARTIFICIAL MAN IS CAPABLE OF ACTUAL DECISION-MAKING, SO LONG AS THOSE DECISIONS ARE TIED INTO A DIRECTIVE.
CLOUD...
AND AT THIS POINT, THE ONLY DIRECTIVES HE FOLLOWS ARE MINE.

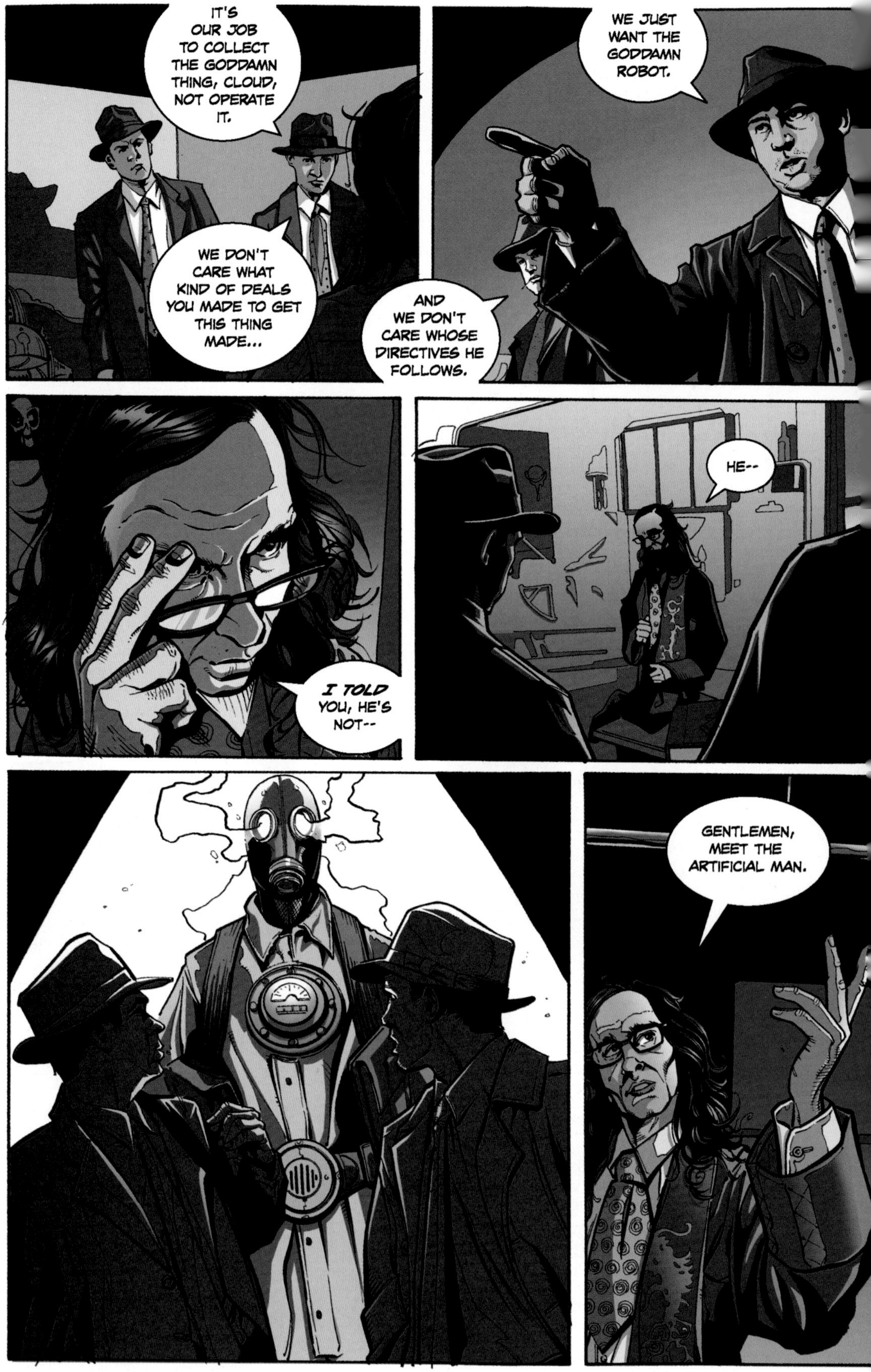
IT'S OUR JOB TO COLLECT THE GODDAMN THING, CLOUD, NOT OPERATE IT.
WE DON'T CARE WHAT KIND OF DEALS YOU MADE TO GET THIS THING MADE...
AND WE DON'T CARE WHOSE DIRECTIVES HE FOLLOWS.
WE JUST WANT THE GODDAMN ROBOT.
I TOLD YOU, HE'S NOT--
HE--
GENTLEMEN, MEET THE ARTIFICIAL MAN.

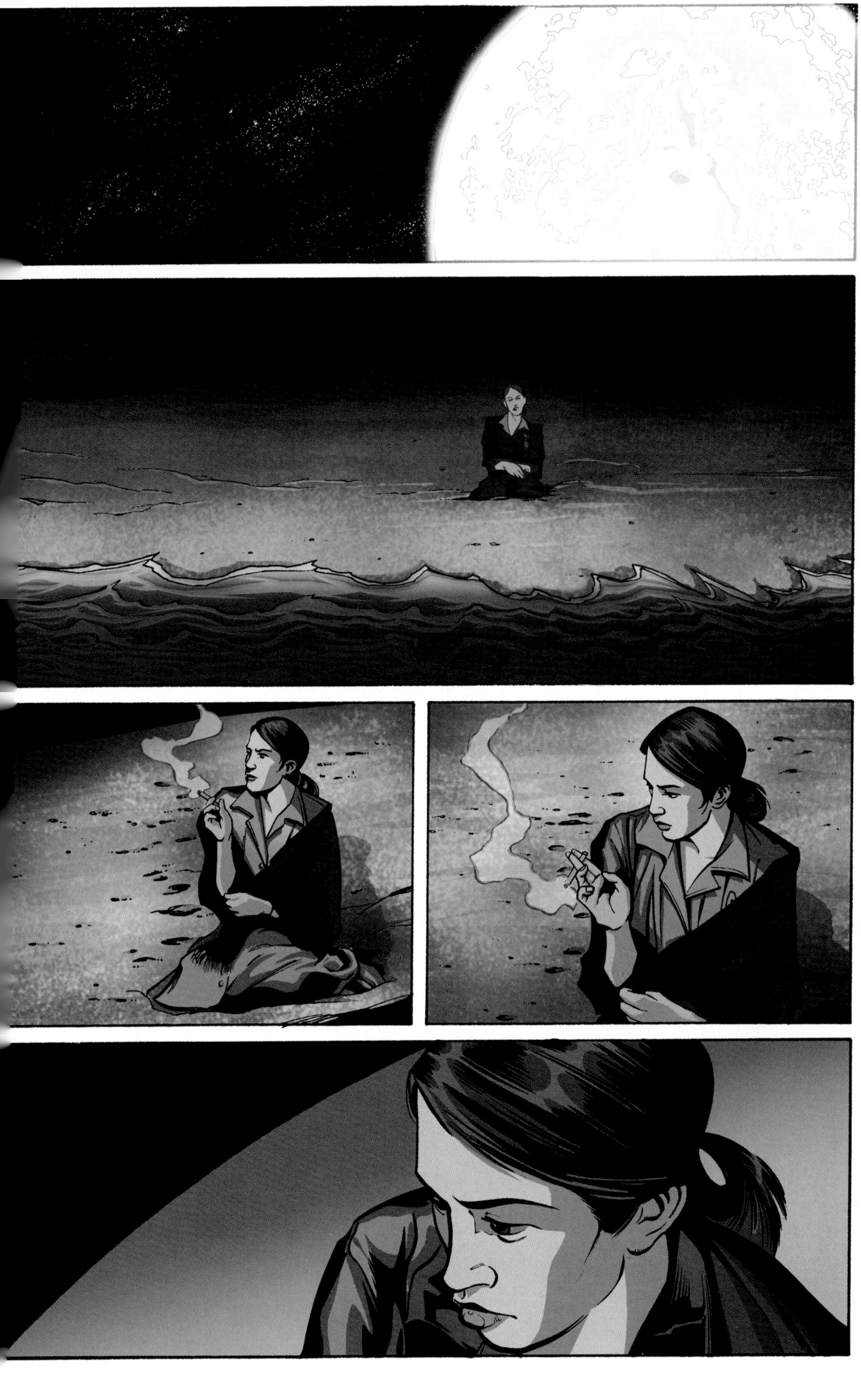

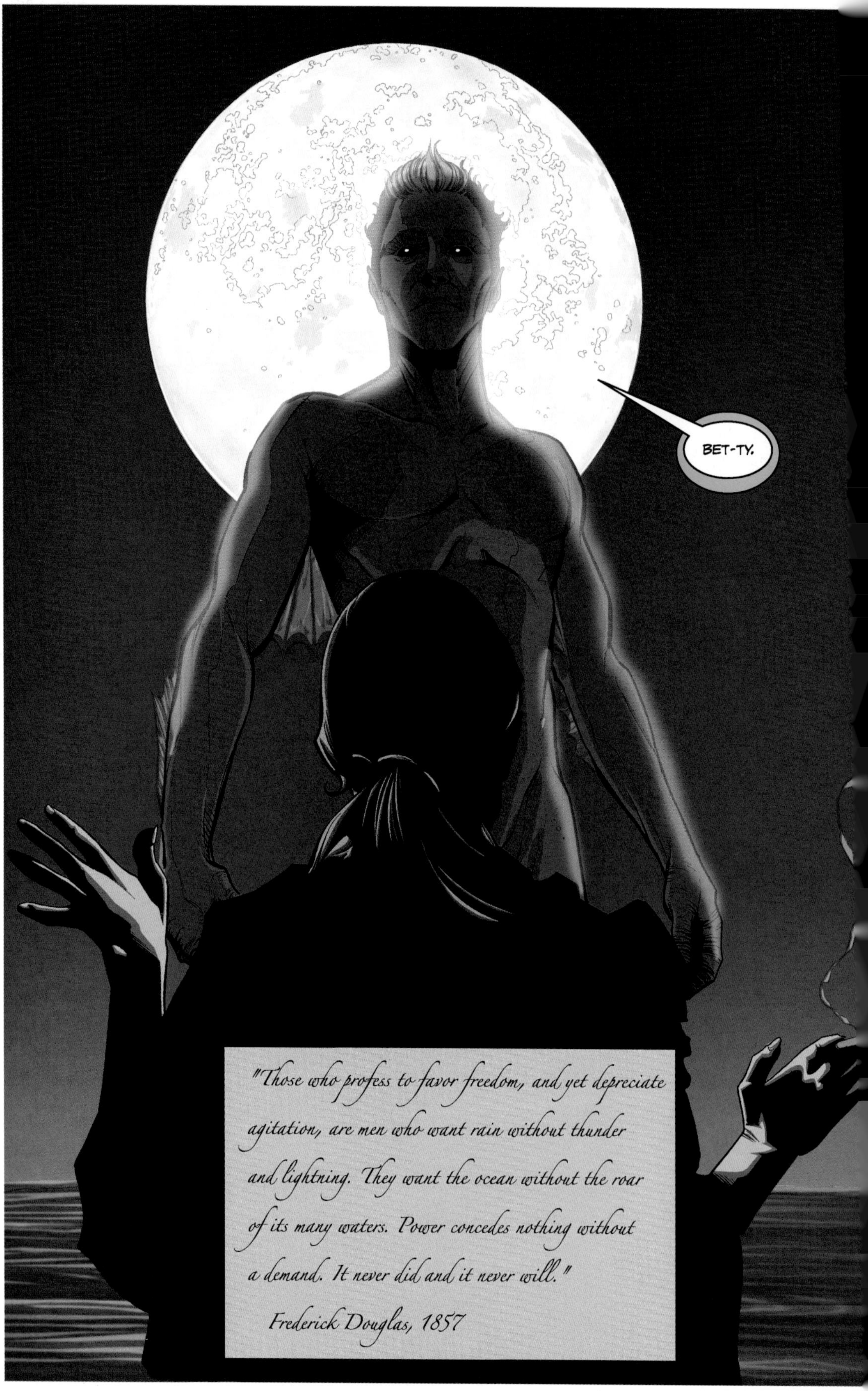
BET-TY.
"Those who profess to favor freedom, and yet depreciate agitation, are men who want rain without thunder and lightning. They want the ocean without the roar of its many waters. Power concedes nothing without a demand. It never did and it never will."
Frederick Douglas, 1857

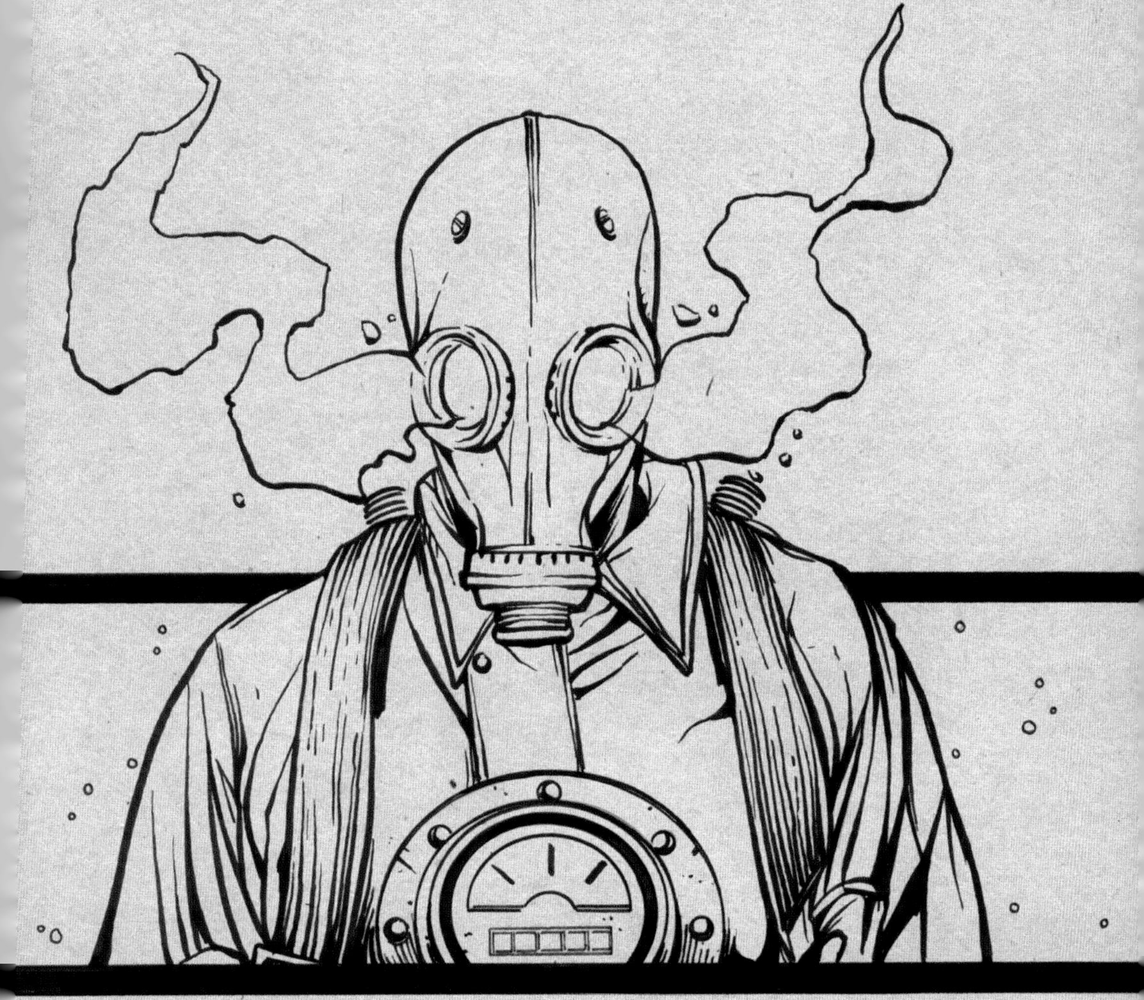

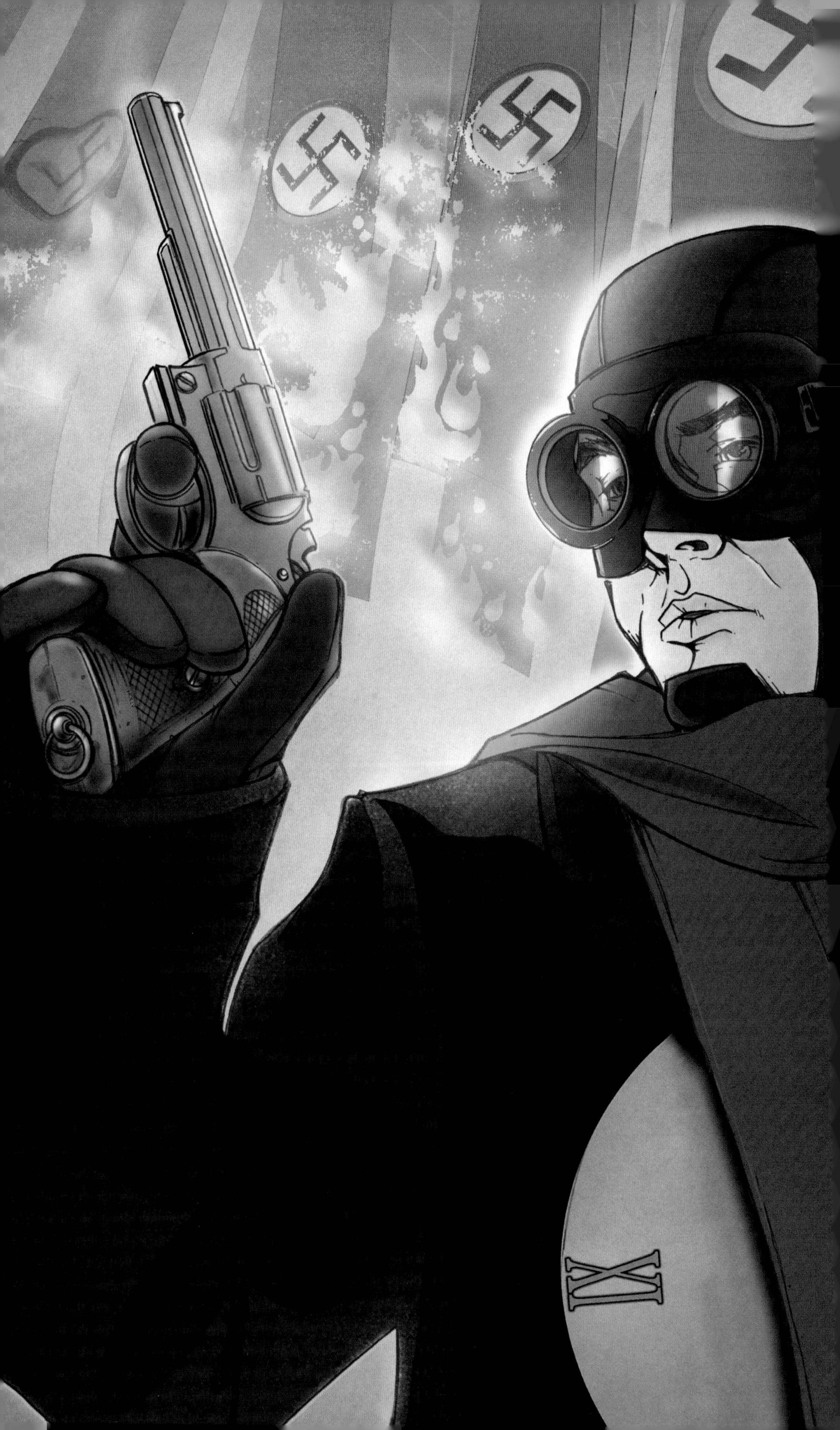

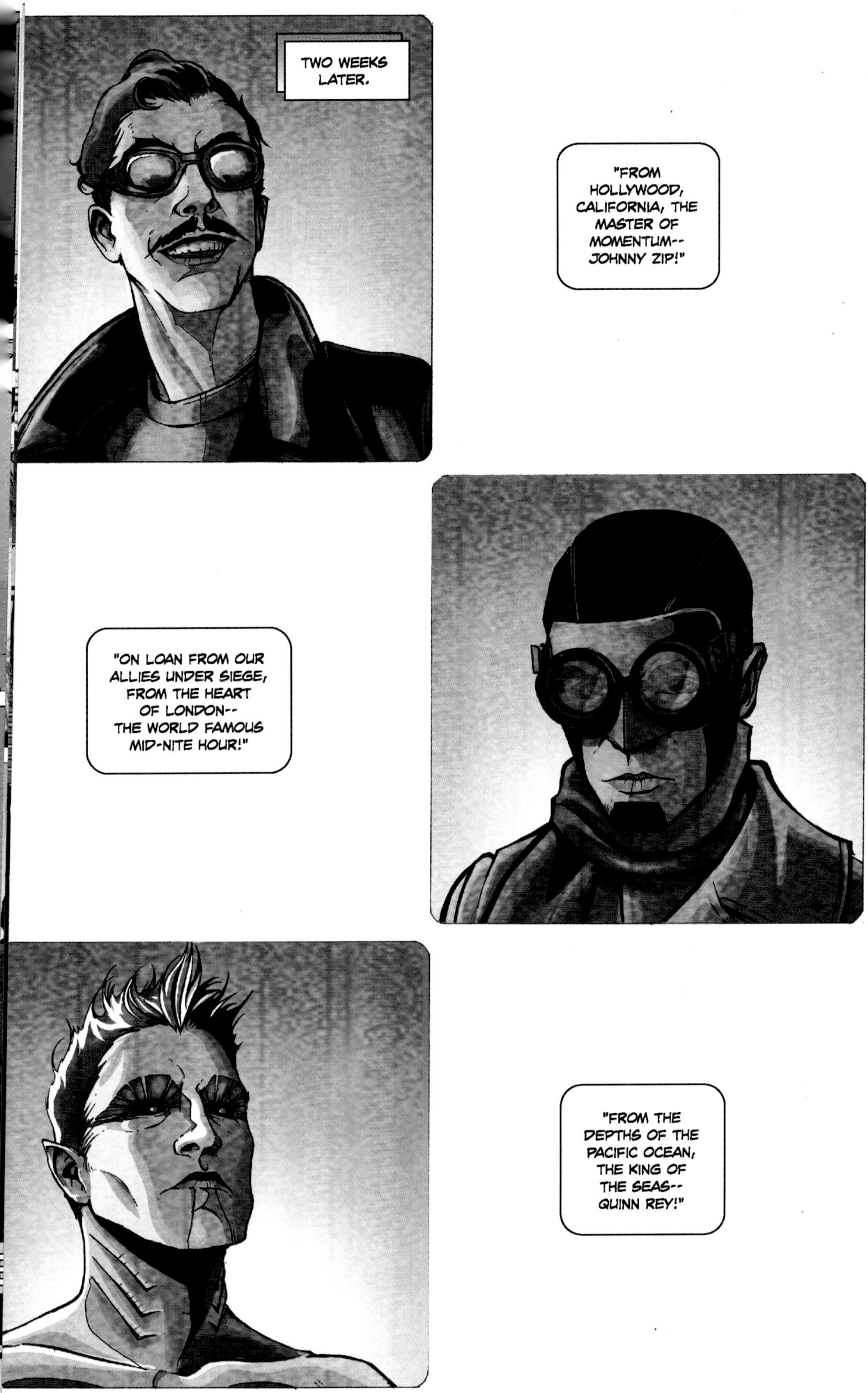
TWO WEEKS LATER.
"FROM HOLLYWOOD, CALIFORNIA, THE MASTER OF MOMENTUM--JOHNNY ZIP!"
"ON LOAN FROM OUR ALLIES UNDER SIEGE, FROM THE HEART OF LONDON--THE WORLD FAMOUS MID-NITE HOUR!"
"FROM THE DEPTHS OF THE PACIFIC OCEAN, THE KING OF THE SEAS--QUINN REY!"

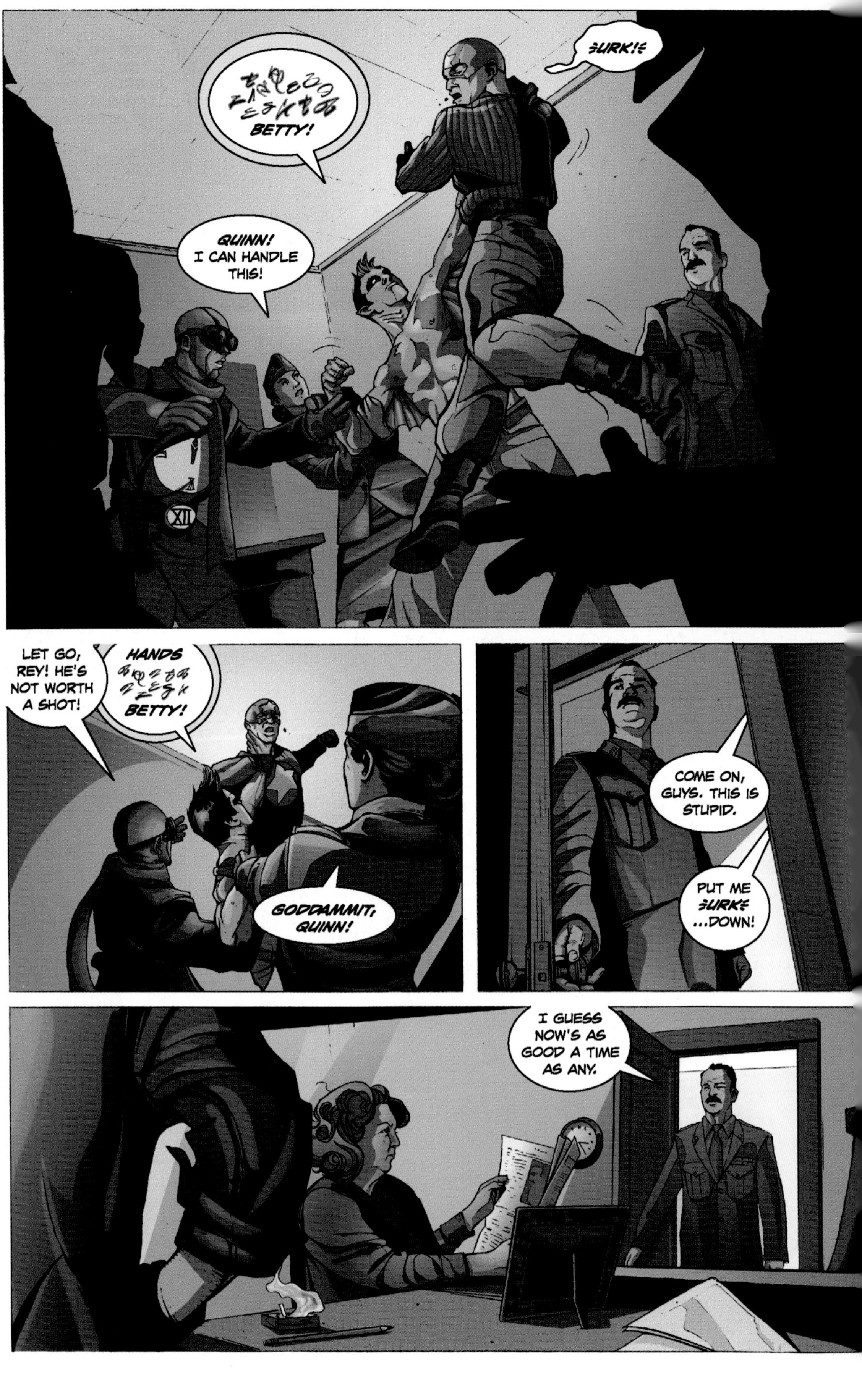

SURK!!
BETTY!
QUINN! I CAN HANDLE THIS!
LET GO, REY! HE'S NOT WORTH A SHOT!
HANDS
BETTY!
GODDAMMIT, QUINN!
COME ON, GUYS. THIS IS STUPID.
PUT ME SURK! ...DOWN!
I GUESS NOW'S AS GOOD A TIME AS ANY.

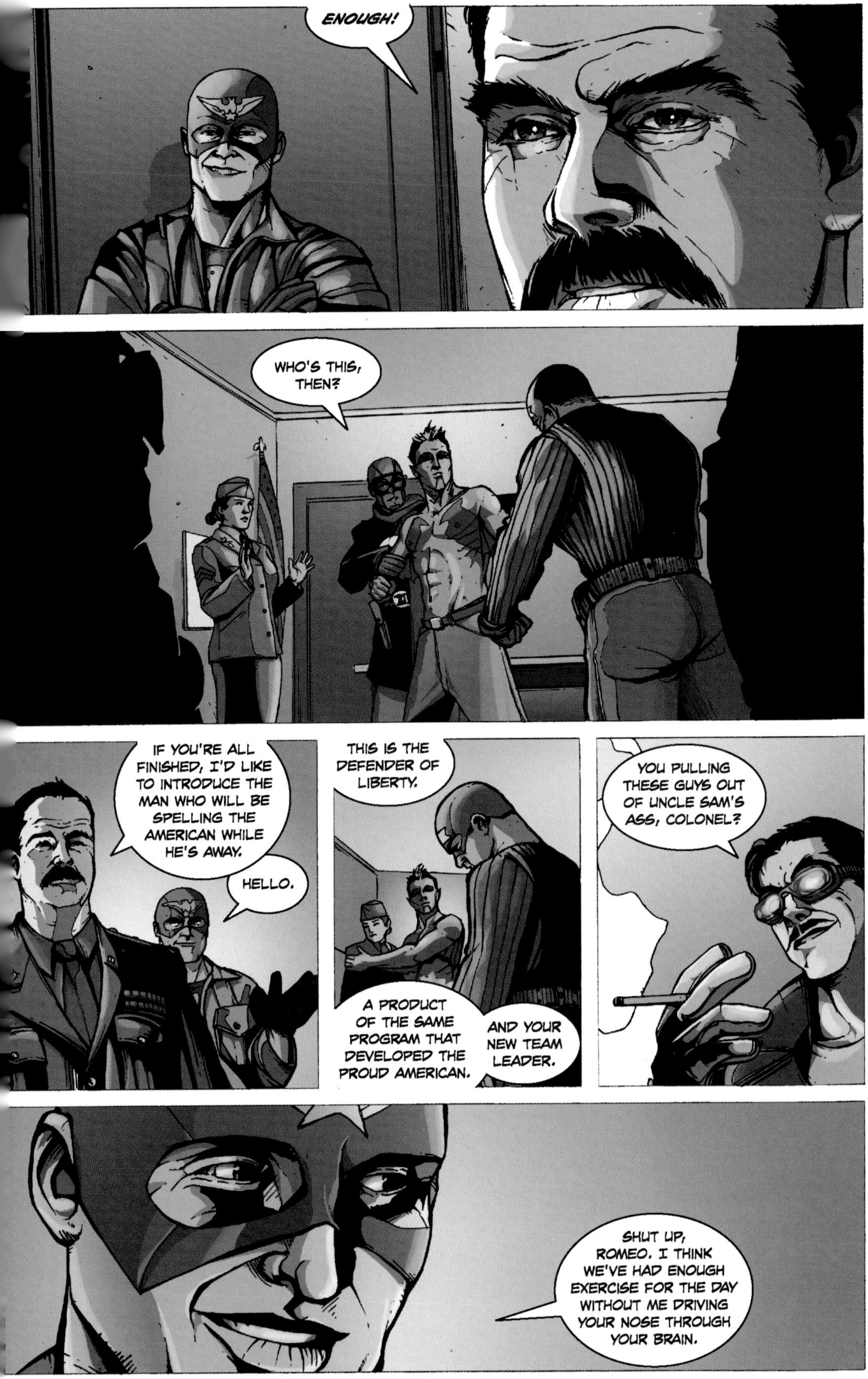
ENOUGH!
WHO'S THIS, THEN?
IF YOU'RE ALL FINISHED, I'D LIKE TO INTRODUCE THE MAN WHO WILL BE SPELLING THE AMERICAN WHILE HE'S AWAY.
HELLO.
THIS IS THE DEFENDER OF LIBERTY.
A PRODUCT OF THE SAME PROGRAM THAT DEVELOPED THE PROUD AMERICAN.
AND YOUR NEW TEAM LEADER.
YOU PULLING THESE GUYS OUT OF UNCLE SAM'S ASS, COLONEL?
SHUT UP, ROMEO. I THINK WE'VE HAD ENOUGH EXERCISE FOR THE DAY WITHOUT ME DRIVING YOUR NOSE THROUGH YOUR BRAIN.

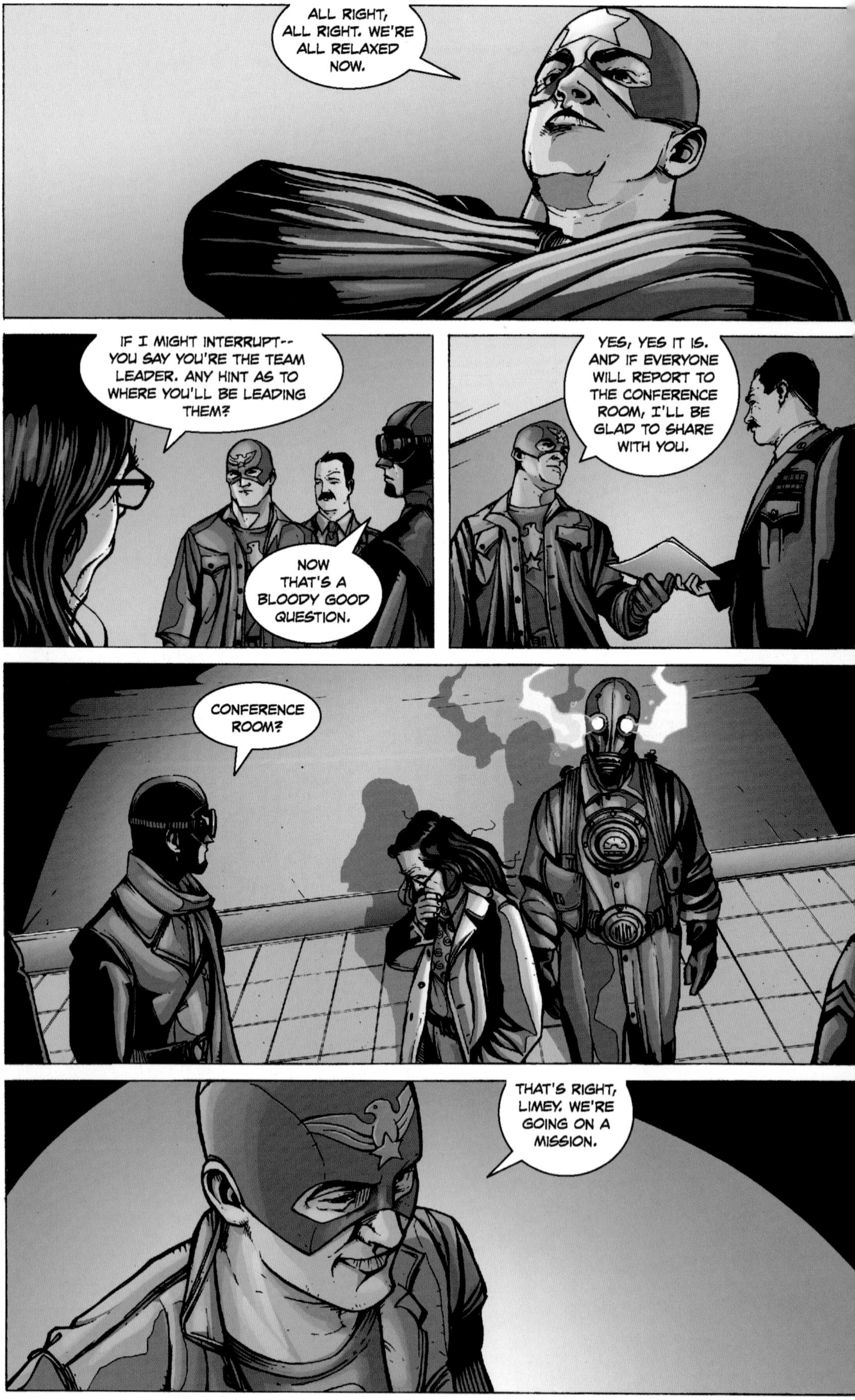
ALL RIGHT, ALL RIGHT. WE'RE ALL RELAXED NOW.
IF I MIGHT INTERRUPT-- YOU SAY YOU'RE THE TEAM LEADER. ANY HINT AS TO WHERE YOU'LL BE LEADING THEM?
NOW THAT'S A BLOODY GOOD QUESTION.
YES, YES IT IS. AND IF EVERYONE WILL REPORT TO THE CONFERENCE ROOM, I'LL BE GLAD TO SHARE WITH YOU.
CONFERENCE ROOM?
THAT'S RIGHT, LIMEY. WE'RE GOING ON A MISSION.

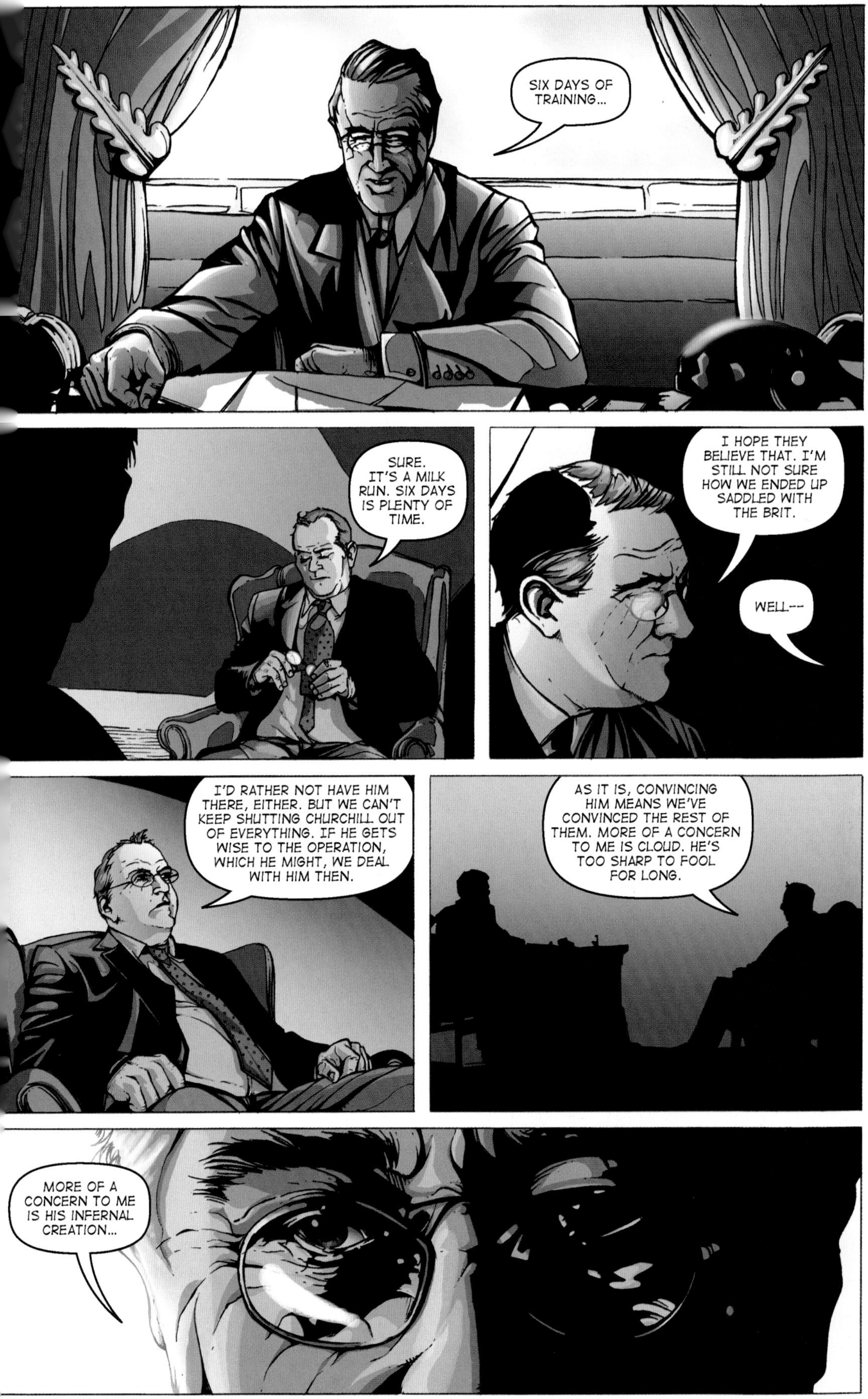
SIX DAYS OF TRAINING...
SURE. IT'S A MILK RUN. SIX DAYS IS PLENTY OF TIME.
I HOPE THEY BELIEVE THAT. I'M STILL NOT SURE HOW WE ENDED UP SADDLED WITH THE BRIT.
WELL---
I'D RATHER NOT HAVE HIM THERE, EITHER. BUT WE CAN'T KEEP SHUTTING CHURCHILL OUT OF EVERYTHING. IF HE GETS WISE TO THE OPERATION, WHICH HE MIGHT, WE DEAL WITH HIM THEN.
AS IT IS, CONVINCING HIM MEANS WE'VE CONVINCED THE REST OF THEM. MORE OF A CONCERN TO ME IS CLOUD. HE'S TOO SHARP TO FOOL FOR LONG.
MORE OF A CONCERN TO ME IS HIS INFERNAL CREATION...

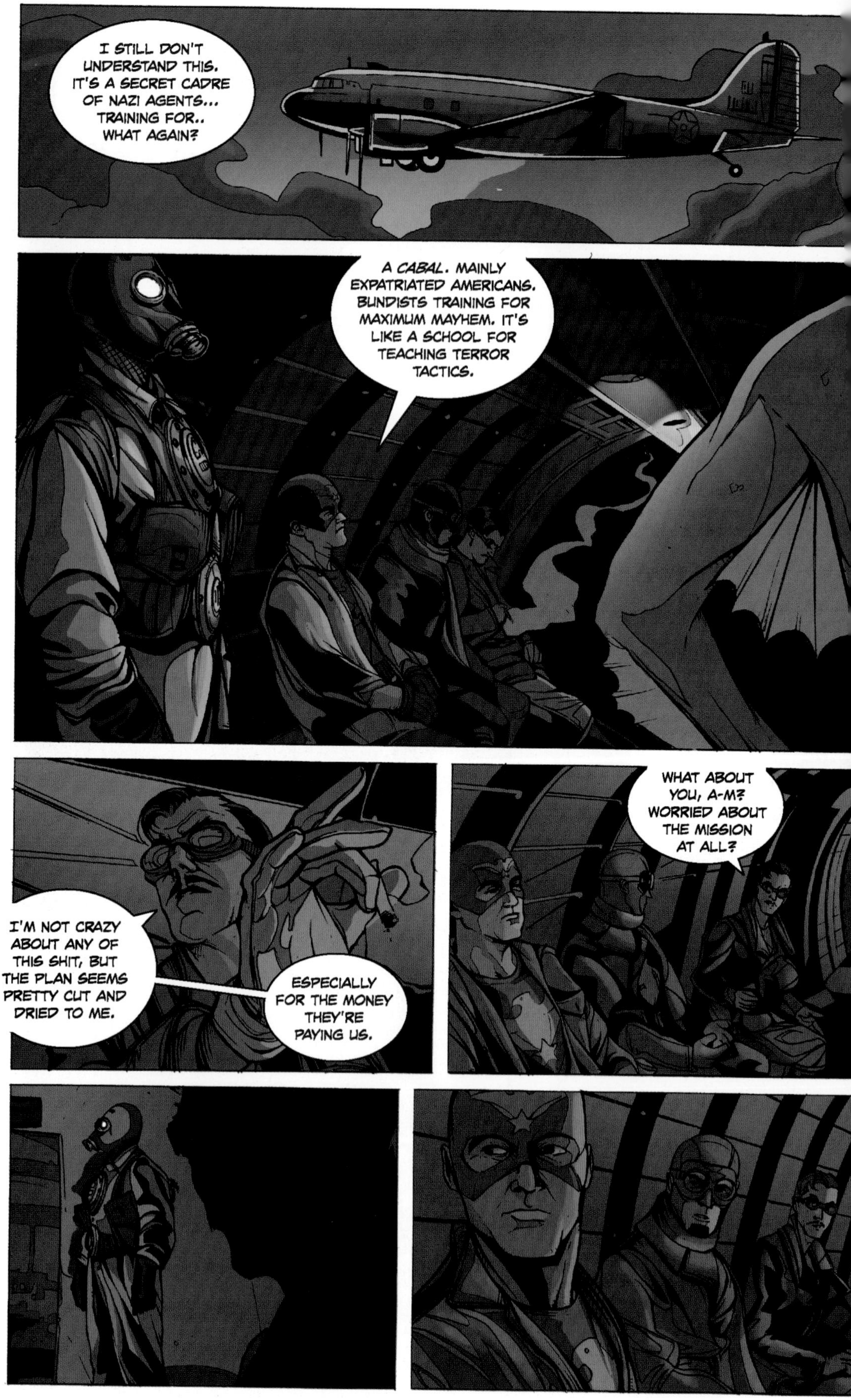
I STILL DON'T UNDERSTAND THIS. IT'S A SECRET CADRE OF NAZI AGENTS... TRAINING FOR.. WHAT AGAIN?
A *CABAL*. MAINLY EXPATRIATED AMERICANS. BUNDISTS TRAINING FOR MAXIMUM MAYHEM. IT'S LIKE A SCHOOL FOR TEACHING TERROR TACTICS.
I'M NOT CRAZY ABOUT ANY OF THIS SHIT, BUT THE PLAN SEEMS PRETTY CUT AND DRIED TO ME.
ESPECIALLY FOR THE MONEY THEY'RE PAYING US.
WHAT ABOUT YOU, A-M? WORRIED ABOUT THE MISSION AT ALL?

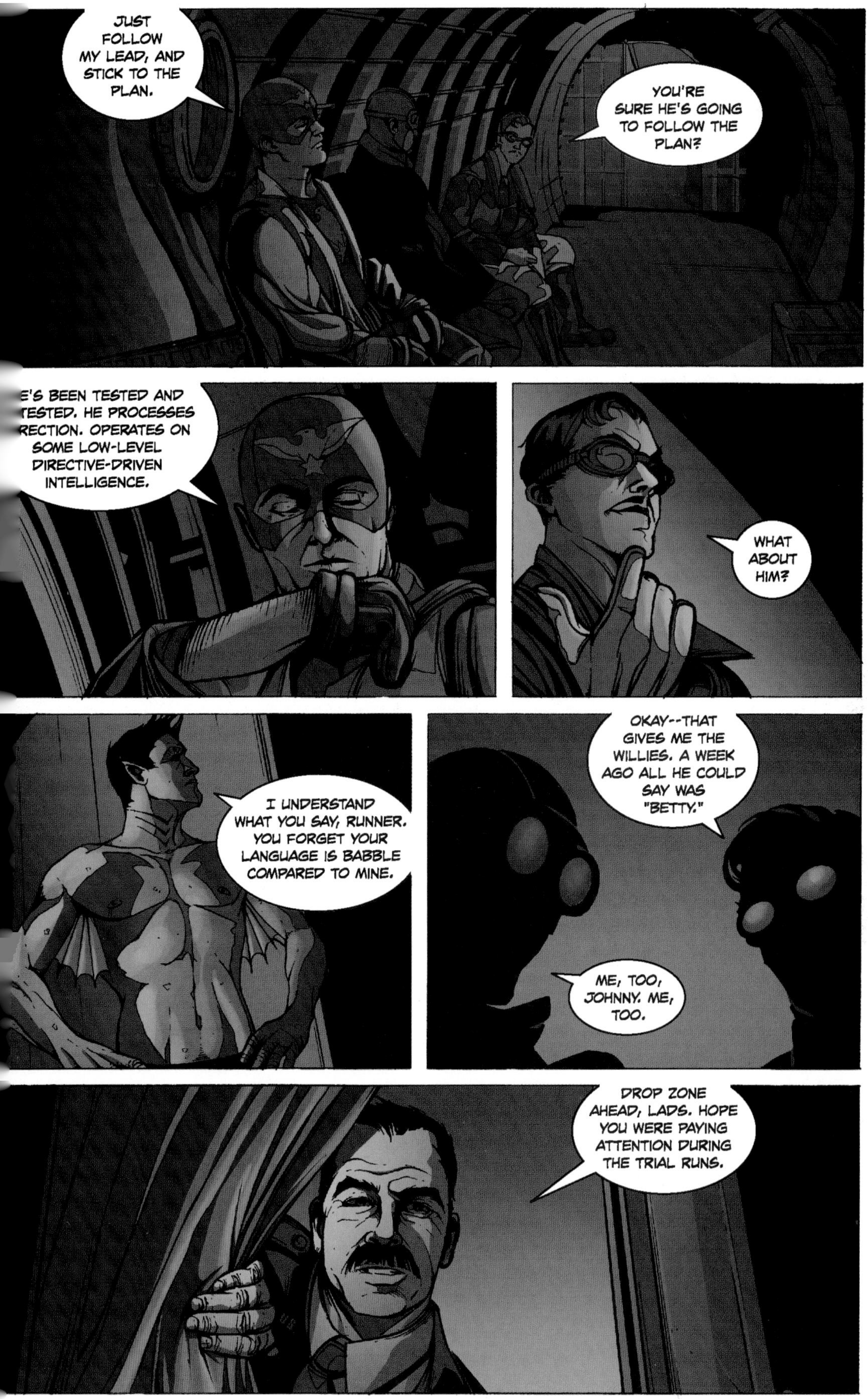
JUST FOLLOW MY LEAD, AND STICK TO THE PLAN.
YOU'RE SURE HE'S GOING TO FOLLOW THE PLAN?
E'S BEEN TESTED AND TESTED. HE PROCESSES RECTION. OPERATES ON SOME LOW-LEVEL DIRECTIVE-DRIVEN INTELLIGENCE.
WHAT ABOUT HIM?
I UNDERSTAND WHAT YOU SAY, RUNNER. YOU FORGET YOUR LANGUAGE IS BABBLE COMPARED TO MINE.
OKAY--THAT GIVES ME THE WILLIES. A WEEK AGO ALL HE COULD SAY WAS "BETTY."
ME, TOO, JOHNNY. ME, TOO.
DROP ZONE AHEAD, LADS. HOPE YOU WERE PAYING ATTENTION DURING THE TRIAL RUNS.

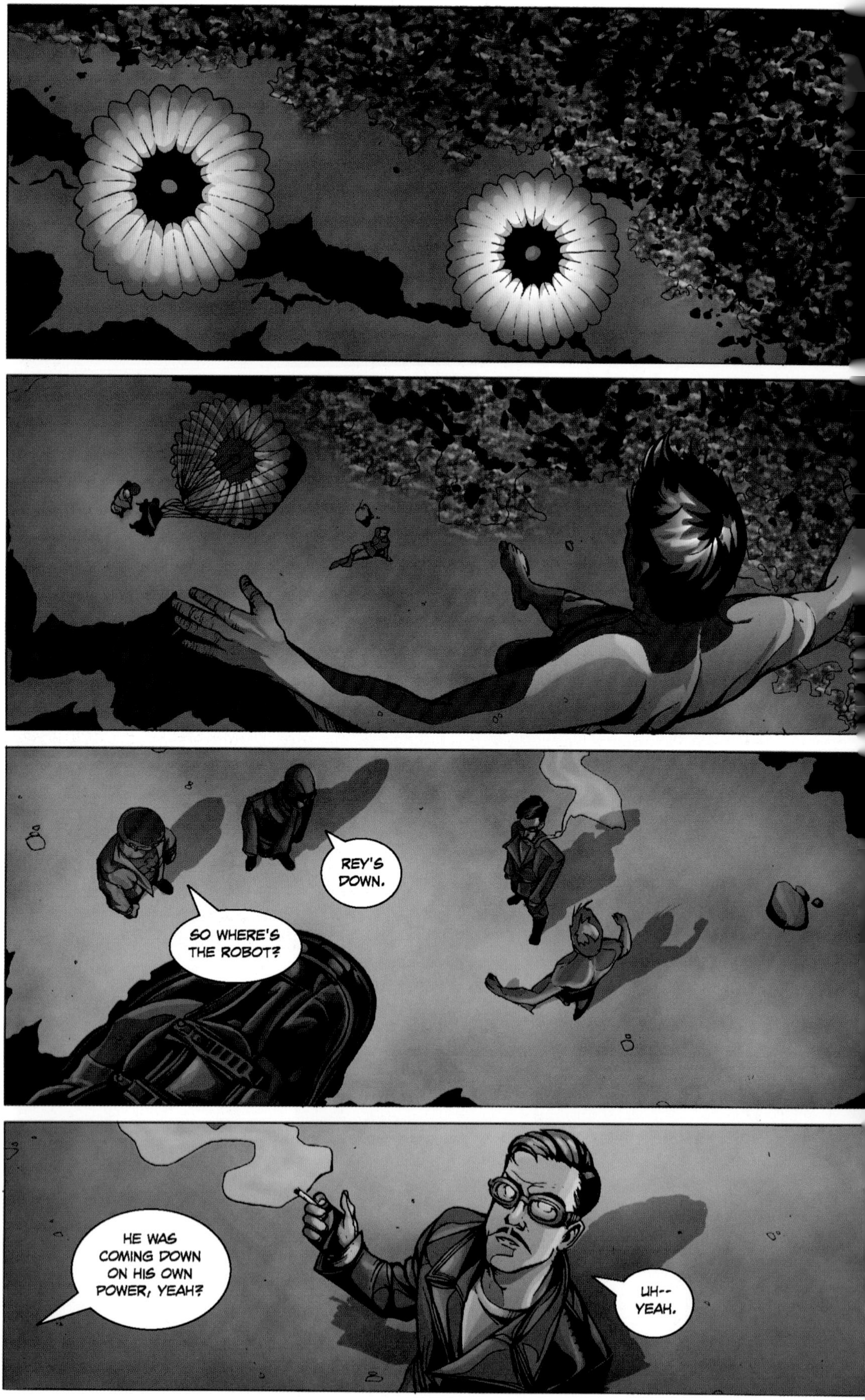
REY'S DOWN.
SO WHERE'S THE ROBOT?
HE WAS COMING DOWN ON HIS OWN POWER, YEAH?
UH-- YEAH.

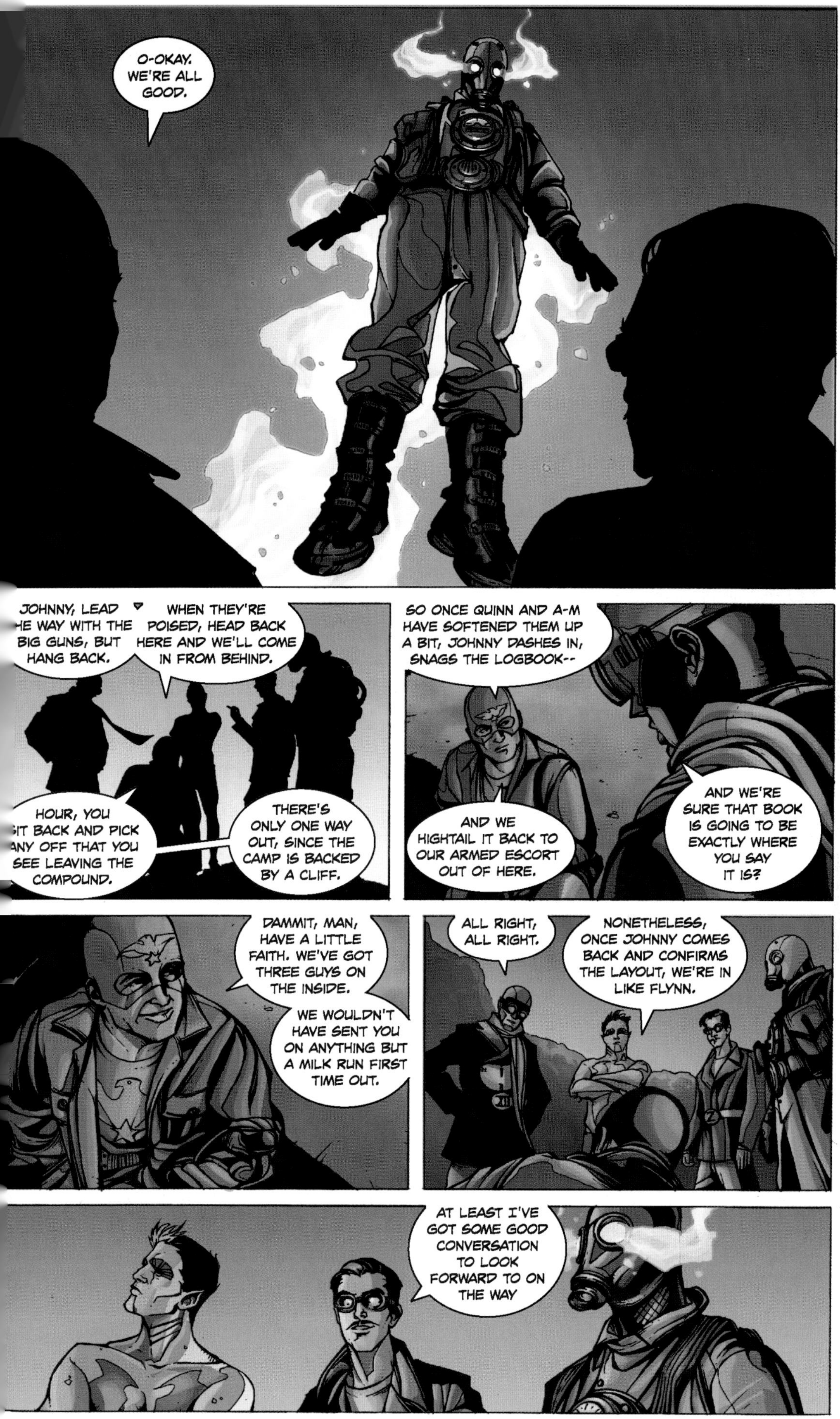
O-OKAY. WE'RE ALL GOOD.
JOHNNY, LEAD HE WAY WITH THE BIG GUNS, BUT HANG BACK.
WHEN THEY'RE POISED, HEAD BACK HERE AND WE'LL COME IN FROM BEHIND.
HOUR, YOU SIT BACK AND PICK ANY OFF THAT YOU SEE LEAVING THE COMPOUND.
THERE'S ONLY ONE WAY OUT, SINCE THE CAMP IS BACKED BY A CLIFF.
SO ONCE QUINN AND A-M HAVE SOFTENED THEM UP A BIT, JOHNNY DASHES IN, SNAGS THE LOGBOOK--
AND WE HIGHTAIL IT BACK TO OUR ARMED ESCORT OUT OF HERE.
AND WE'RE SURE THAT BOOK IS GOING TO BE EXACTLY WHERE YOU SAY IT IS?
DAMMIT, MAN, HAVE A LITTLE FAITH. WE'VE GOT THREE GUYS ON THE INSIDE.
WE WOULDN'T HAVE SENT YOU ON ANYTHING BUT A MILK RUN FIRST TIME OUT.
ALL RIGHT, ALL RIGHT.
NONETHELESS, ONCE JOHNNY COMES BACK AND CONFIRMS THE LAYOUT, WE'RE IN LIKE FLYNN.
AT LEAST I'VE GOT SOME GOOD CONVERSATION TO LOOK FORWARD TO ON THE WAY

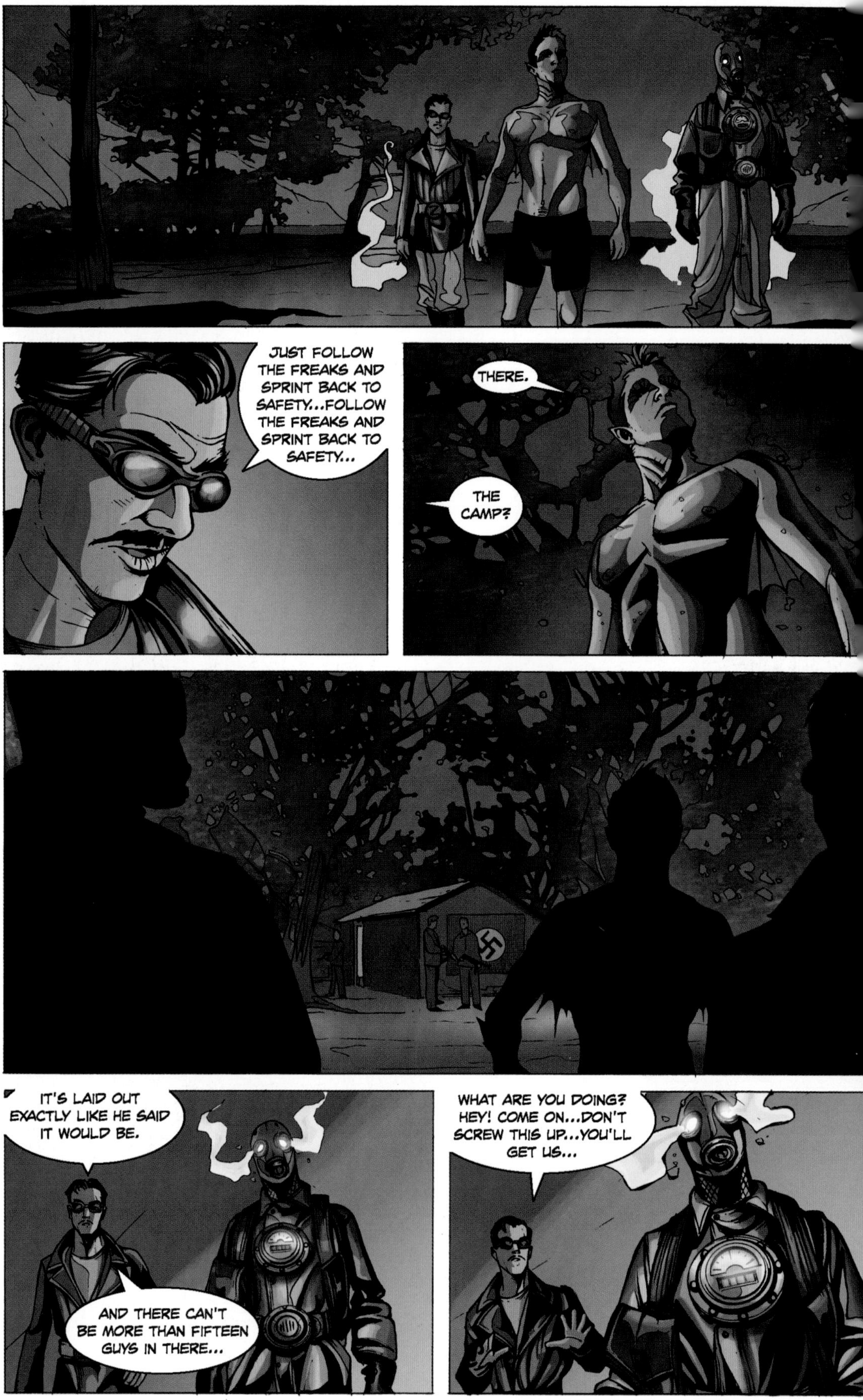
JUST FOLLOW THE FREAKS AND SPRINT BACK TO SAFETY...FOLLOW THE FREAKS AND SPRINT BACK TO SAFETY...
THERE.
THE CAMP?
IT'S LAID OUT EXACTLY LIKE HE SAID IT WOULD BE.
AND THERE CAN'T BE MORE THAN FIFTEEN GUYS IN THERE...
WHAT ARE YOU DOING? HEY! COME ON...DON'T SCREW THIS UP...YOU'LL GET US...

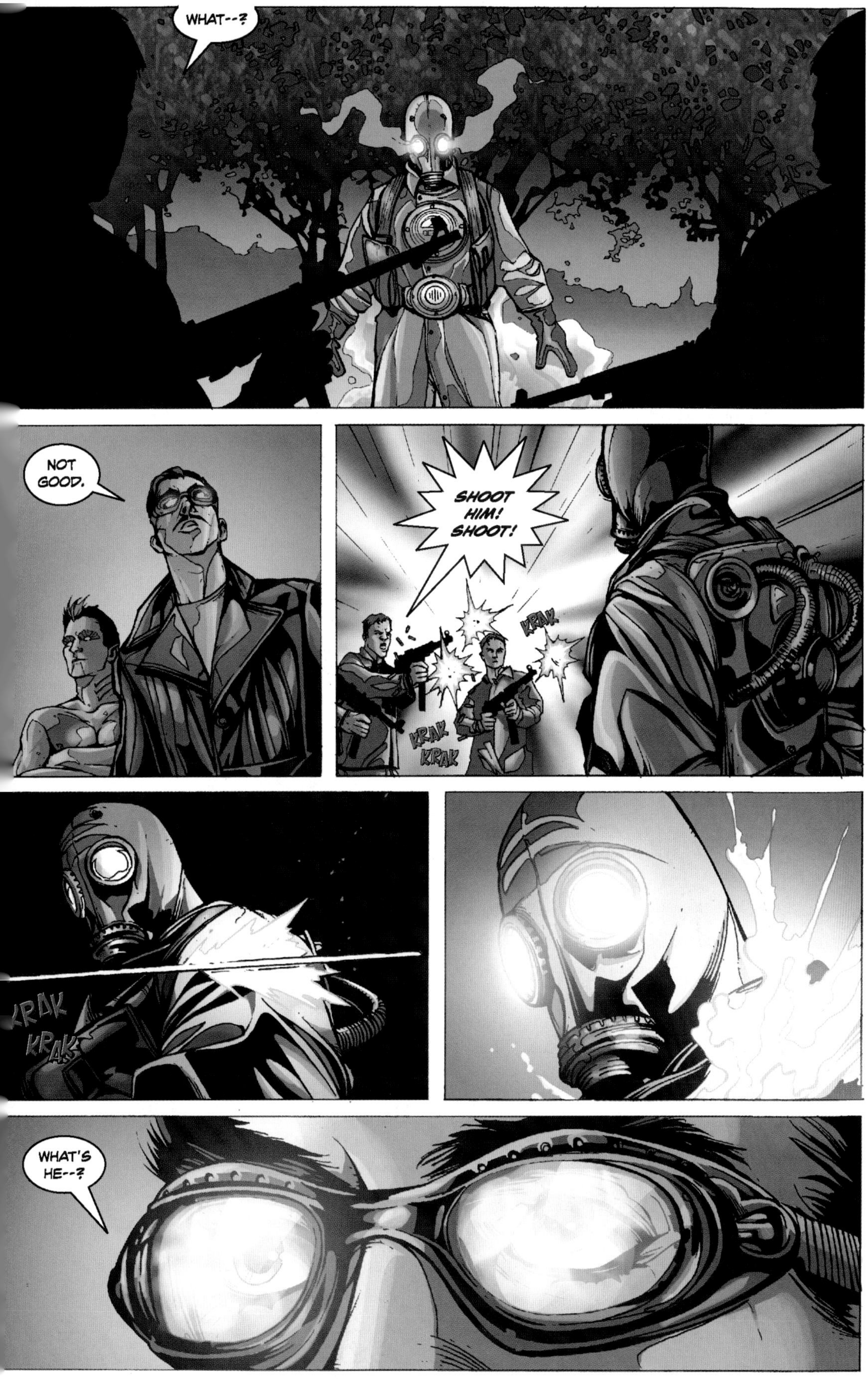
WHAT--?
NOT GOOD.
SHOOT HIM! SHOOT!
KRAK
KRAK KRAK
KRAK KRAK
WHAT'S HE--?

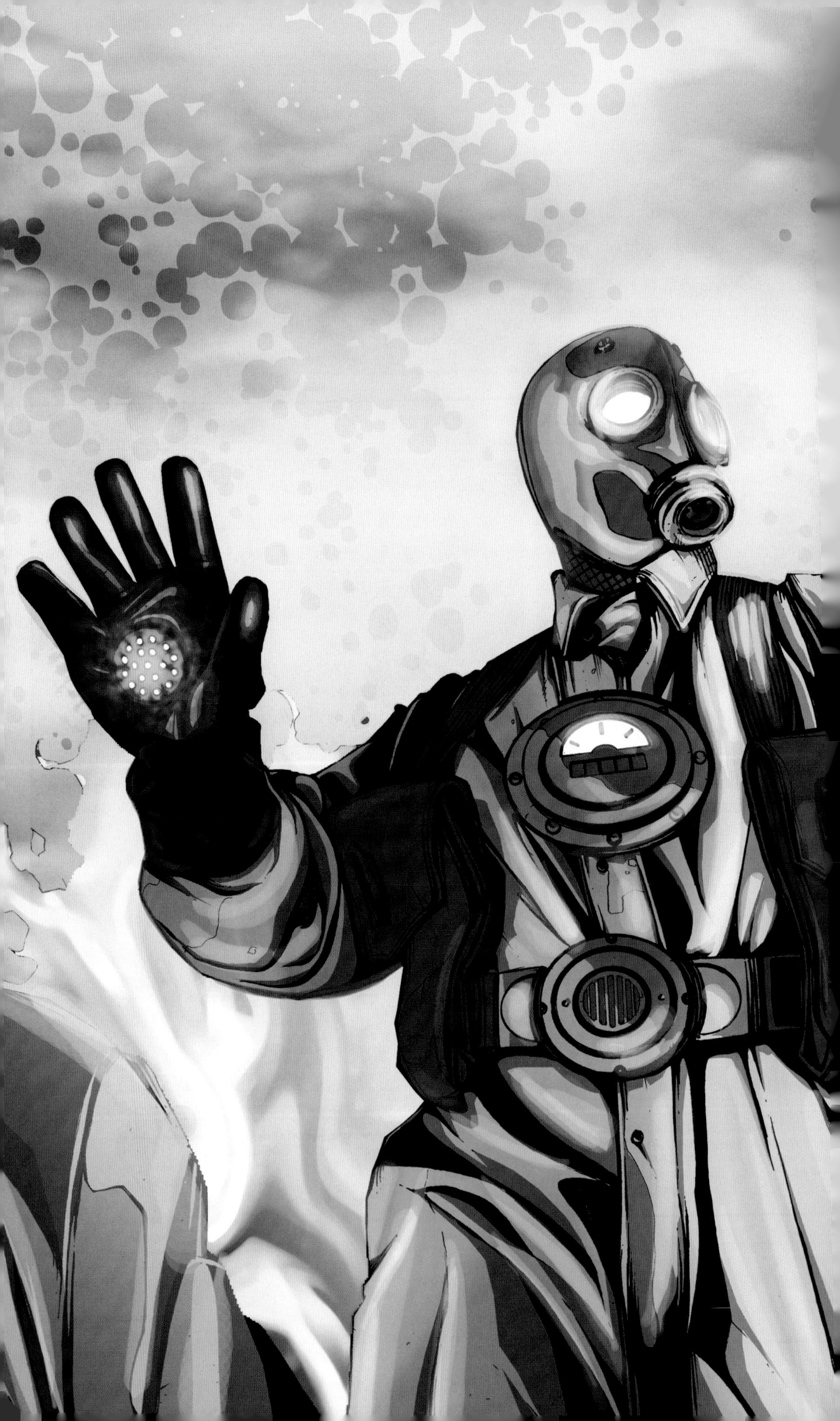

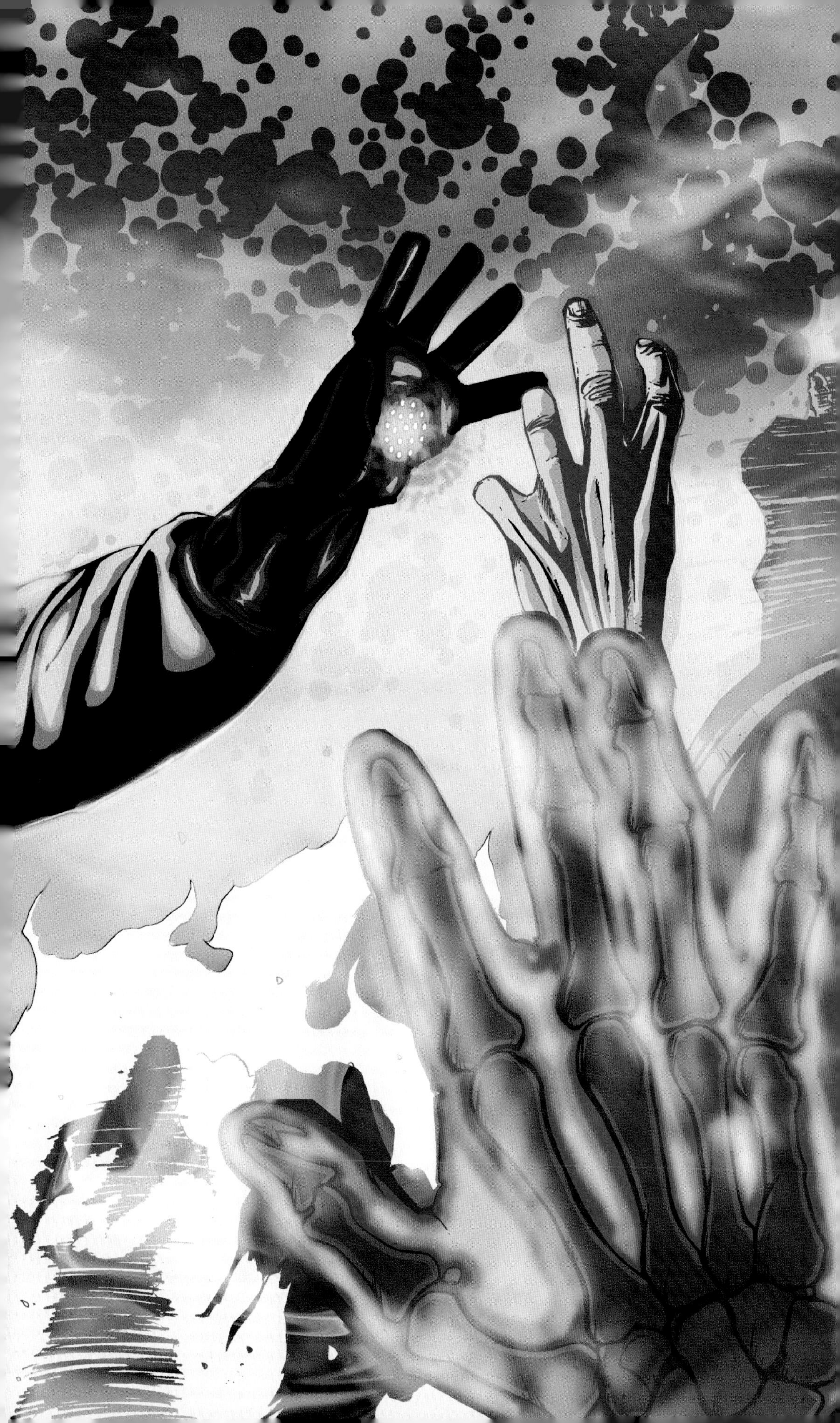

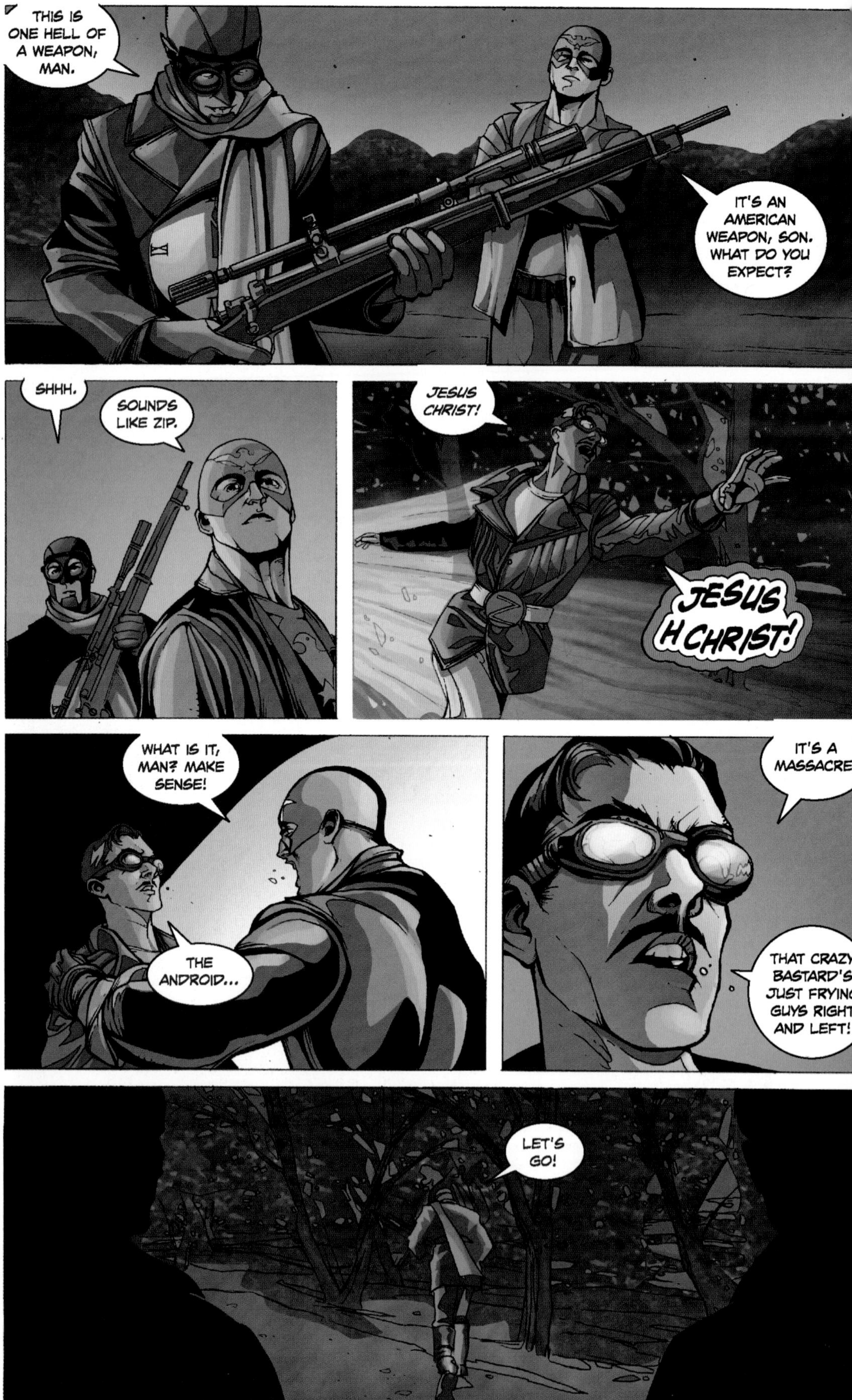
THIS IS ONE HELL OF A WEAPON, MAN.
IT'S AN AMERICAN WEAPON, SON. WHAT DO YOU EXPECT?
SHHH.
SOUNDS LIKE ZIP.
JESUS CHRIST!
JESUS H CHRIST!
WHAT IS IT, MAN? MAKE SENSE!
THE ANDROID...
IT'S A MASSACRE!
THAT CRAZY BASTARD'S JUST FRYING GUYS RIGHT AND LEFT!
LET'S GO!

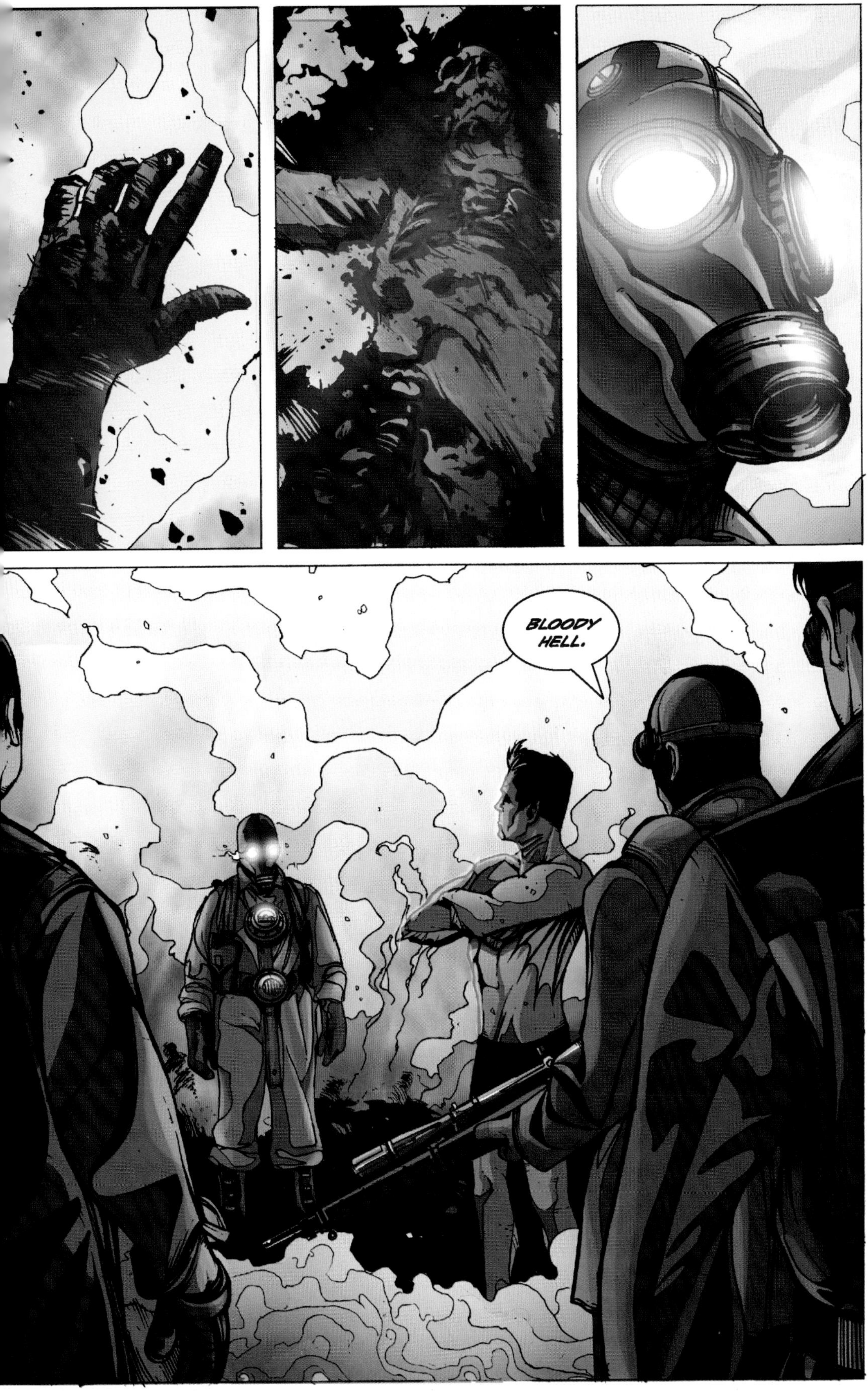
BLOODY HELL.

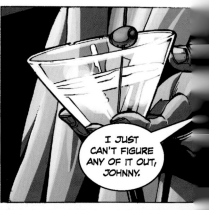

I JUST CAN'T FIGURE ANY OF IT OUT, JOHNNY.

DON'T KNOW WHAT THEY'RE PAYING YOU, MID-NITE, BUT A LOT OF MONEY MAKES A LOT OF WORRIES DISAPPEAR.

YEAH.

AND, FOR THE RECORD, THEY'RE NOT PAYING ME ANYTHING.

SEE, NOW I'M WORRIED ABOUT YOU, SUPER SPY.

EVEN IF THOSE NAZIS WEREN'T SHOOTING BACK AT US--

I WOULDN'T RISK IT FOR FREE.

I'M SURE YOU WOULDN'T.

HELL, NO.

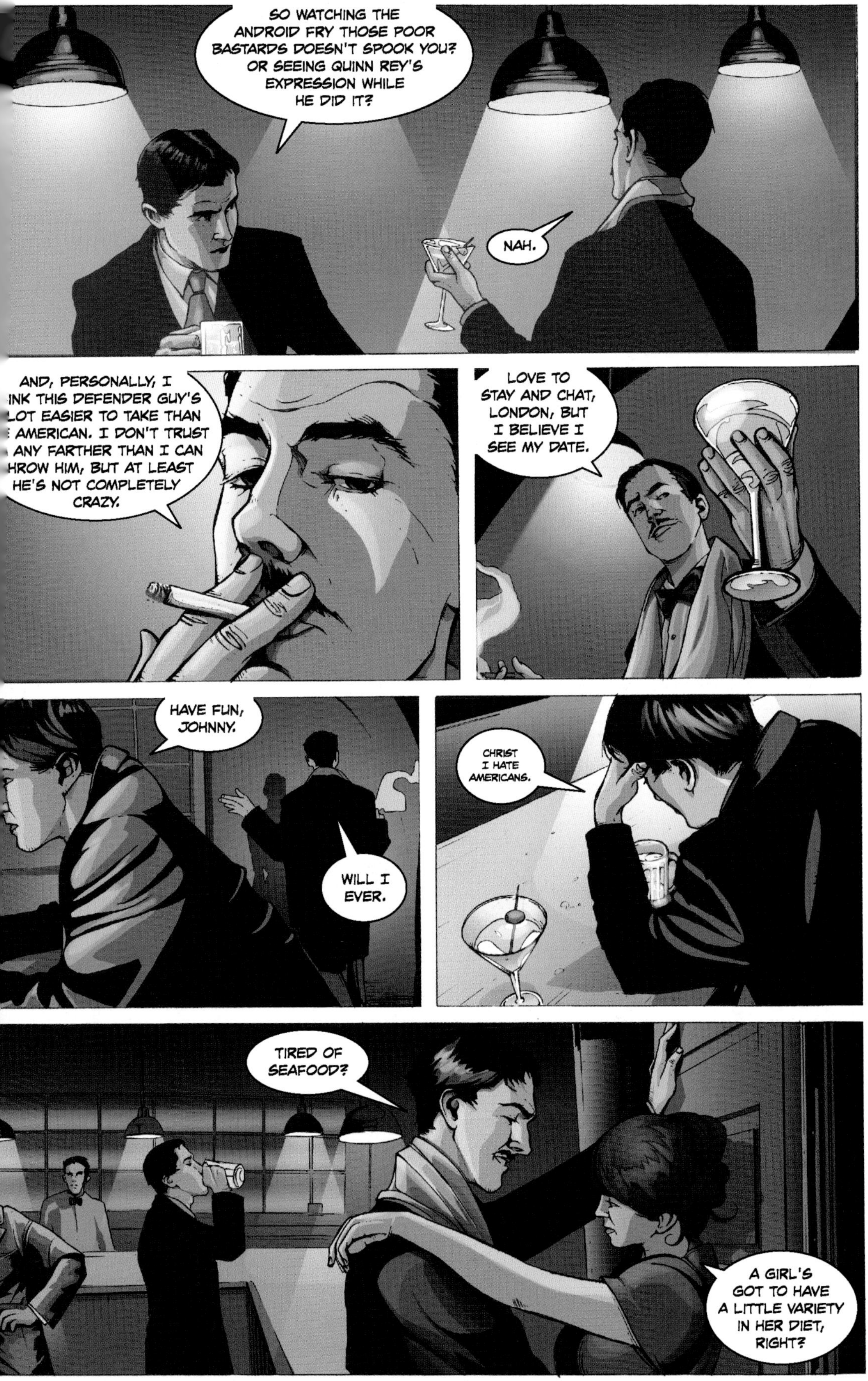
SO WATCHING THE ANDROID FRY THOSE POOR BASTARDS DOESN'T SPOOK YOU? OR SEEING QUINN REY'S EXPRESSION WHILE HE DID IT?
NAH.
AND, PERSONALLY, I INK THIS DEFENDER GUY'S LOT EASIER TO TAKE THAN AMERICAN. I DON'T TRUST ANY FARTHER THAN I CAN HROW HIM, BUT AT LEAST HE'S NOT COMPLETELY CRAZY.
LOVE TO STAY AND CHAT, LONDON, BUT I BELIEVE I SEE MY DATE.
HAVE FUN, JOHNNY.
WILL I EVER.
CHRIST I HATE AMERICANS.
TIRED OF SEAFOOD?
A GIRL'S GOT TO HAVE A LITTLE VARIETY IN HER DIET, RIGHT?

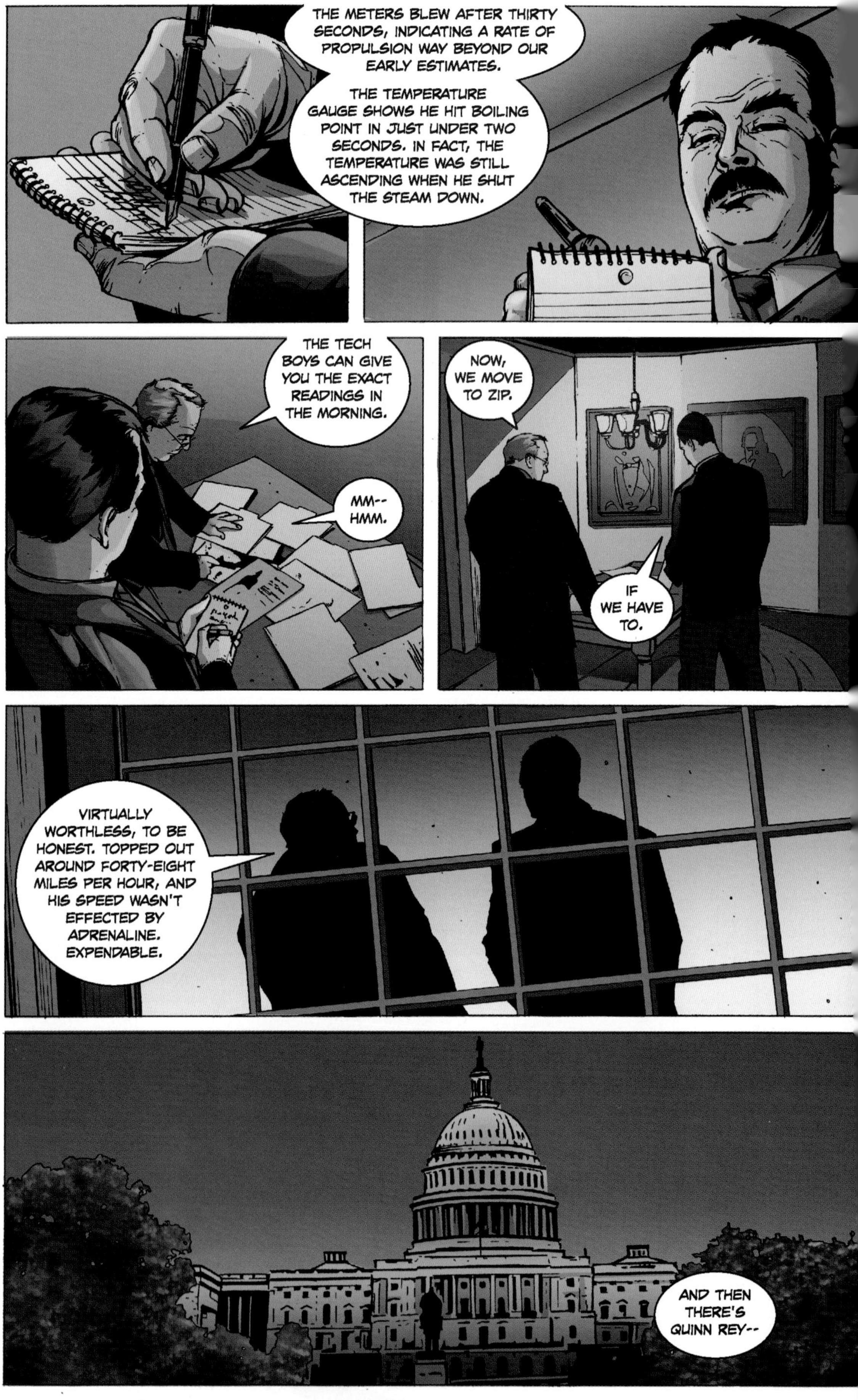
THE METERS BLEW AFTER THIRTY SECONDS, INDICATING A RATE OF PROPULSION WAY BEYOND OUR EARLY ESTIMATES.
THE TEMPERATURE GAUGE SHOWS HE HIT BOILING POINT IN JUST UNDER TWO SECONDS. IN FACT, THE TEMPERATURE WAS STILL ASCENDING WHEN HE SHUT THE STEAM DOWN.
THE TECH BOYS CAN GIVE YOU THE EXACT READINGS IN THE MORNING.
MM-- HMM.
NOW, WE MOVE TO ZIP.
IF WE HAVE TO.
VIRTUALLY WORTHLESS, TO BE HONEST. TOPPED OUT AROUND FORTY-EIGHT MILES PER HOUR, AND HIS SPEED WASN'T EFFECTED BY ADRENALINE. EXPENDABLE.
AND THEN THERE'S QUINN REY--

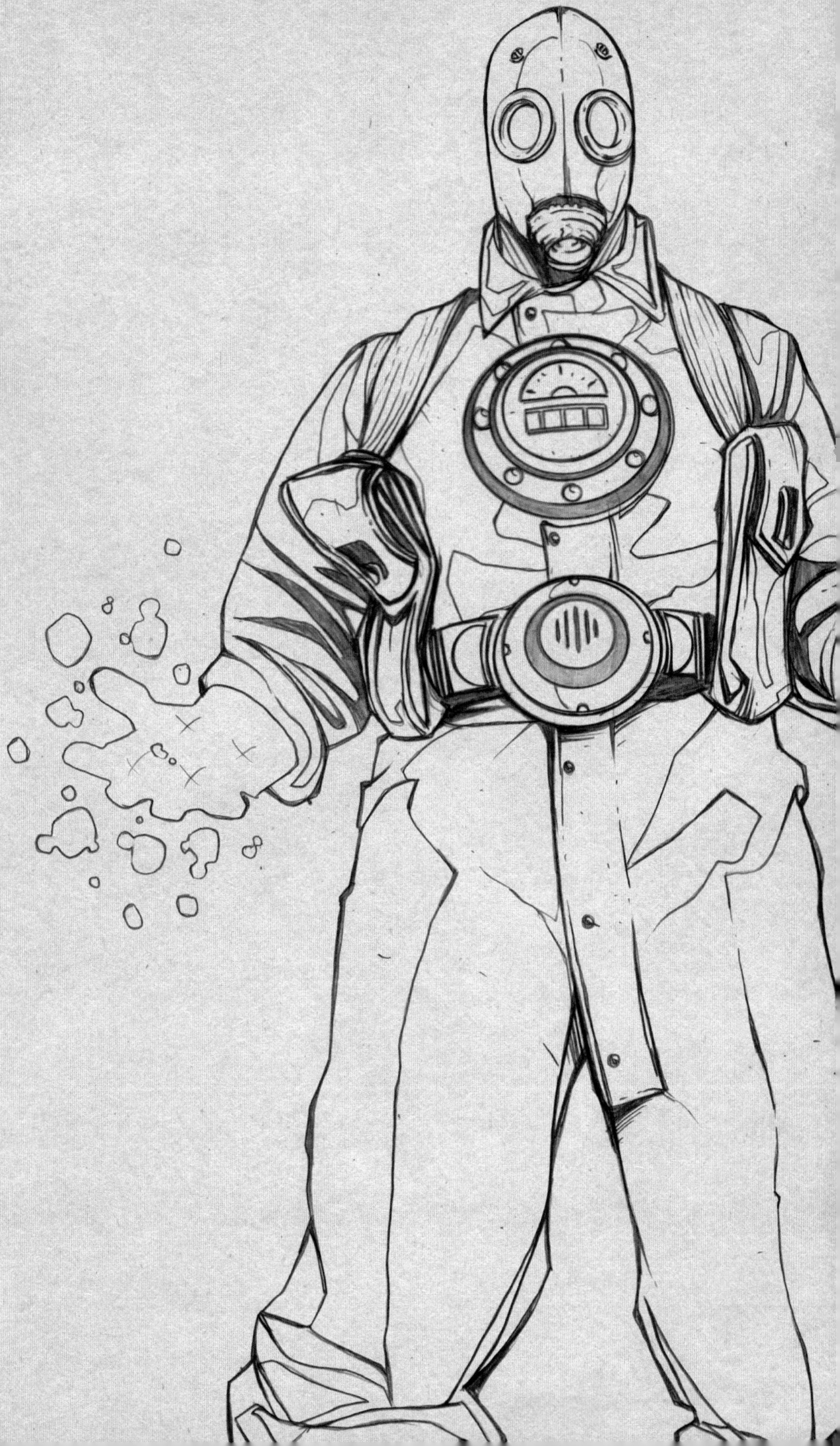

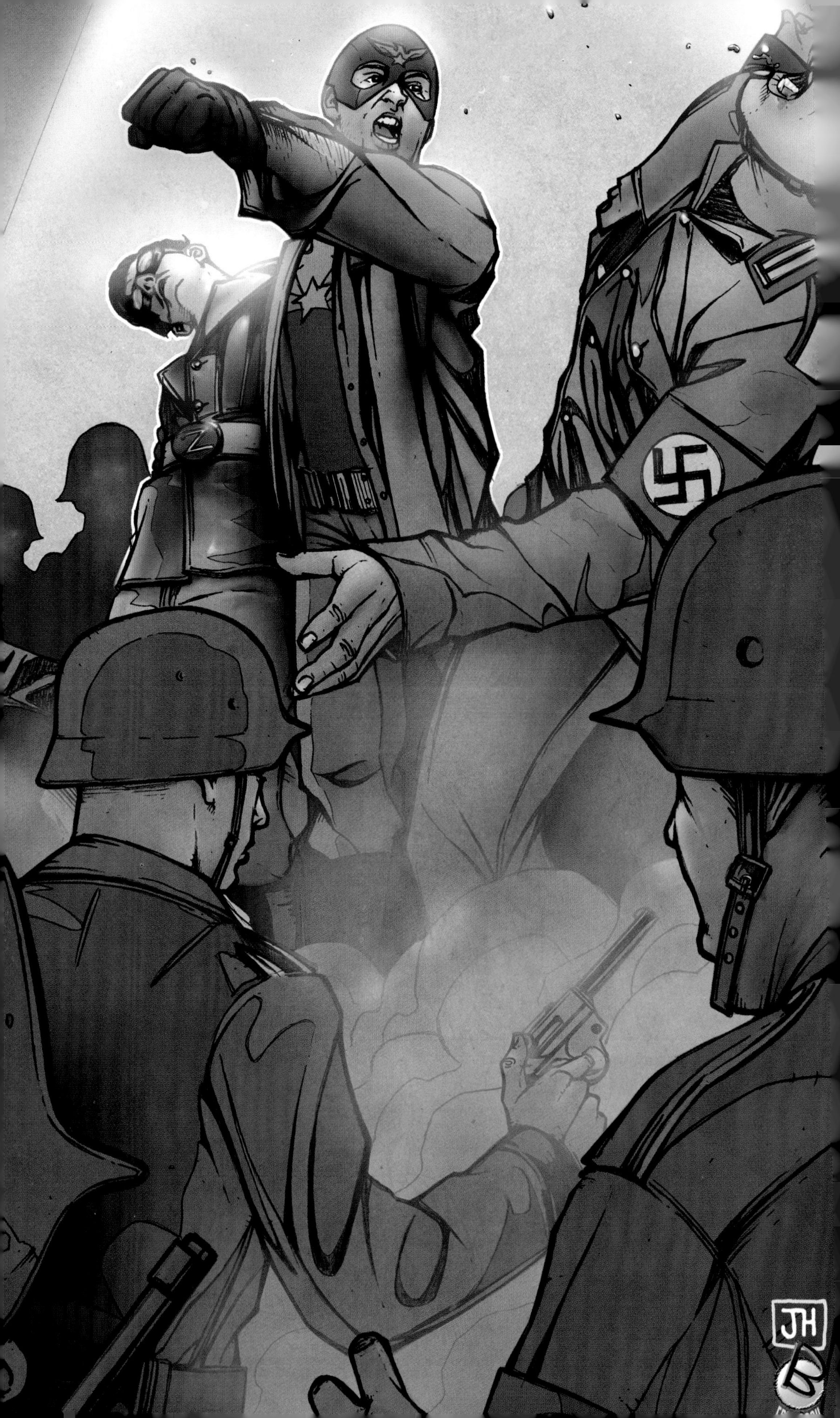

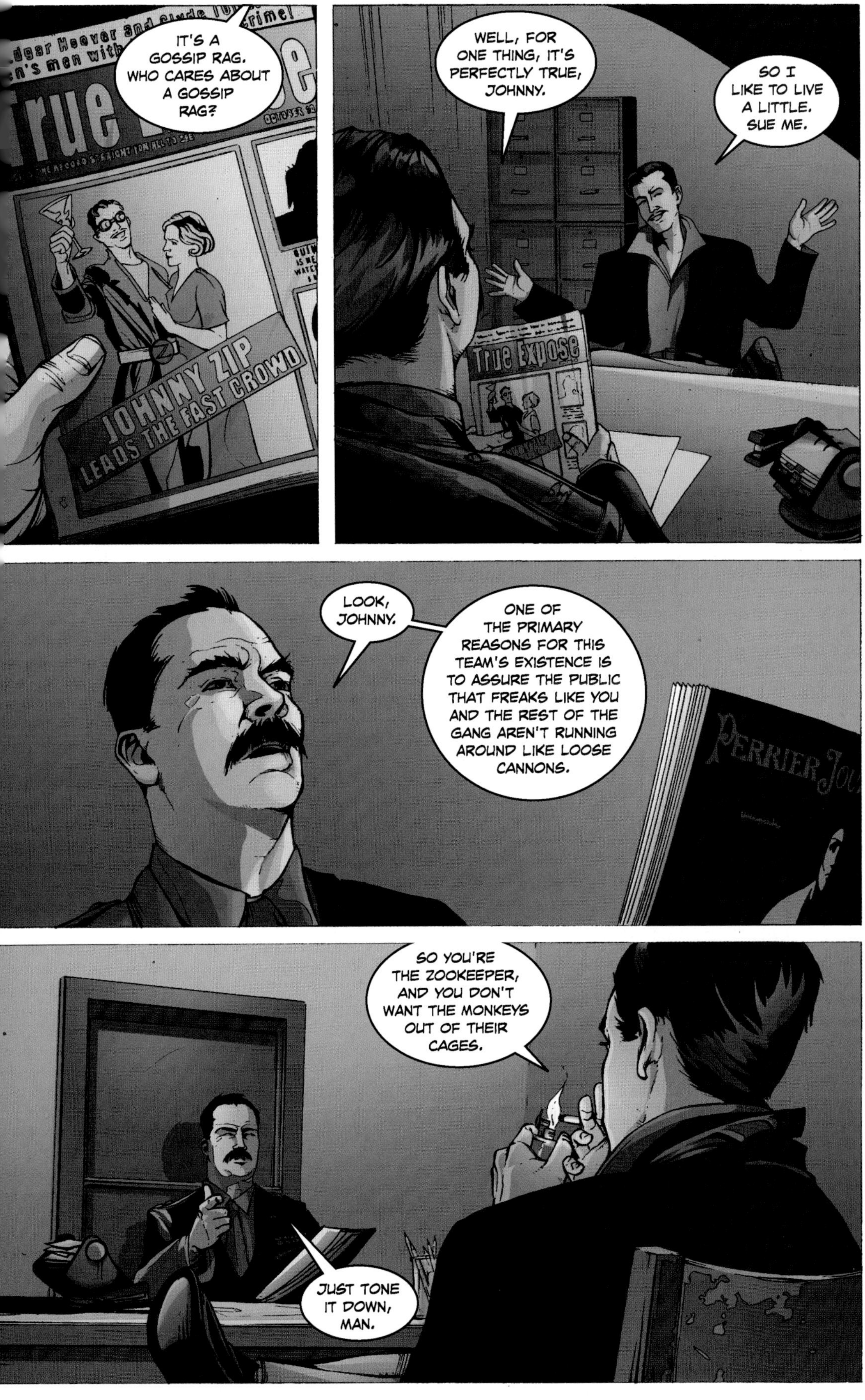
IT'S A GOSSIP RAG. WHO CARES ABOUT A GOSSIP RAG?
JOHNNY ZIP LEADS THE FAST CROWD
WELL, FOR ONE THING, IT'S PERFECTLY TRUE, JOHNNY.
SO I LIKE TO LIVE A LITTLE. SUE ME.
True Expose
LOOK, JOHNNY.
ONE OF THE PRIMARY REASONS FOR THIS TEAM'S EXISTENCE IS TO ASSURE THE PUBLIC THAT FREAKS LIKE YOU AND THE REST OF THE GANG AREN'T RUNNING AROUND LIKE LOOSE CANNONS.
SO YOU'RE THE ZOOKEEPER, AND YOU DON'T WANT THE MONKEYS OUT OF THEIR CAGES.
JUST TONE IT DOWN, MAN.

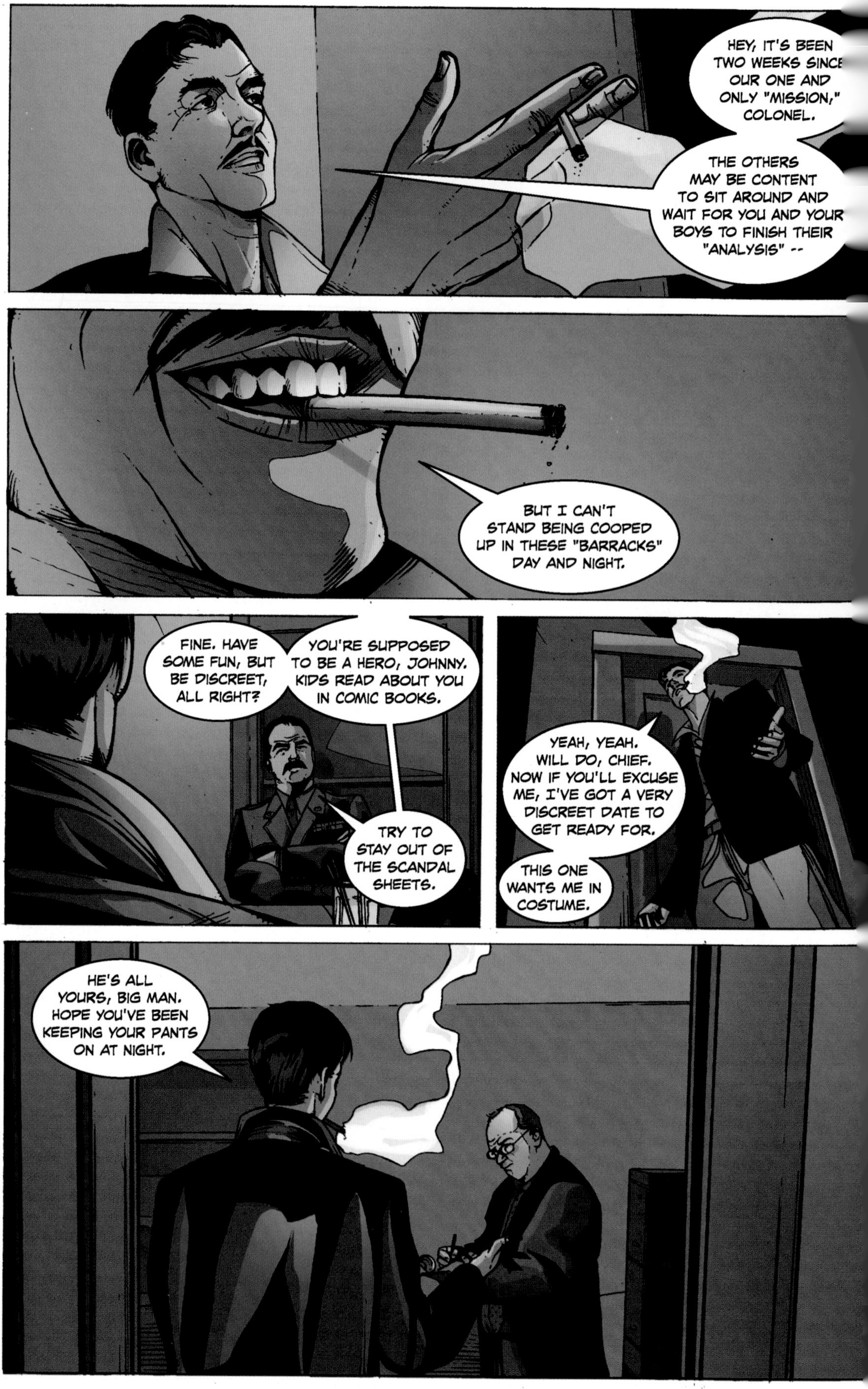
HEY, IT'S BEEN TWO WEEKS SINCE OUR ONE AND ONLY "MISSION," COLONEL.
THE OTHERS MAY BE CONTENT TO SIT AROUND AND WAIT FOR YOU AND YOUR BOYS TO FINISH THEIR "ANALYSIS" --
BUT I CAN'T STAND BEING COOPED UP IN THESE "BARRACKS" DAY AND NIGHT.
FINE. HAVE SOME FUN, BUT BE DISCREET, ALL RIGHT?
YOU'RE SUPPOSED TO BE A HERO, JOHNNY. KIDS READ ABOUT YOU IN COMIC BOOKS.
TRY TO STAY OUT OF THE SCANDAL SHEETS.
YEAH, YEAH. WILL DO, CHIEF. NOW IF YOU'LL EXCUSE ME, I'VE GOT A VERY DISCREET DATE TO GET READY FOR.
THIS ONE WANTS ME IN COSTUME.
HE'S ALL YOURS, BIG MAN. HOPE YOU'VE BEEN KEEPING YOUR PANTS ON AT NIGHT.

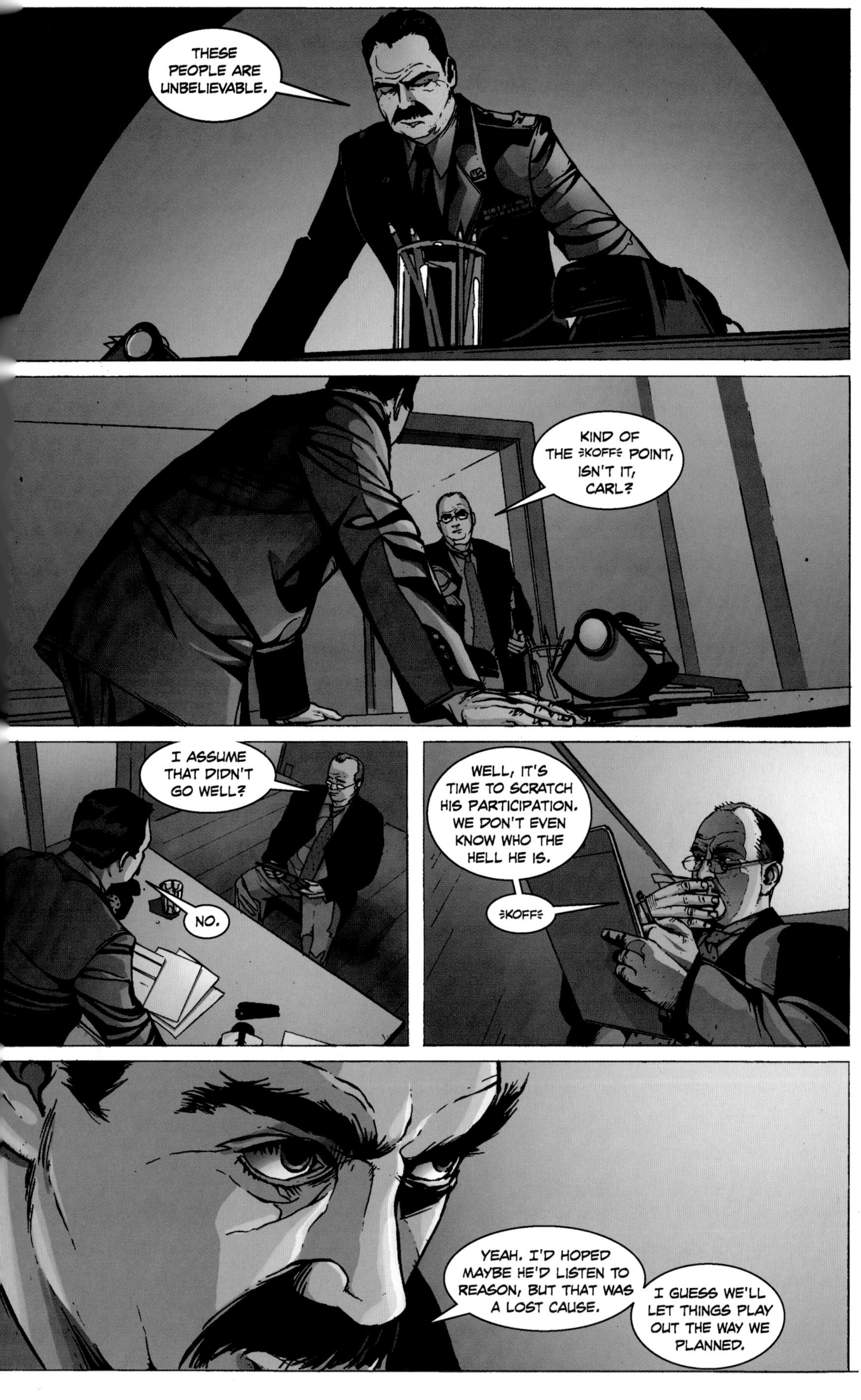
THESE PEOPLE ARE UNBELIEVABLE.
KIND OF THE *KOFF* POINT, ISN'T IT, CARL?
I ASSUME THAT DIDN'T GO WELL?
NO.
WELL, IT'S TIME TO SCRATCH HIS PARTICIPATION. WE DON'T EVEN KNOW WHO THE HELL HE IS.
KOFF
YEAH. I'D HOPED MAYBE HE'D LISTEN TO REASON, BUT THAT WAS A LOST CAUSE.
I GUESS WE'LL LET THINGS PLAY OUT THE WAY WE PLANNED.

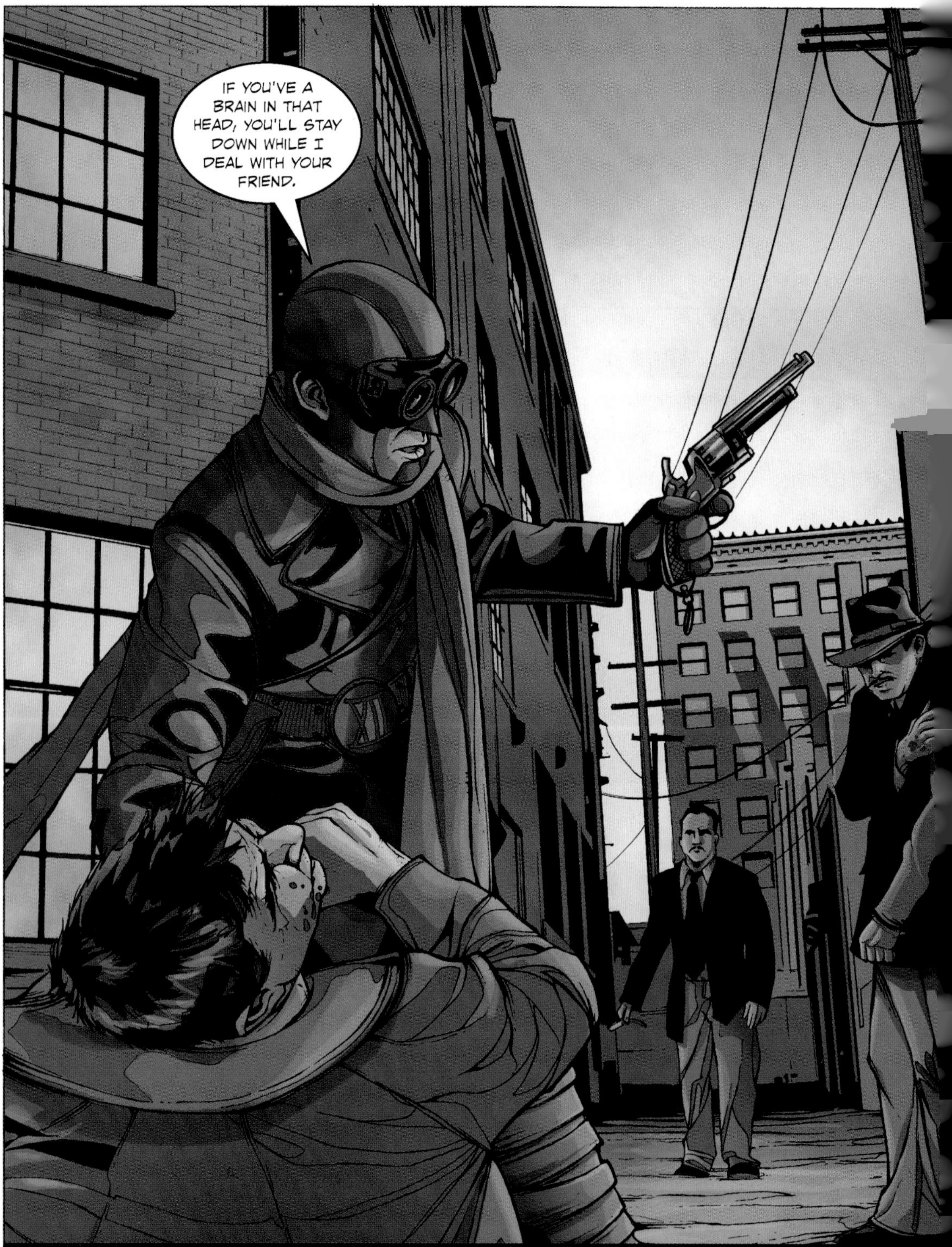
IF YOU'VE A BRAIN IN THAT HEAD, YOU'LL STAY DOWN WHILE I DEAL WITH YOUR FRIEND.

BATTLE HYMN:

Book Three

"THE TRIPWIRE"

Written by B. Clay Moore
Art by Jeremy Haun
Colors by Dave Bryant
Letters by Greg Thompson

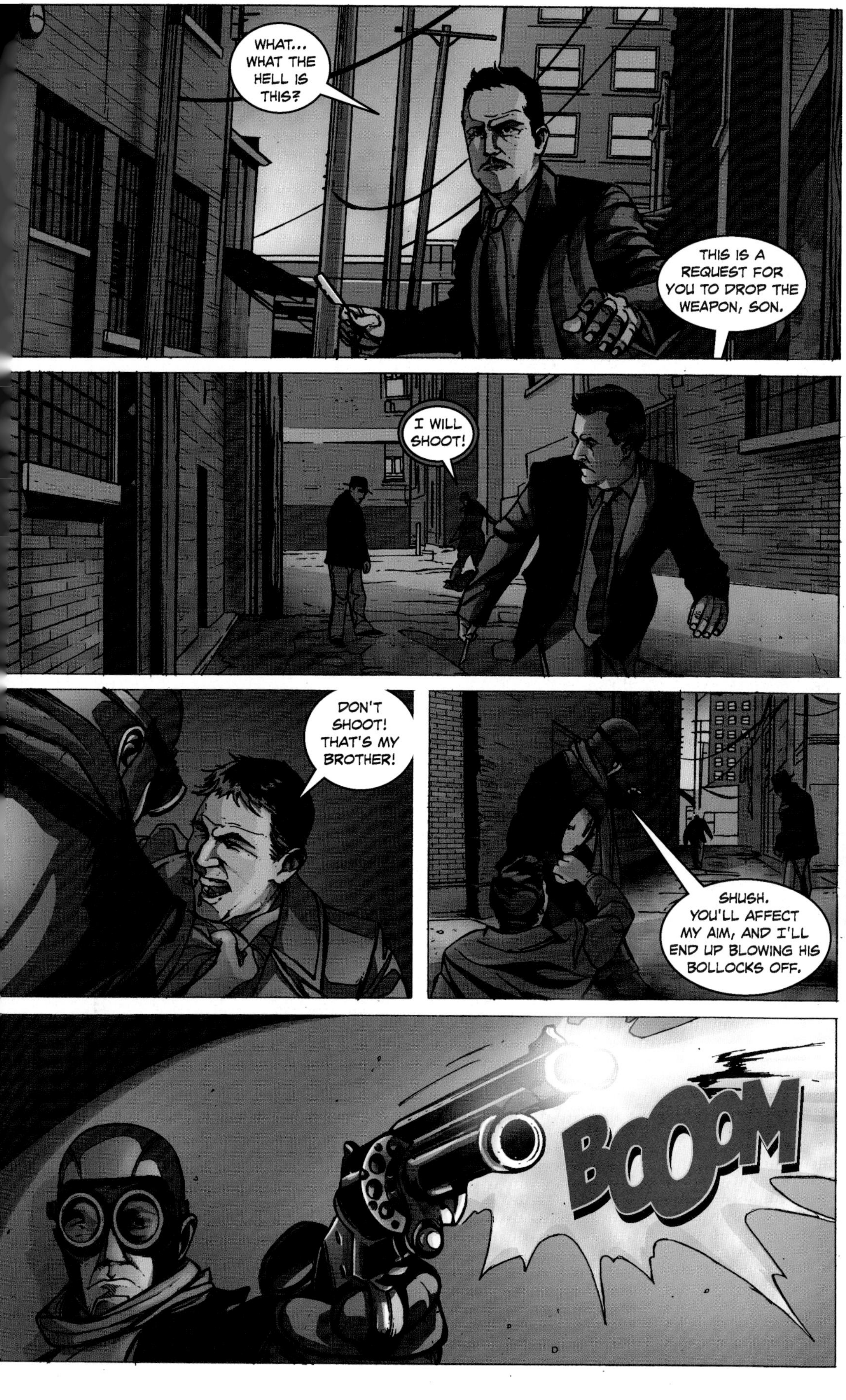
WHAT... WHAT THE HELL IS THIS?
THIS IS A REQUEST FOR YOU TO DROP THE WEAPON, SON.
I WILL SHOOT!
DON'T SHOOT! THAT'S MY BROTHER!
SHUSH. YOU'LL AFFECT MY AIM, AND I'LL END UP BLOWING HIS BOLLOCKS OFF.
BOOOM

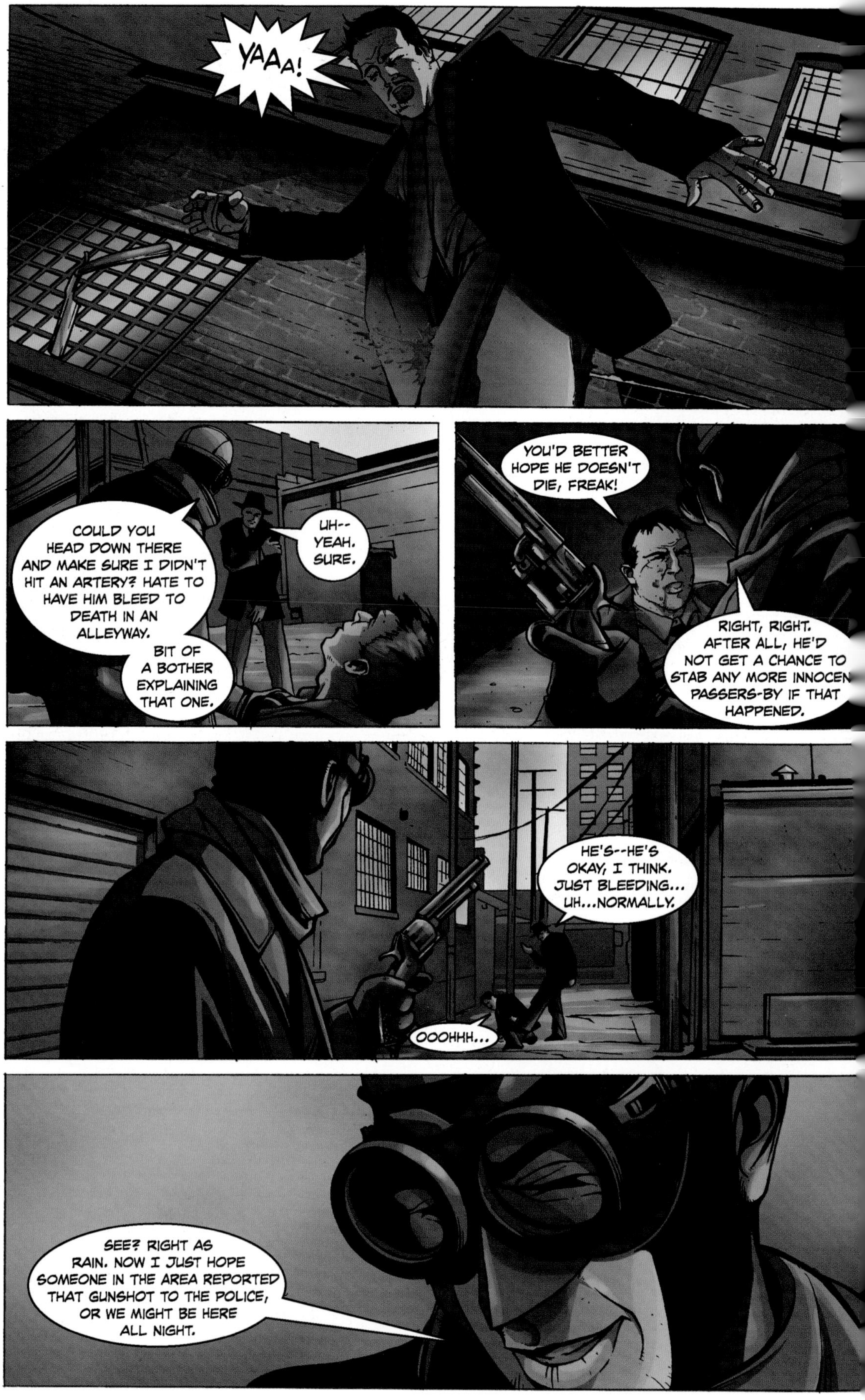
YAAA!
COULD YOU HEAD DOWN THERE AND MAKE SURE I DIDN'T HIT AN ARTERY? HATE TO HAVE HIM BLEED TO DEATH IN AN ALLEYWAY.
BIT OF A BOTHER EXPLAINING THAT ONE.
UH--YEAH. SURE.
YOU'D BETTER HOPE HE DOESN'T DIE, FREAK!
RIGHT, RIGHT. AFTER ALL, HE'D NOT GET A CHANCE TO STAB ANY MORE INNOCEN PASSERS-BY IF THAT HAPPENED.
HE'S--HE'S OKAY, I THINK. JUST BLEEDING... UH...NORMALLY.
OOOHHH...
SEE? RIGHT AS RAIN. NOW I JUST HOPE SOMEONE IN THE AREA REPORTED THAT GUNSHOT TO THE POLICE, OR WE MIGHT BE HERE ALL NIGHT.

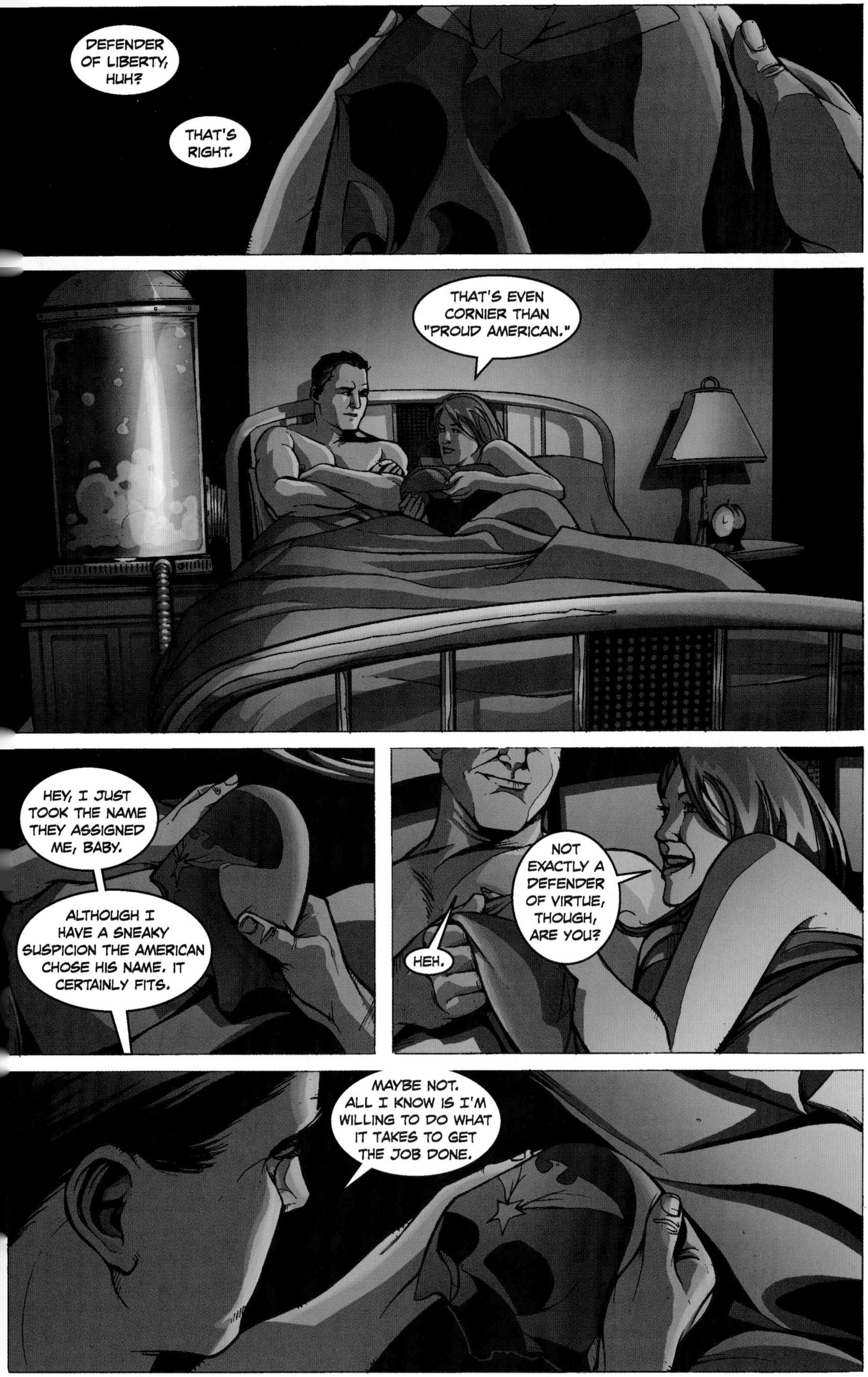
DEFENDER OF LIBERTY, HUH?
THAT'S RIGHT.
THAT'S EVEN CORNIER THAN "PROUD AMERICAN."
HEY, I JUST TOOK THE NAME THEY ASSIGNED ME, BABY.
ALTHOUGH I HAVE A SNEAKY SUSPICION THE AMERICAN CHOSE HIS NAME. IT CERTAINLY FITS.
NOT EXACTLY A DEFENDER OF VIRTUE, THOUGH, ARE YOU?
HEH.
MAYBE NOT. ALL I KNOW IS I'M WILLING TO DO WHAT IT TAKES TO GET THE JOB DONE.

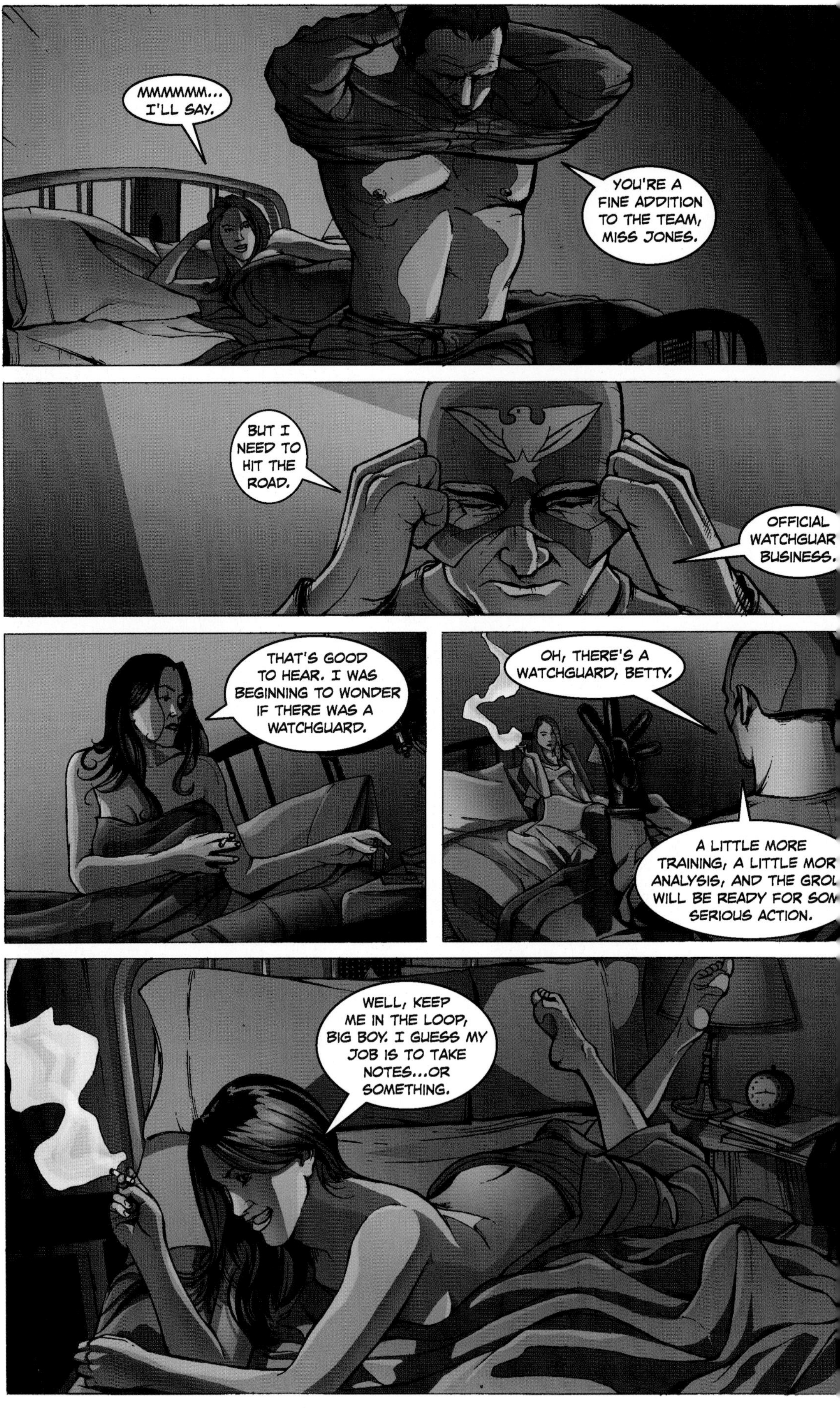

MMMMMM... I'LL SAY.
YOU'RE A FINE ADDITION TO THE TEAM, MISS JONES.
BUT I NEED TO HIT THE ROAD.
OFFICIAL WATCHGUAR BUSINESS.
THAT'S GOOD TO HEAR. I WAS BEGINNING TO WONDER IF THERE WAS A WATCHGUARD.
OH, THERE'S A WATCHGUARD, BETTY.
A LITTLE MORE TRAINING, A LITTLE MOR ANALYSIS, AND THE GROU WILL BE READY FOR SOM SERIOUS ACTION.
WELL, KEEP ME IN THE LOOP, BIG BOY. I GUESS MY JOB IS TO TAKE NOTES...OR SOMETHING.

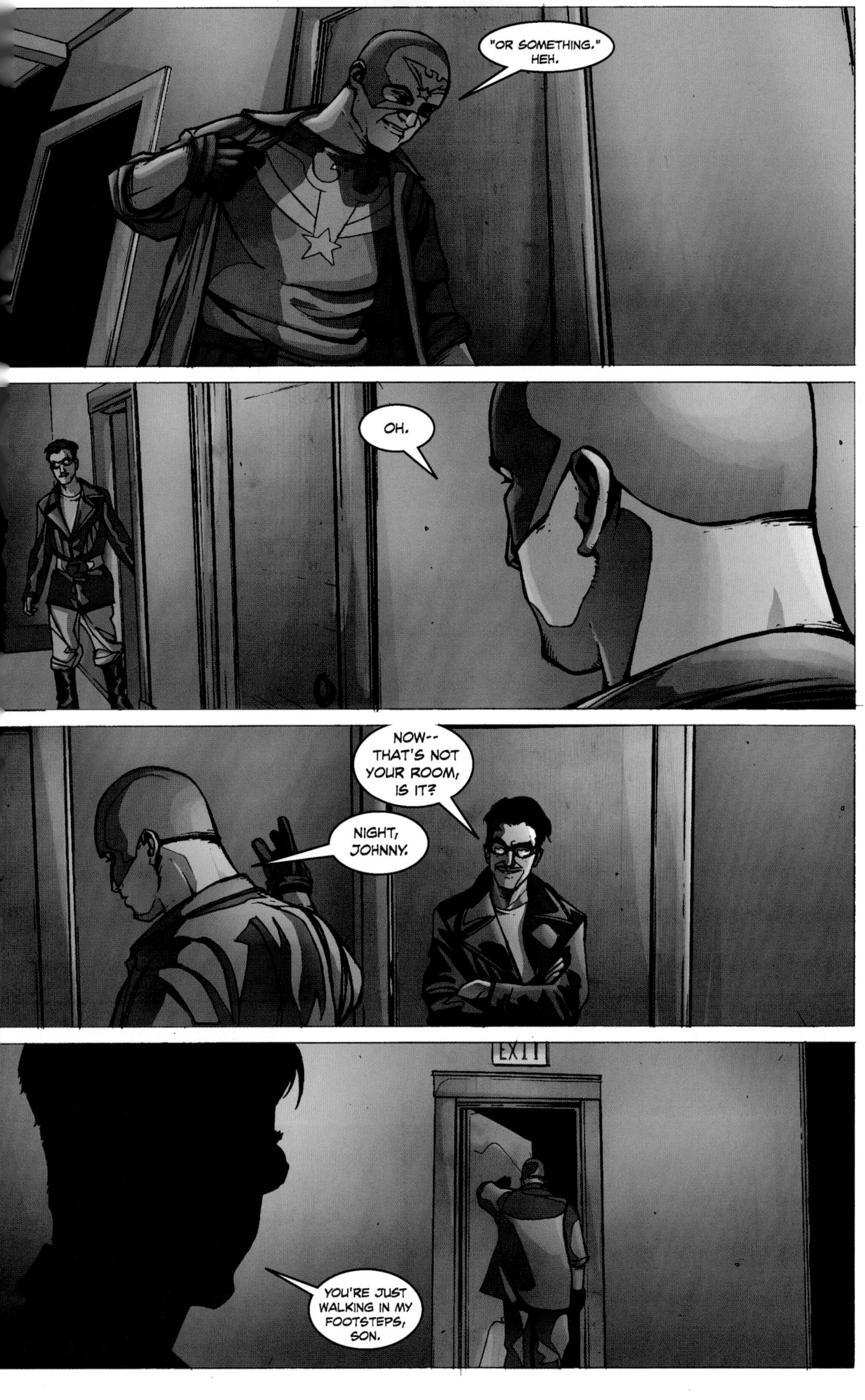
"OR SOMETHING." HEH.
OH.
NOW-- THAT'S NOT YOUR ROOM, IS IT?
NIGHT, JOHNNY.
EXIT
YOU'RE JUST WALKING IN MY FOOTSTEPS, SON.

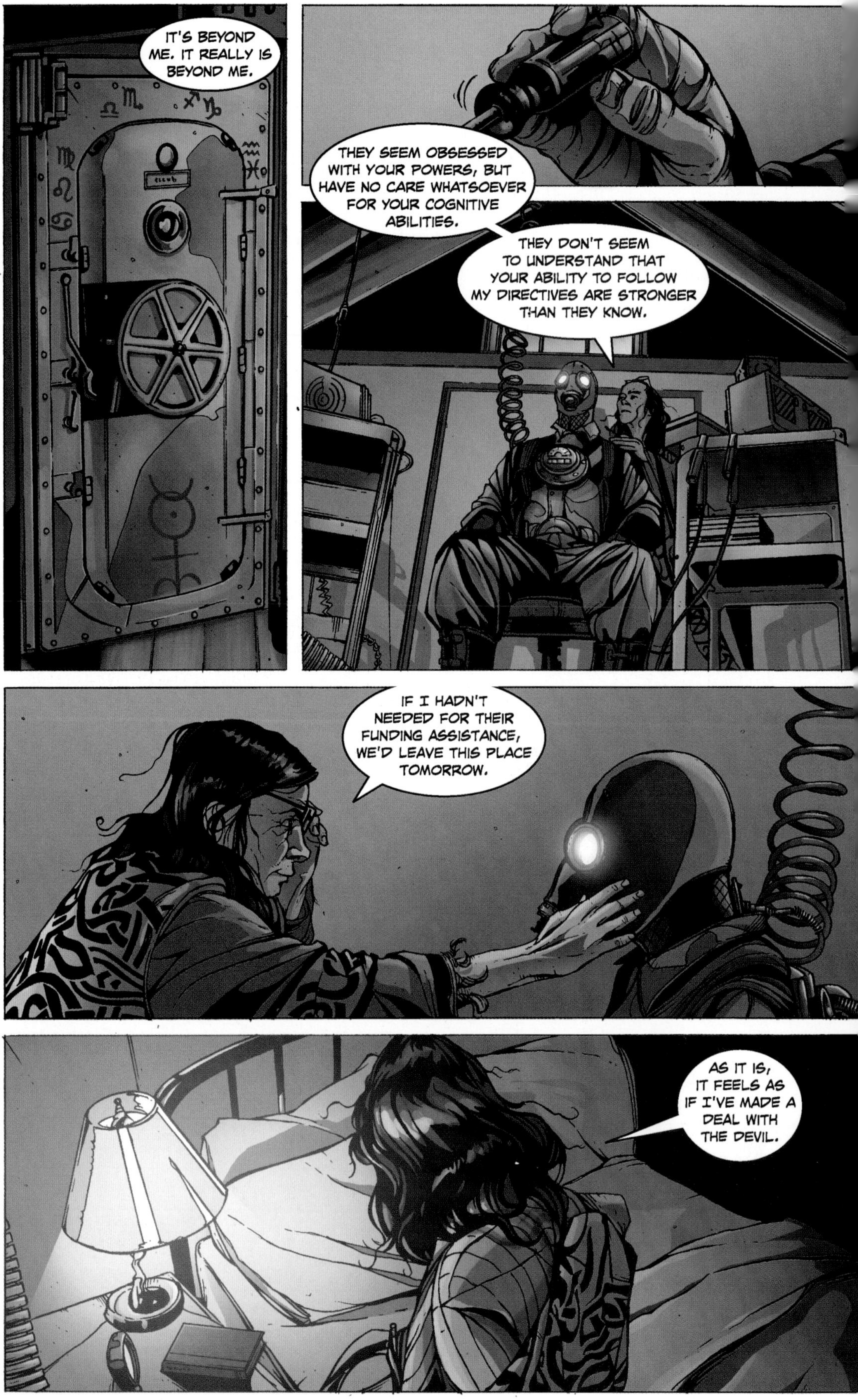
IT'S BEYOND ME. IT REALLY IS BEYOND ME.
THEY SEEM OBSESSED WITH YOUR POWERS, BUT HAVE NO CARE WHATSOEVER FOR YOUR COGNITIVE ABILITIES.
THEY DON'T SEEM TO UNDERSTAND THAT YOUR ABILITY TO FOLLOW MY DIRECTIVES ARE STRONGER THAN THEY KNOW.
IF I HADN'T NEEDED FOR THEIR FUNDING ASSISTANCE, WE'D LEAVE THIS PLACE TOMORROW.
AS IT IS, IT FEELS AS IF I'VE MADE A DEAL WITH THE DEVIL.

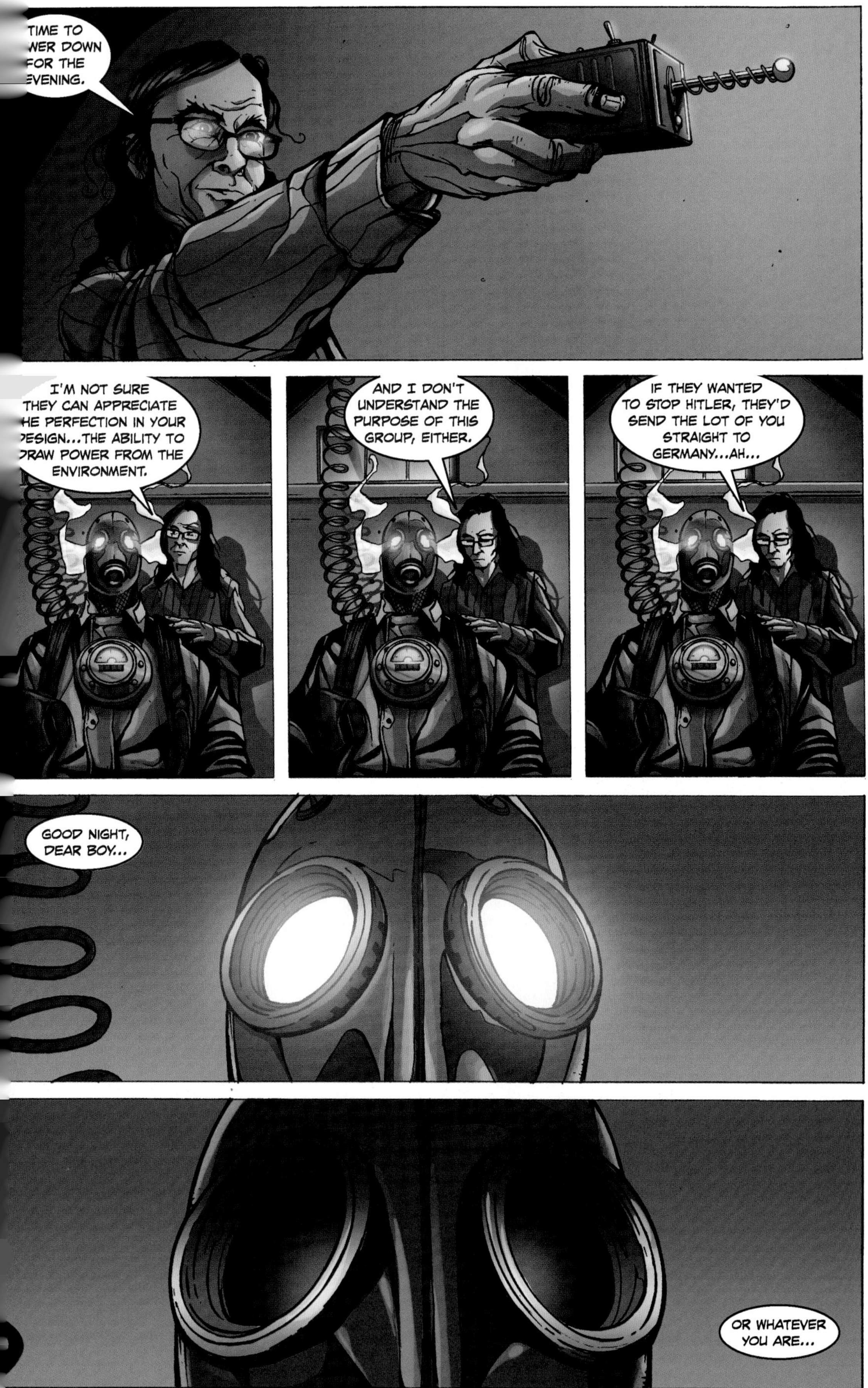
TIME TO
WER DOWN
FOR THE
EVENING.
I'M NOT SURE THEY CAN APPRECIATE HE PERFECTION IN YOUR ESIGN...THE ABILITY TO RAW POWER FROM THE ENVIRONMENT.
AND I DON'T UNDERSTAND THE PURPOSE OF THIS GROUP, EITHER.
IF THEY WANTED TO STOP HITLER, THEY'D SEND THE LOT OF YOU STRAIGHT TO GERMANY...AH...
GOOD NIGHT, DEAR BOY...
OR WHATEVER YOU ARE...

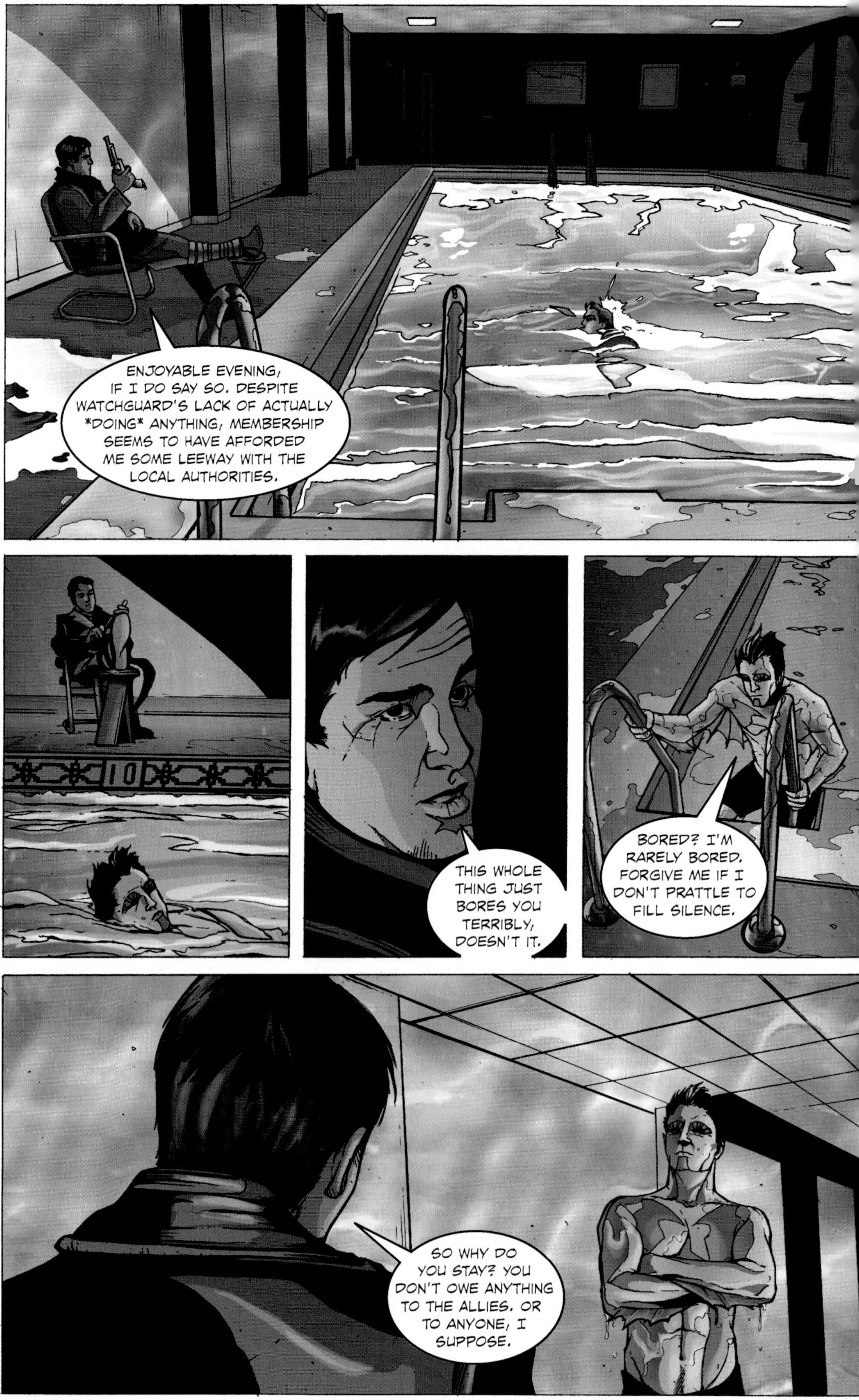
ENJOYABLE EVENING, IF I DO SAY SO. DESPITE WATCHGUARD'S LACK OF ACTUALLY *DOING* ANYTHING, MEMBERSHIP SEEMS TO HAVE AFFORDED ME SOME LEEWAY WITH THE LOCAL AUTHORITIES.
10
THIS WHOLE THING JUST BORES YOU TERRIBLY, DOESN'T IT.
BORED? I'M RARELY BORED. FORGIVE ME IF I DON'T PRATTLE TO FILL SILENCE.
SO WHY DO YOU STAY? YOU DON'T OWE ANYTHING TO THE ALLIES. OR TO ANYONE, I SUPPOSE.

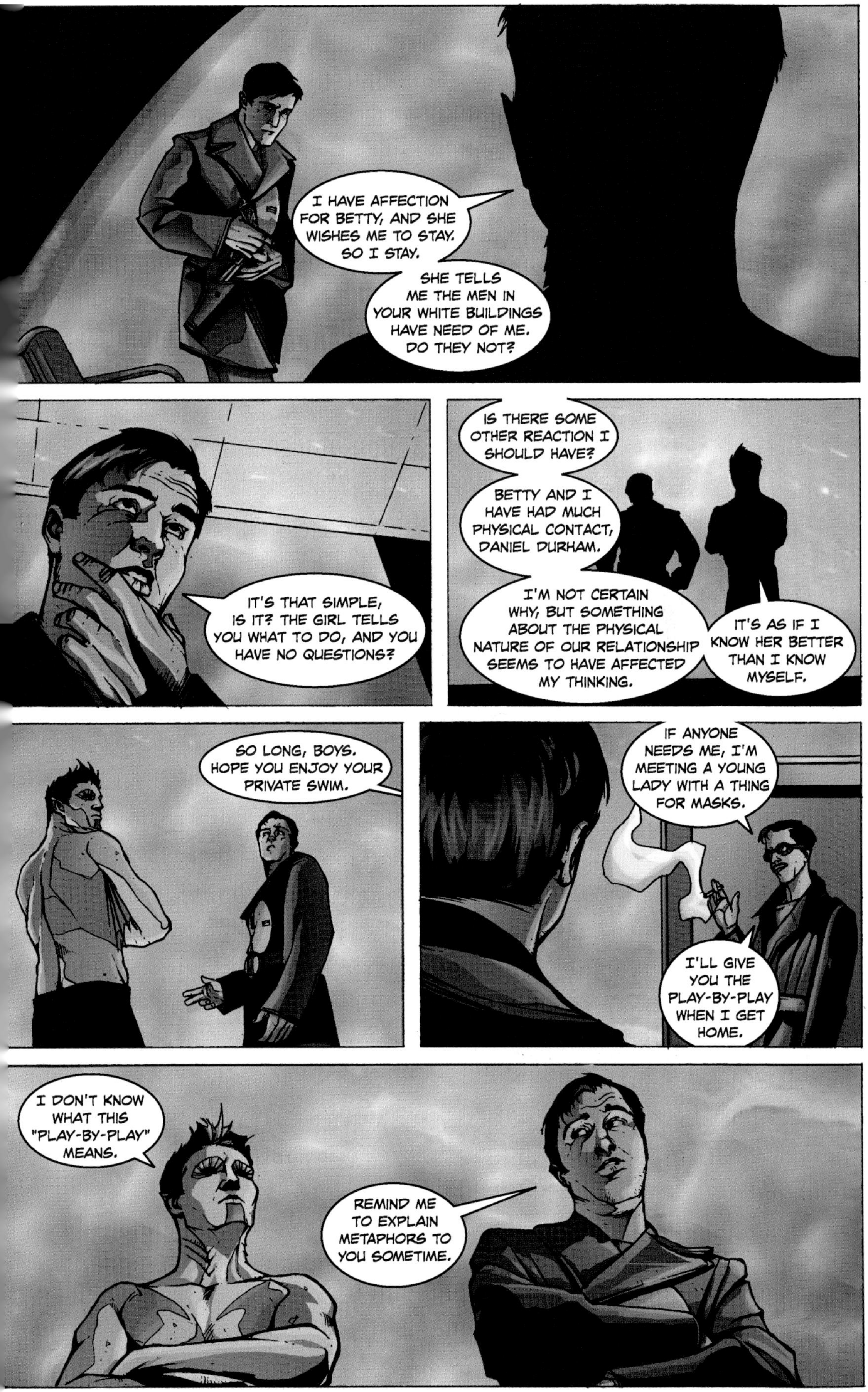
I HAVE AFFECTION FOR BETTY, AND SHE WISHES ME TO STAY. SO I STAY.
SHE TELLS ME THE MEN IN YOUR WHITE BUILDINGS HAVE NEED OF ME. DO THEY NOT?
IT'S THAT SIMPLE, IS IT? THE GIRL TELLS YOU WHAT TO DO, AND YOU HAVE NO QUESTIONS?
IS THERE SOME OTHER REACTION I SHOULD HAVE?
BETTY AND I HAVE HAD MUCH PHYSICAL CONTACT, DANIEL DURHAM.
I'M NOT CERTAIN WHY, BUT SOMETHING ABOUT THE PHYSICAL NATURE OF OUR RELATIONSHIP SEEMS TO HAVE AFFECTED MY THINKING.
IT'S AS IF I KNOW HER BETTER THAN I KNOW MYSELF.
SO LONG, BOYS. HOPE YOU ENJOY YOUR PRIVATE SWIM.
IF ANYONE NEEDS ME, I'M MEETING A YOUNG LADY WITH A THING FOR MASKS.
I'LL GIVE YOU THE PLAY-BY-PLAY WHEN I GET HOME.
I DON'T KNOW WHAT THIS "PLAY-BY-PLAY" MEANS.
REMIND ME TO EXPLAIN METAPHORS TO YOU SOMETIME.

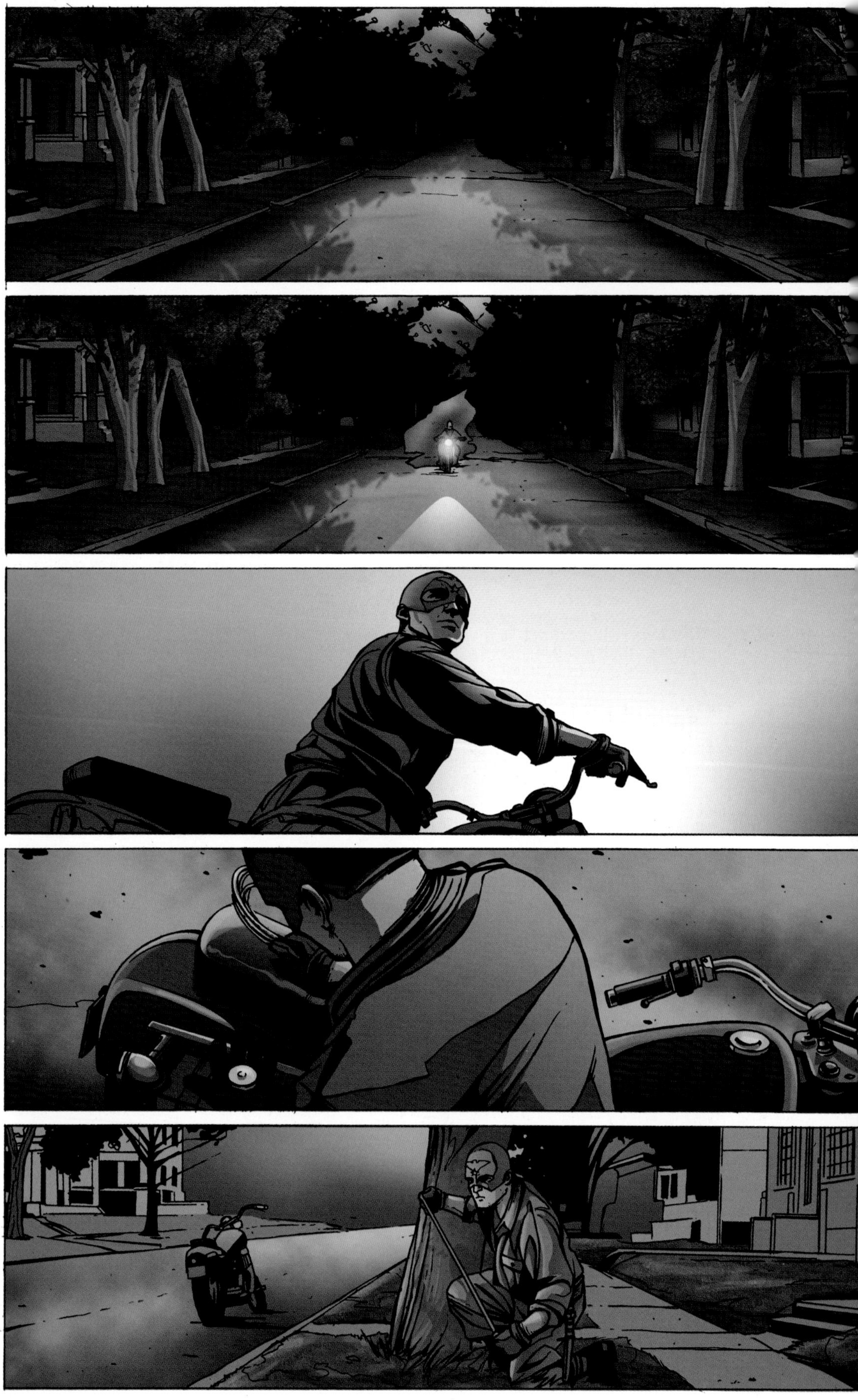

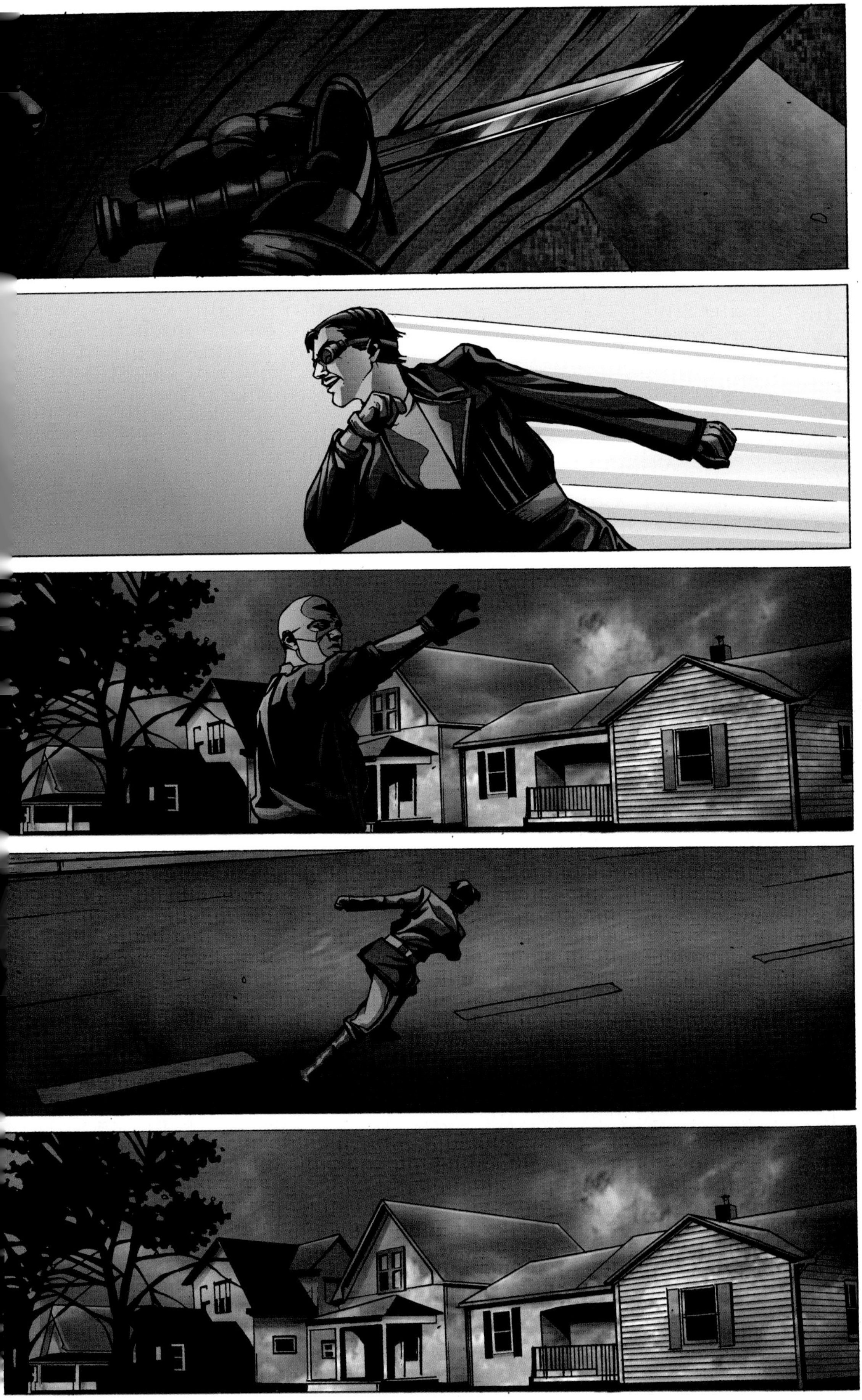

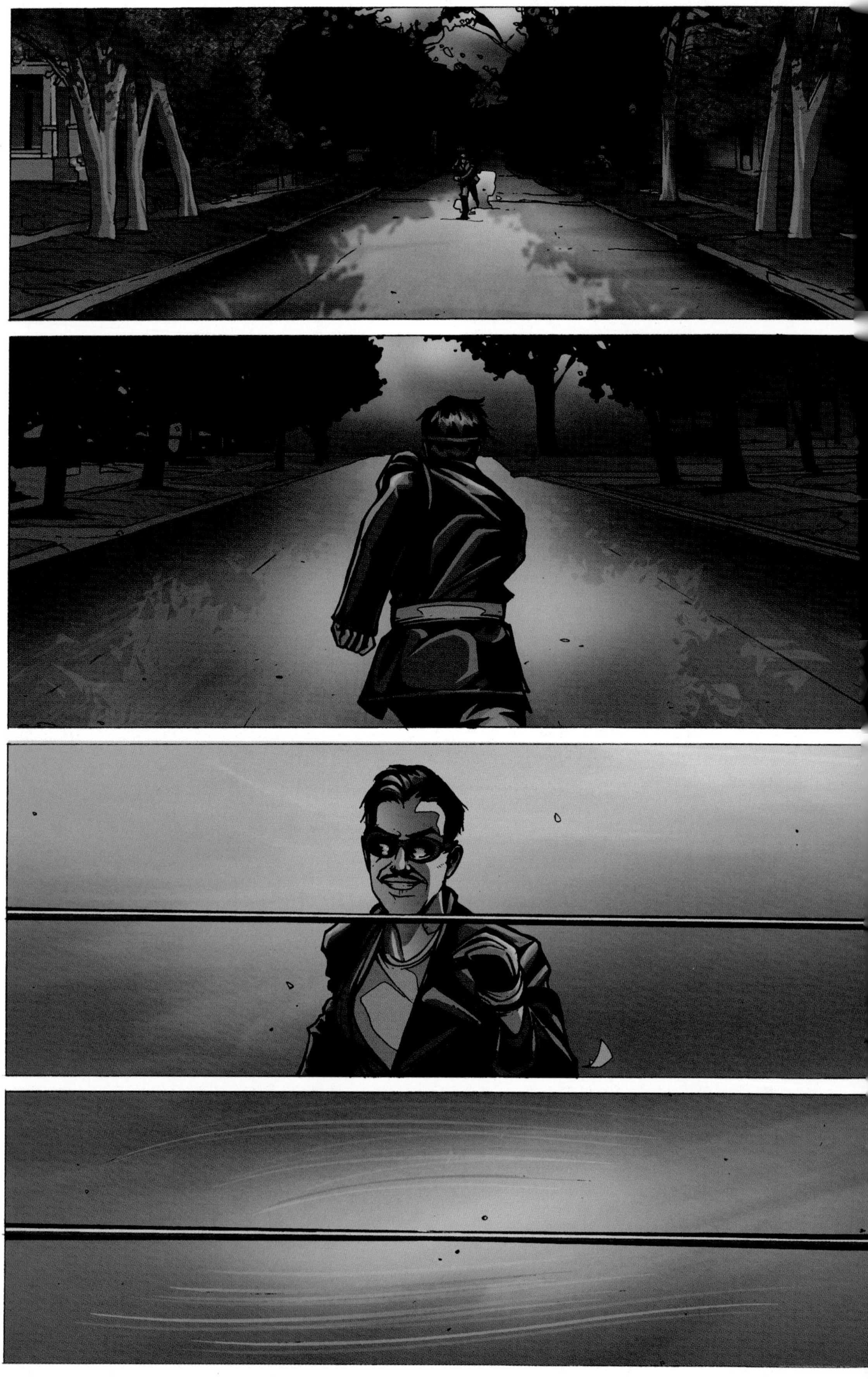

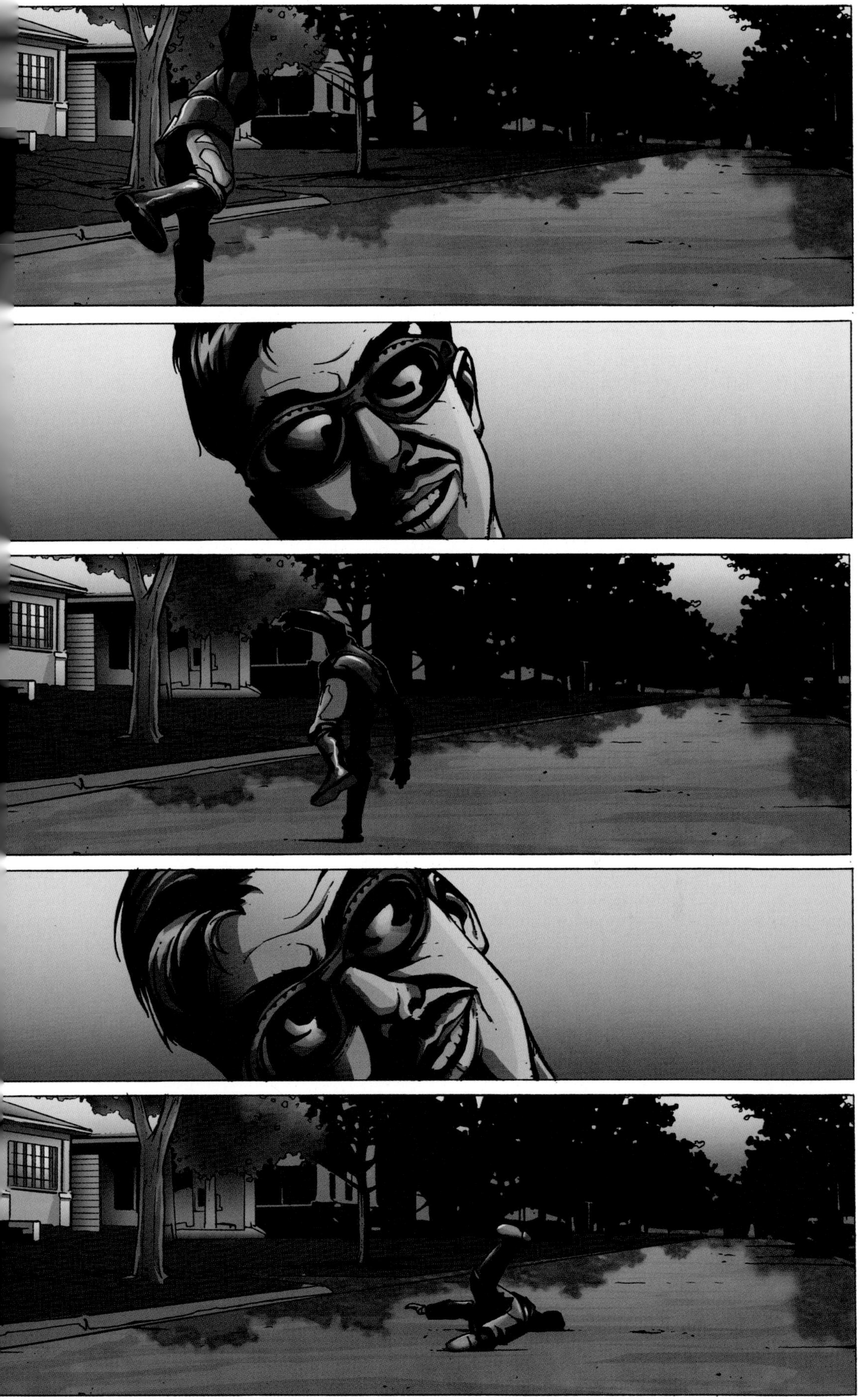

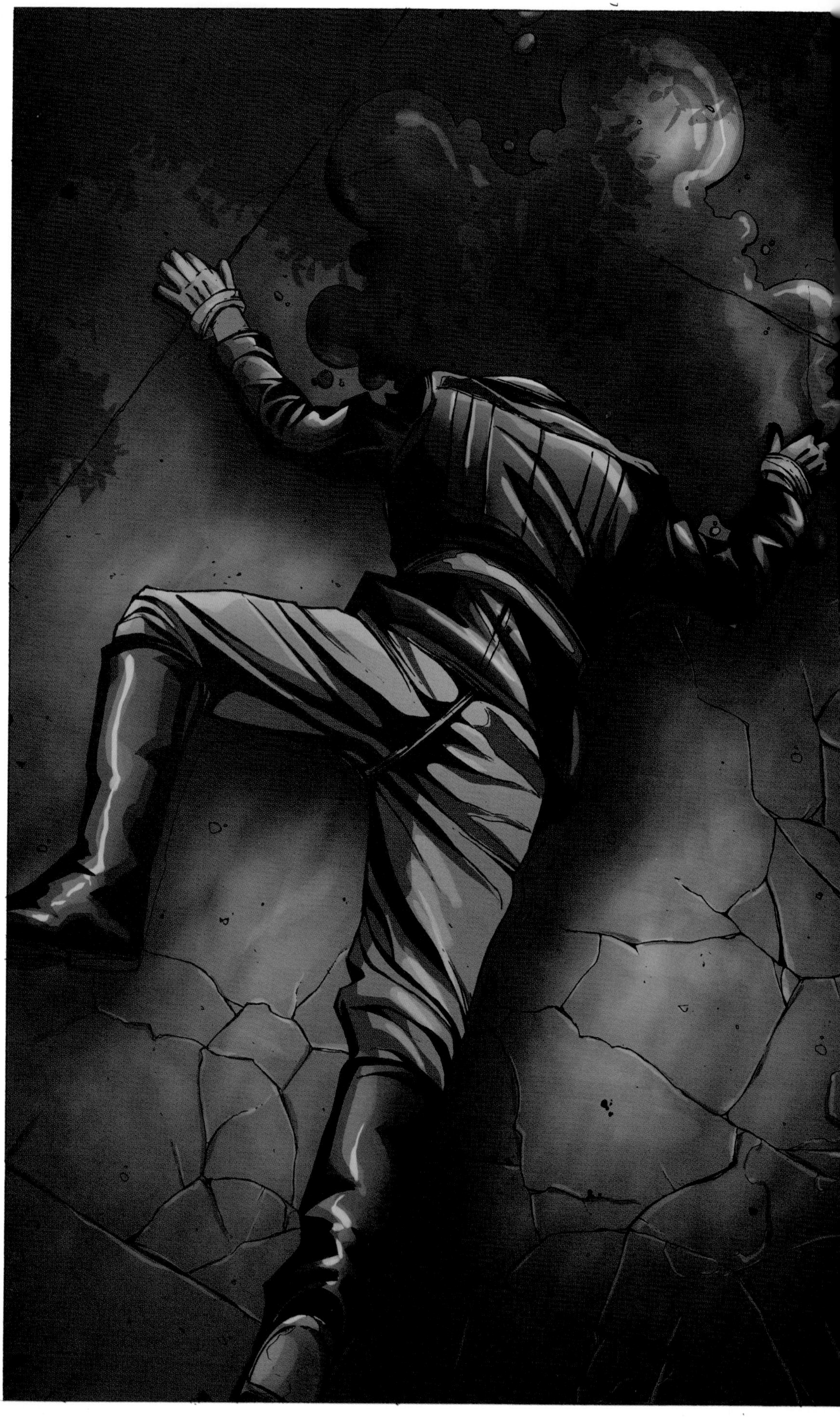

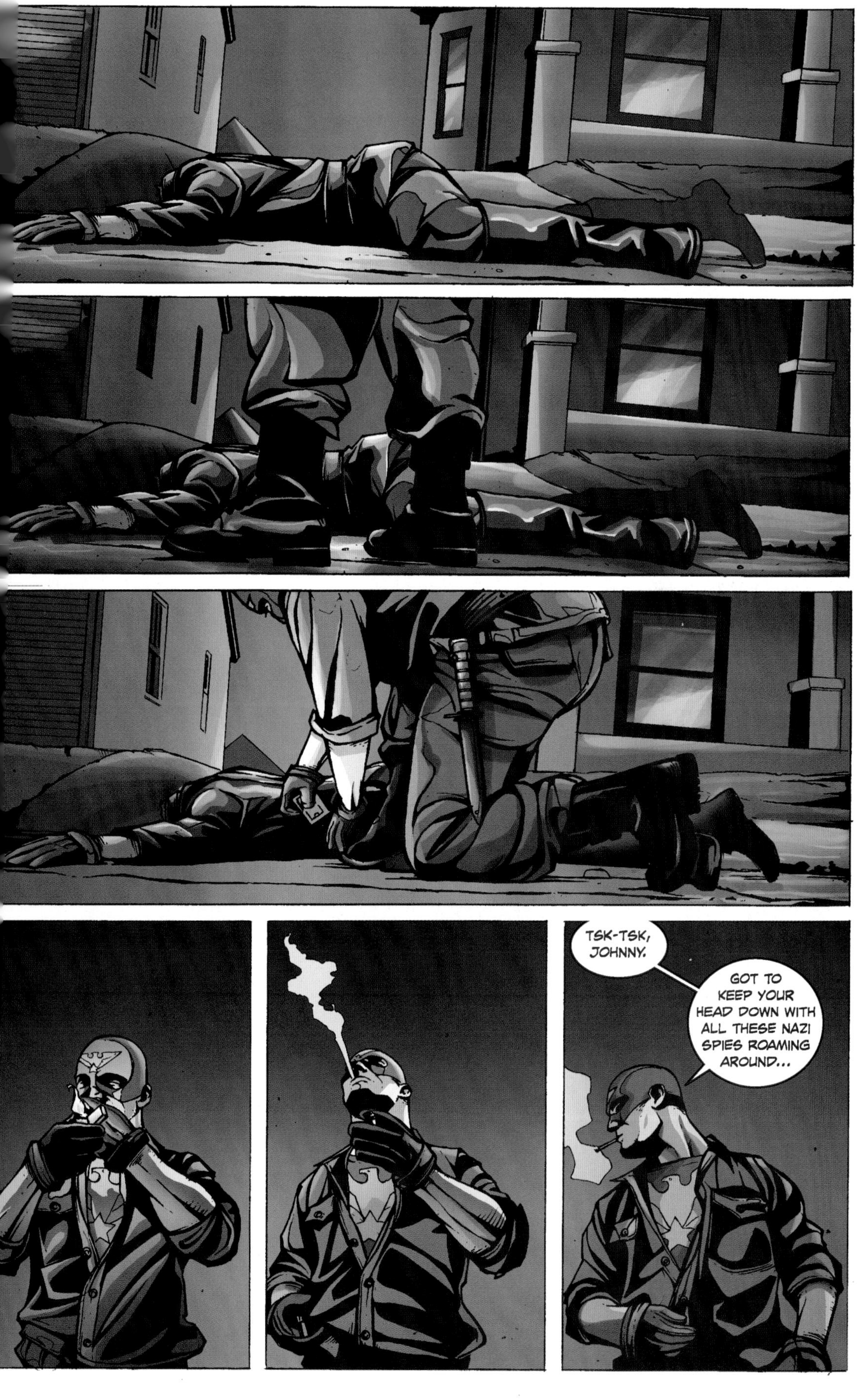
TSK-TSK, JOHNNY.
GOT TO KEEP YOUR HEAD DOWN WITH ALL THESE NAZI SPIES ROAMING AROUND...

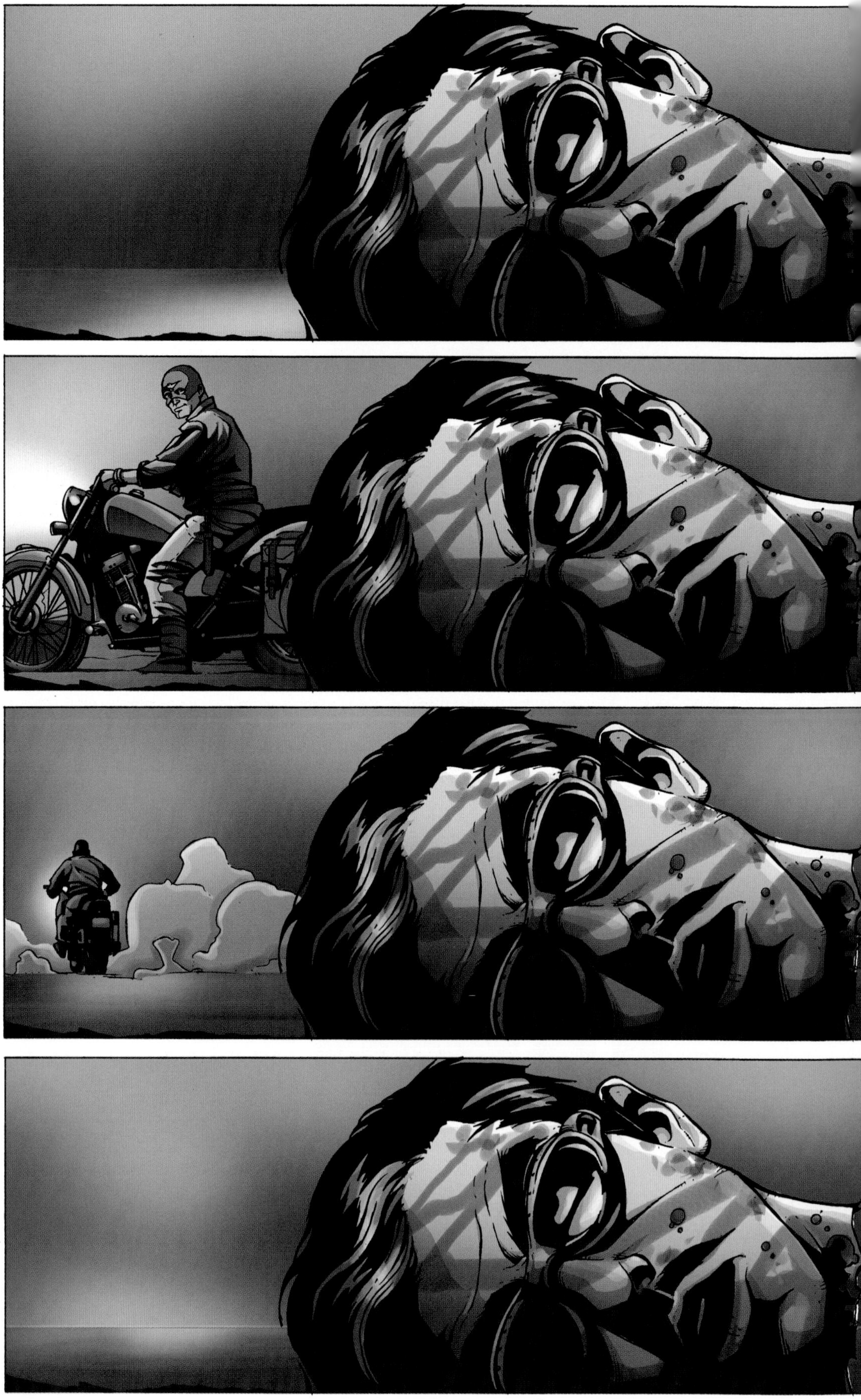

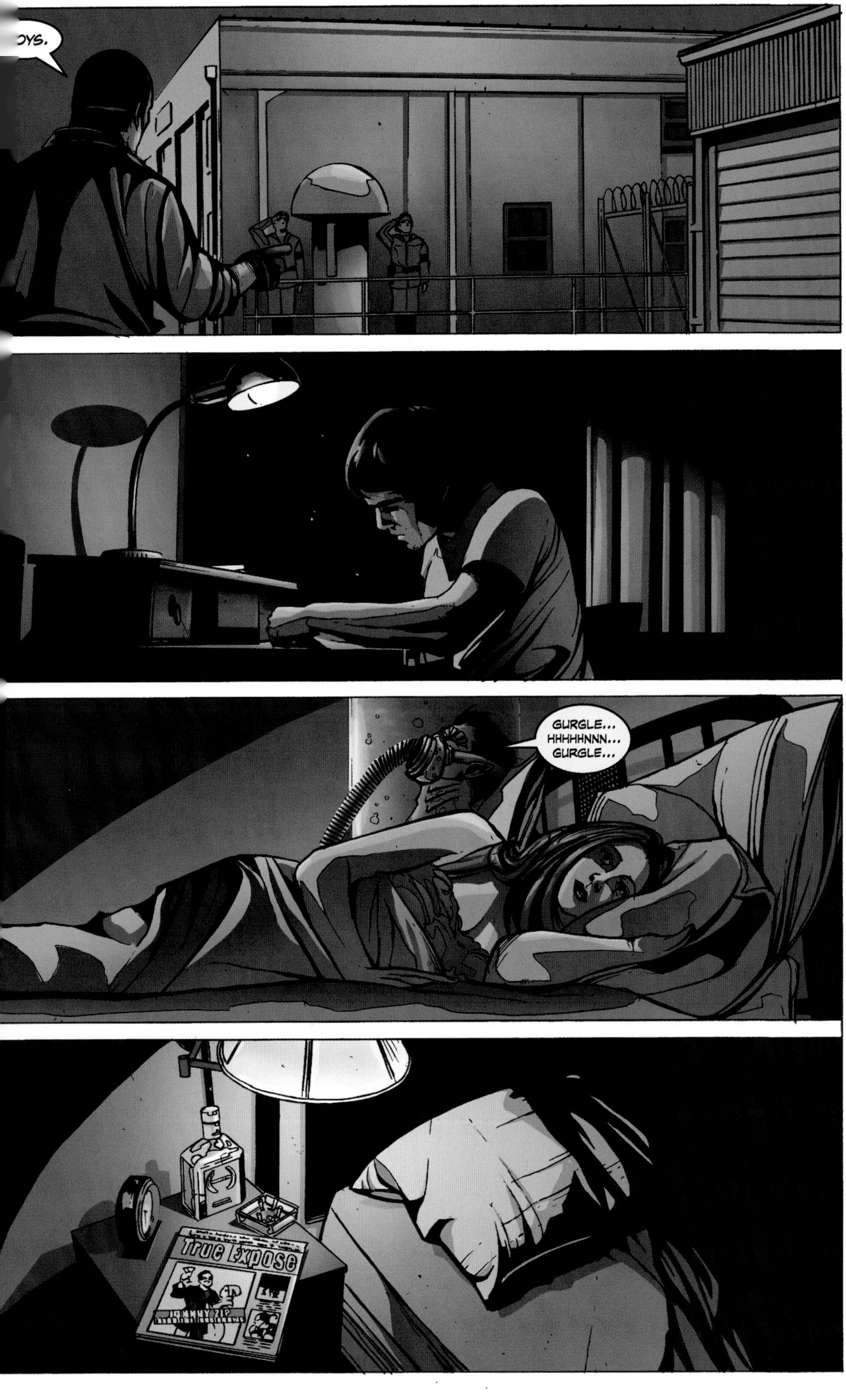
OYS.
GURGLE... HHHHHNNN... GURGLE...
True Expose

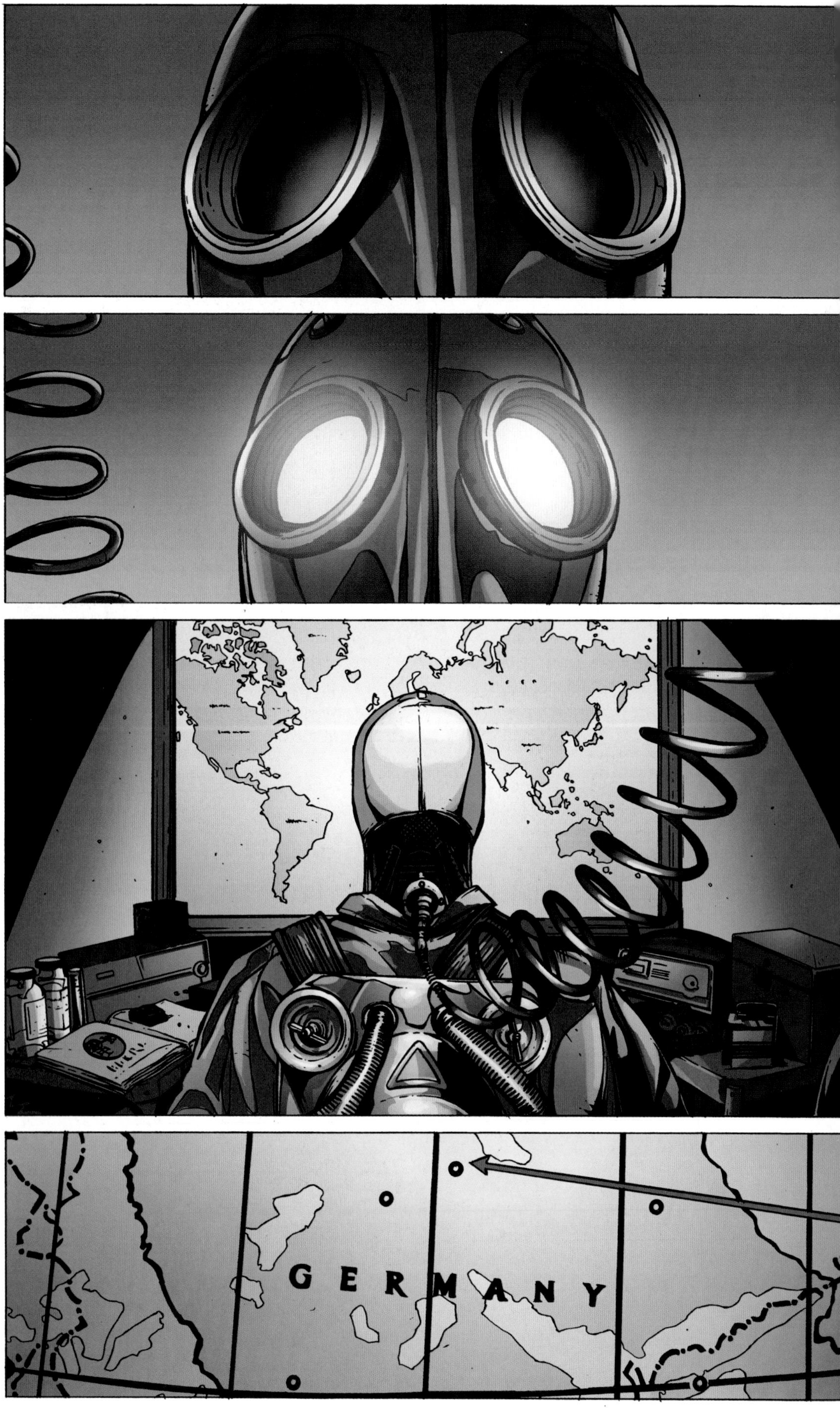
GERMANY

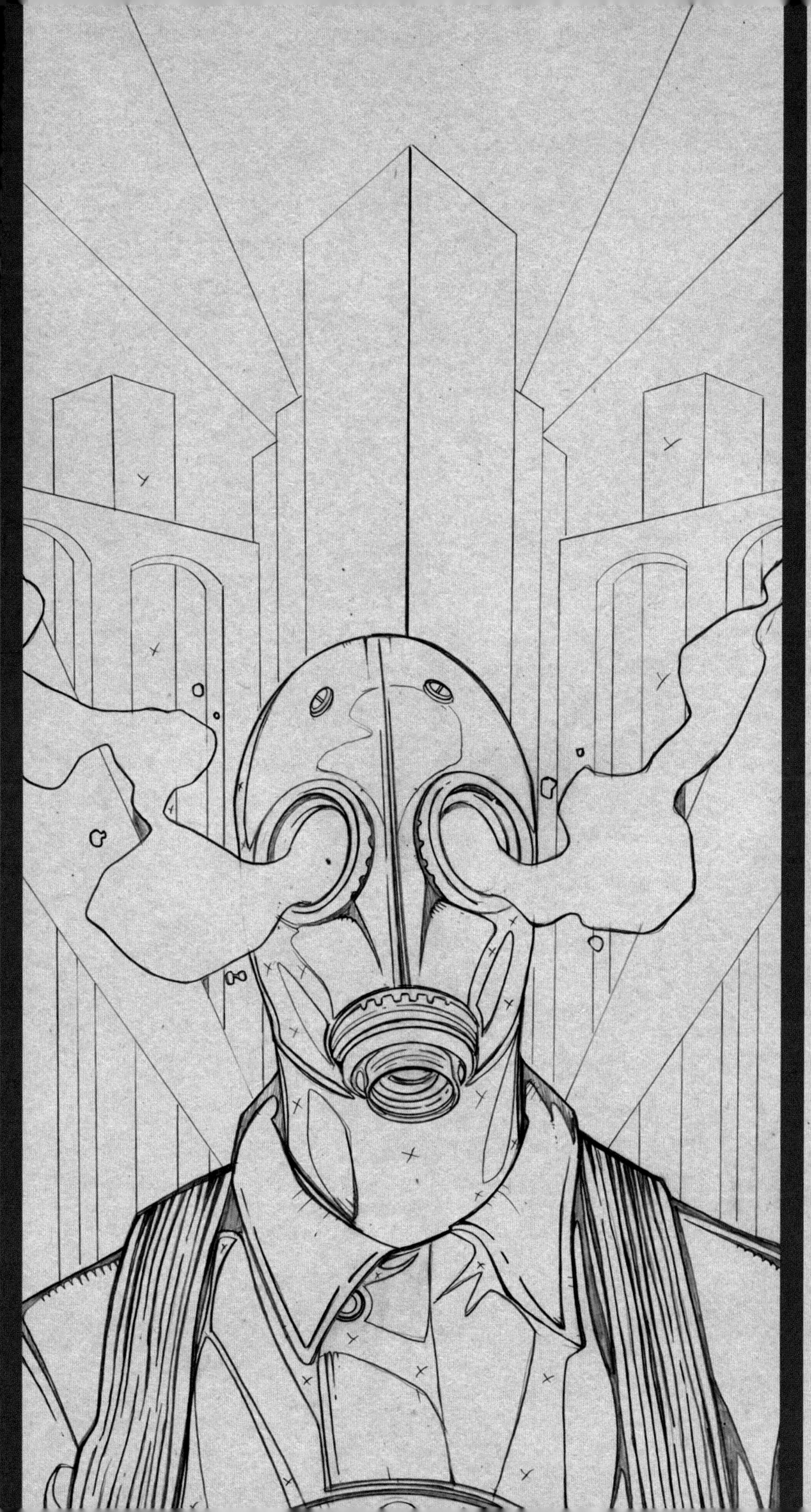

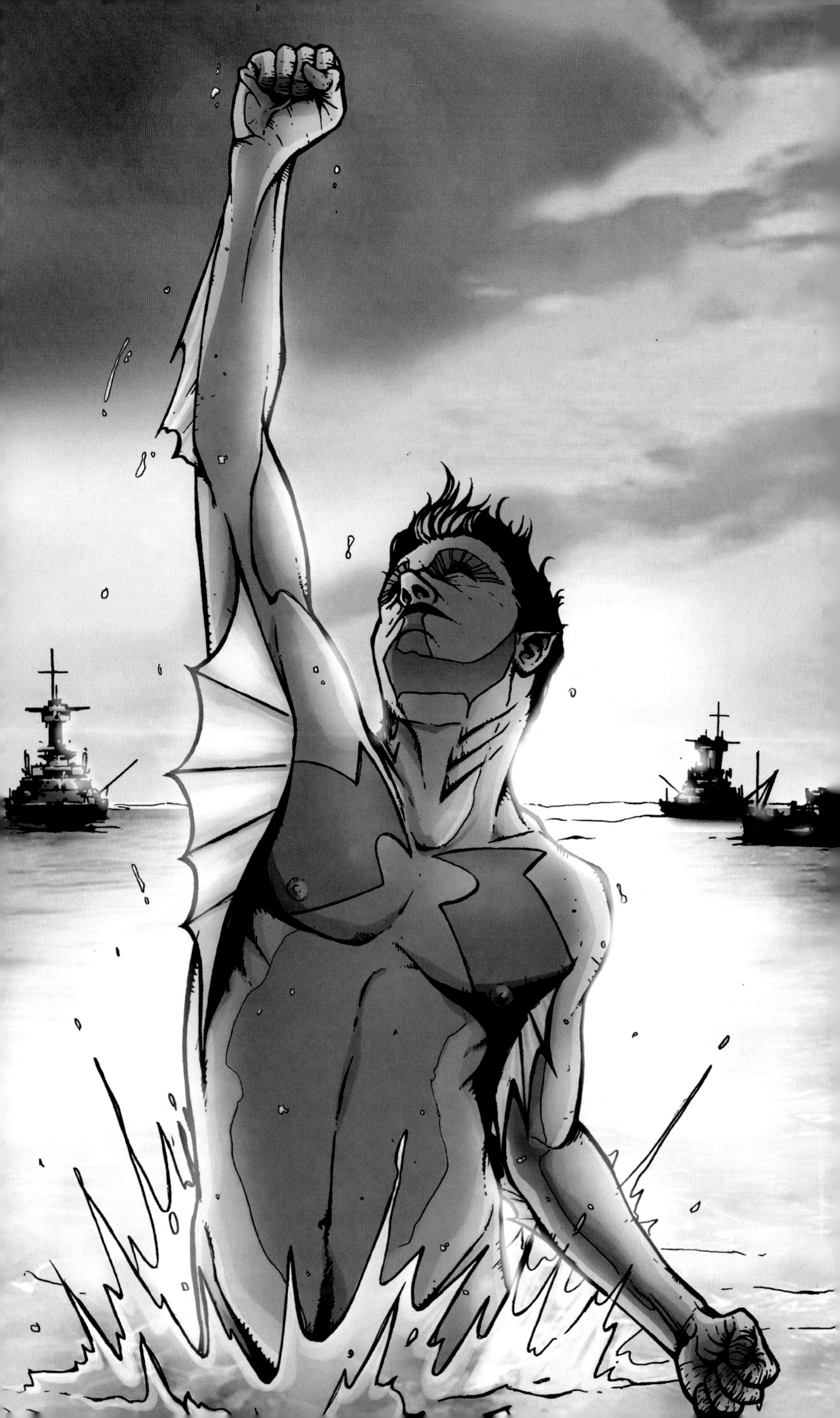

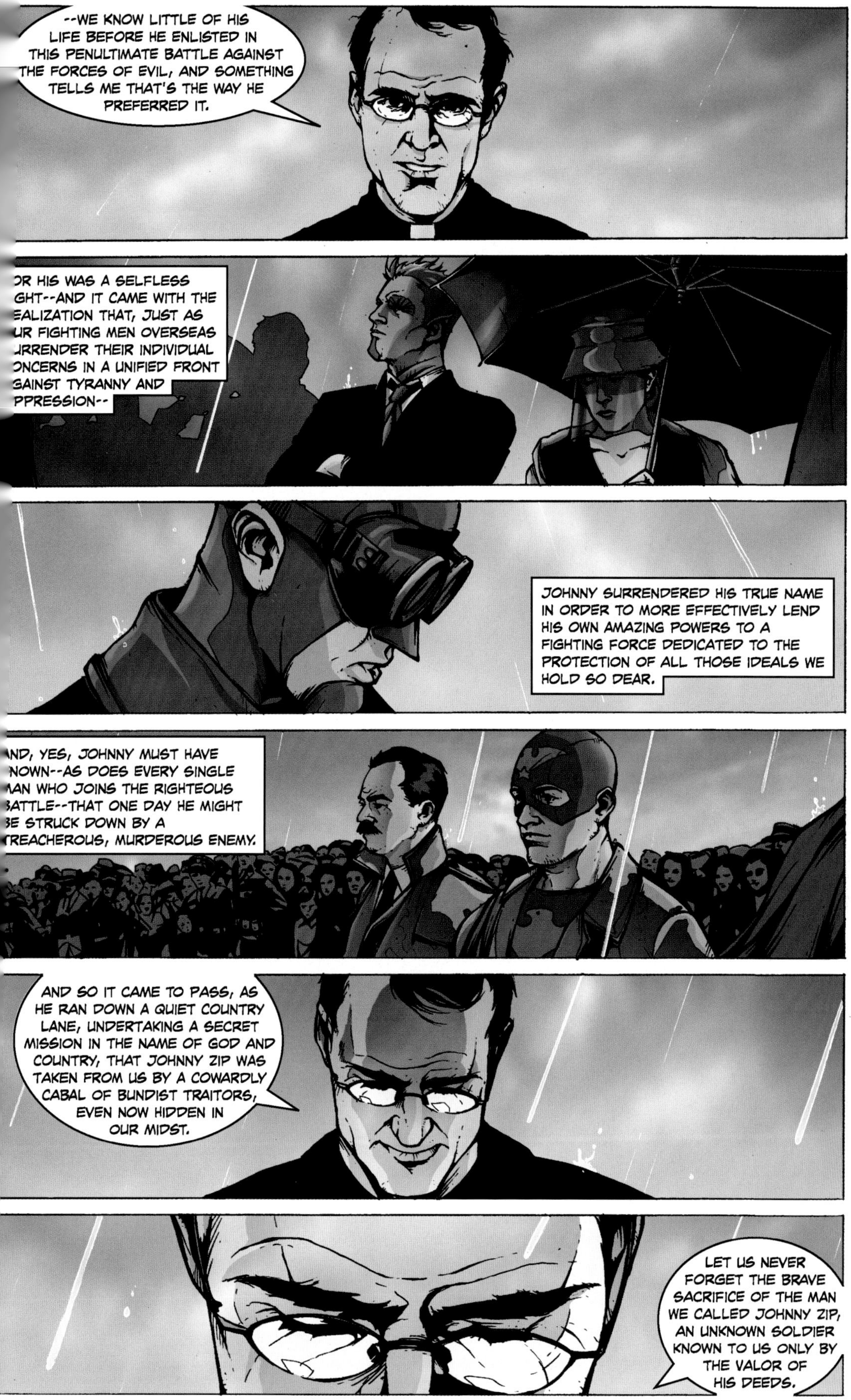
--WE KNOW LITTLE OF HIS LIFE BEFORE HE ENLISTED IN THIS PENULTIMATE BATTLE AGAINST THE FORCES OF EVIL, AND SOMETHING TELLS ME THAT'S THE WAY HE PREFERRED IT.
OR HIS WAS A SELFLESS GHT--AND IT CAME WITH THE EALIZATION THAT, JUST AS UR FIGHTING MEN OVERSEAS URRENDER THEIR INDIVIDUAL ONCERNS IN A UNIFIED FRONT GAINST TYRANNY AND PPRESSION--
JOHNNY SURRENDERED HIS TRUE NAME IN ORDER TO MORE EFFECTIVELY LEND HIS OWN AMAZING POWERS TO A FIGHTING FORCE DEDICATED TO THE PROTECTION OF ALL THOSE IDEALS WE HOLD SO DEAR.
ND, YES, JOHNNY MUST HAVE NOWN--AS DOES EVERY SINGLE AN WHO JOINS THE RIGHTEOUS ATTLE--THAT ONE DAY HE MIGHT E STRUCK DOWN BY A TREACHEROUS, MURDEROUS ENEMY.
AND SO IT CAME TO PASS, AS HE RAN DOWN A QUIET COUNTRY LANE, UNDERTAKING A SECRET MISSION IN THE NAME OF GOD AND COUNTRY, THAT JOHNNY ZIP WAS TAKEN FROM US BY A COWARDLY CABAL OF BUNDIST TRAITORS, EVEN NOW HIDDEN IN OUR MIDST.
LET US NEVER FORGET THE BRAVE SACRIFICE OF THE MAN WE CALLED JOHNNY ZIP, AN UNKNOWN SOLDIER KNOWN TO US ONLY BY THE VALOR OF HIS DEEDS.

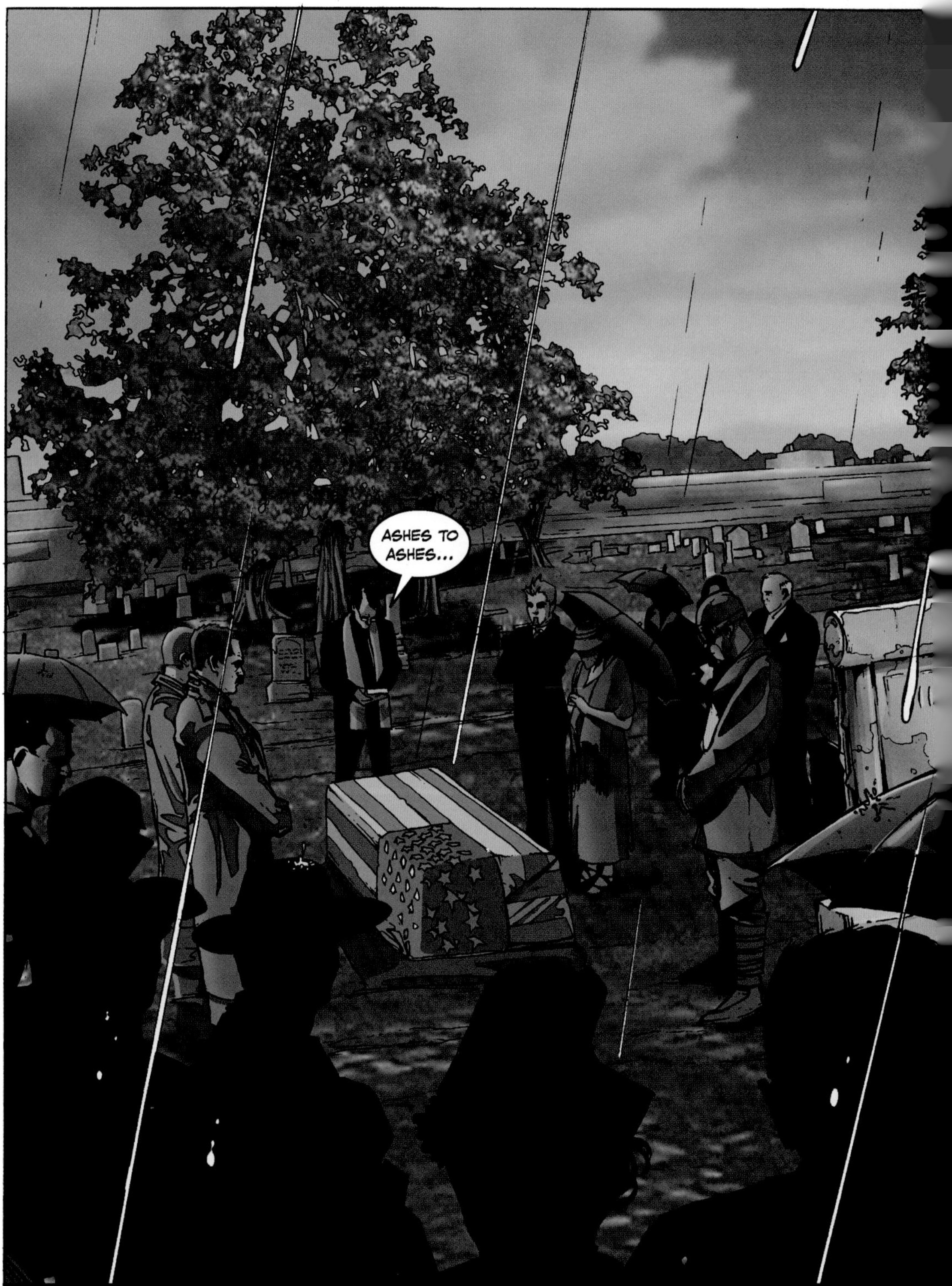
ASHES TO ASHES...

BATTLE HYMN:

Book Four

"OVER THERE"

Written by B. Clay Moore
Colors by Dave Bryant

Art by Jeremy Haun
Letters by Greg Thompson

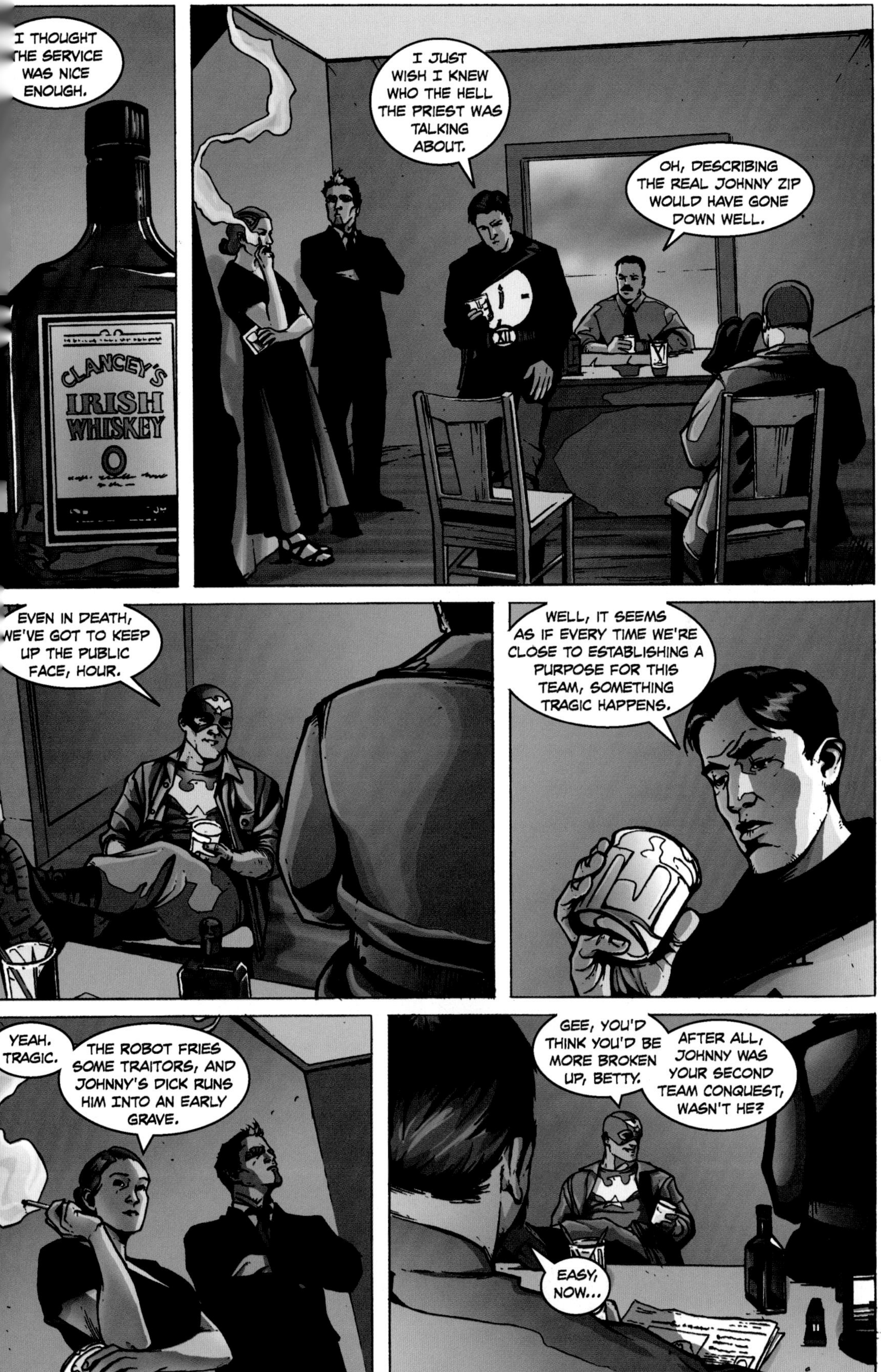
I THOUGHT THE SERVICE WAS NICE ENOUGH.
CLANCEY'S IRISH WHISKEY
I JUST WISH I KNEW WHO THE HELL THE PRIEST WAS TALKING ABOUT.
OH, DESCRIBING THE REAL JOHNNY ZIP WOULD HAVE GONE DOWN WELL.
EVEN IN DEATH, WE'VE GOT TO KEEP UP THE PUBLIC FACE, HOUR.
WELL, IT SEEMS AS IF EVERY TIME WE'RE CLOSE TO ESTABLISHING A PURPOSE FOR THIS TEAM, SOMETHING TRAGIC HAPPENS.
YEAH. TRAGIC.
THE ROBOT FRIES SOME TRAITORS, AND JOHNNY'S DICK RUNS HIM INTO AN EARLY GRAVE.
GEE, YOU'D THINK YOU'D BE MORE BROKEN UP, BETTY.
AFTER ALL, JOHNNY WAS YOUR SECOND TEAM CONQUEST, WASN'T HE?
EASY, NOW...

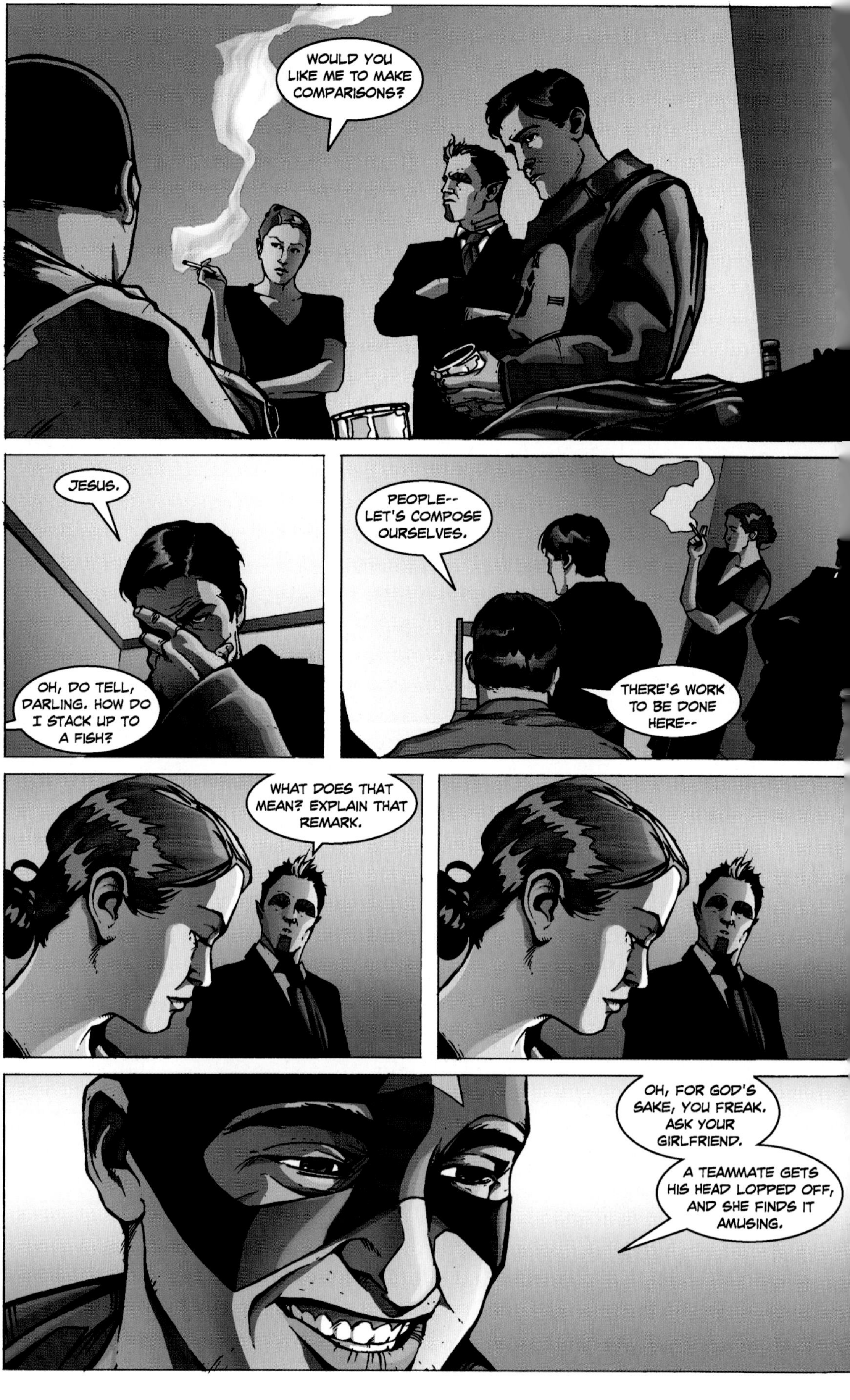
WOULD YOU LIKE ME TO MAKE COMPARISONS?
JESUS.
OH, DO TELL, DARLING. HOW DO I STACK UP TO A FISH?
PEOPLE-- LET'S COMPOSE OURSELVES.
THERE'S WORK TO BE DONE HERE--
WHAT DOES THAT MEAN? EXPLAIN THAT REMARK.
OH, FOR GOD'S SAKE, YOU FREAK. ASK YOUR GIRLFRIEND.
A TEAMMATE GETS HIS HEAD LOPPED OFF, AND SHE FINDS IT AMUSING.

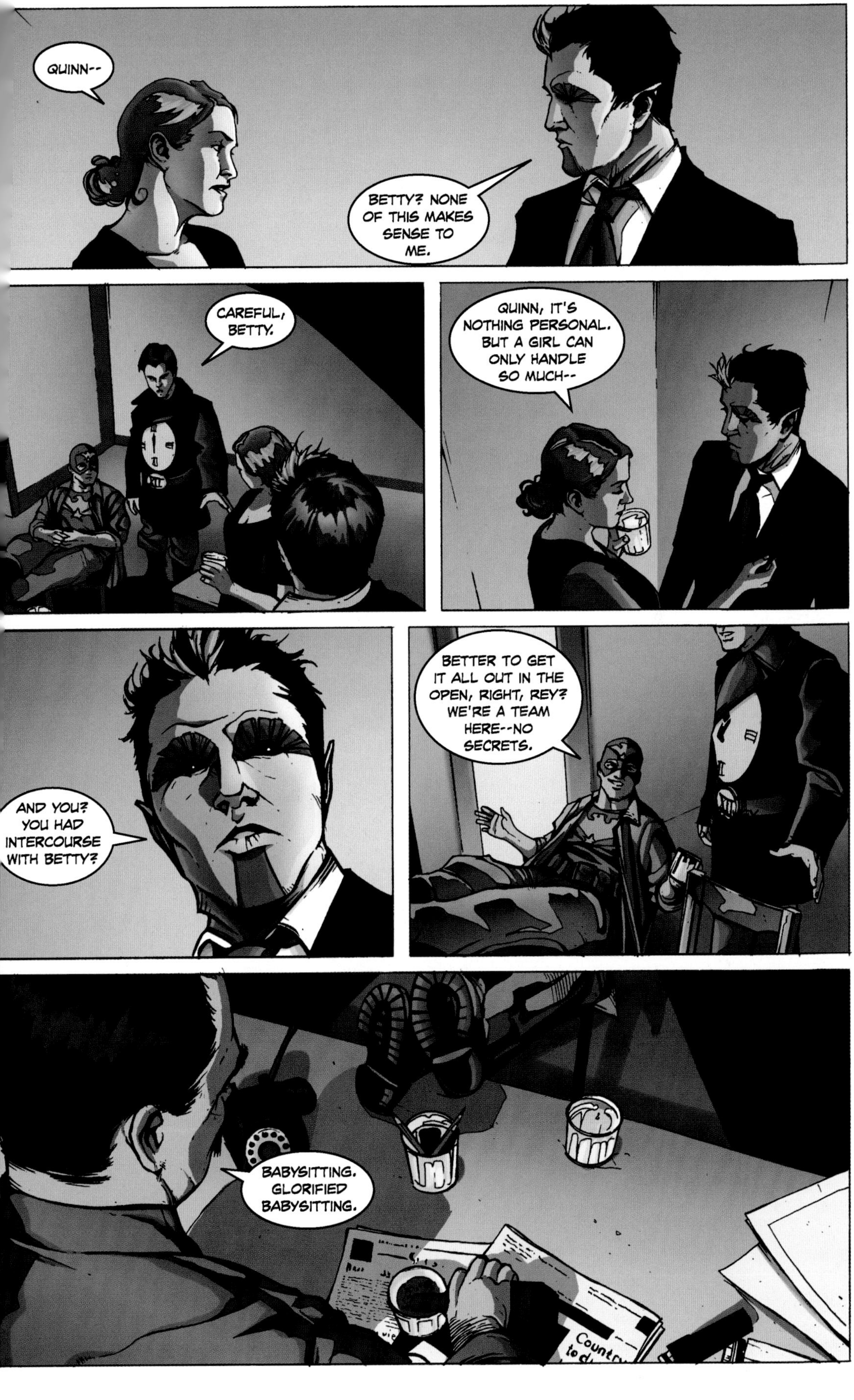
QUINN--
BETTY? NONE OF THIS MAKES SENSE TO ME.
CAREFUL, BETTY.
QUINN, IT'S NOTHING PERSONAL. BUT A GIRL CAN ONLY HANDLE SO MUCH--
AND YOU? YOU HAD INTERCOURSE WITH BETTY?
BETTER TO GET IT ALL OUT IN THE OPEN, RIGHT, REY? WE'RE A TEAM HERE--NO SECRETS.
BABYSITTING. GLORIFIED BABYSITTING.

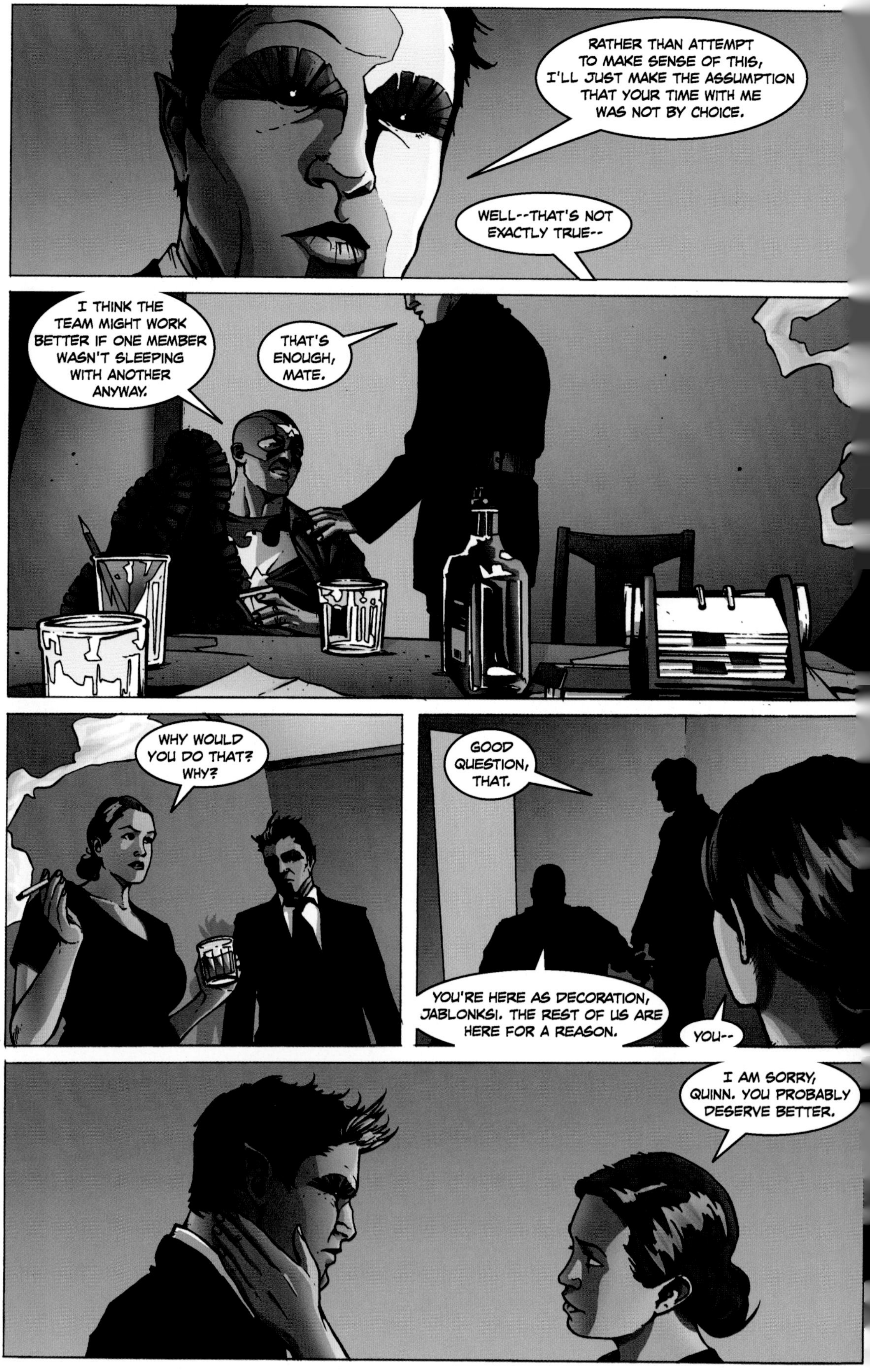

RATHER THAN ATTEMPT TO MAKE SENSE OF THIS, I'LL JUST MAKE THE ASSUMPTION THAT YOUR TIME WITH ME WAS NOT BY CHOICE.
WELL--THAT'S NOT EXACTLY TRUE--
I THINK THE TEAM MIGHT WORK BETTER IF ONE MEMBER WASN'T SLEEPING WITH ANOTHER ANYWAY.
THAT'S ENOUGH, MATE.
WHY WOULD YOU DO THAT? WHY?
GOOD QUESTION, THAT.
YOU'RE HERE AS DECORATION, JABLONKSI. THE REST OF US ARE HERE FOR A REASON.
YOU--
I AM SORRY, QUINN. YOU PROBABLY DESERVE BETTER.

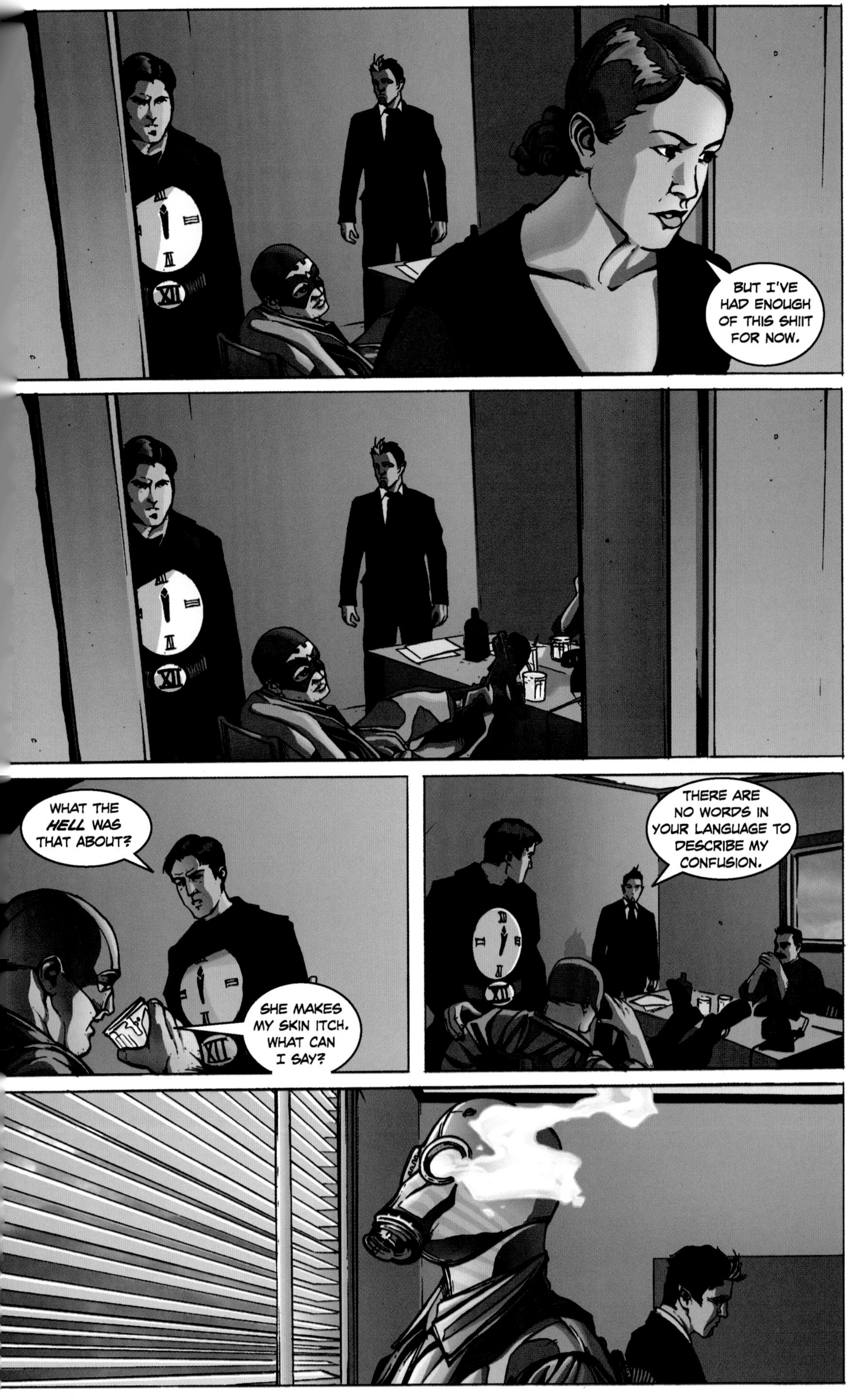
BUT I'VE HAD ENOUGH OF THIS SHIIT FOR NOW.
WHAT THE *HELL* WAS THAT ABOUT?
SHE MAKES MY SKIN ITCH. WHAT CAN I SAY?
THERE ARE NO WORDS IN YOUR LANGUAGE TO DESCRIBE MY CONFUSION.

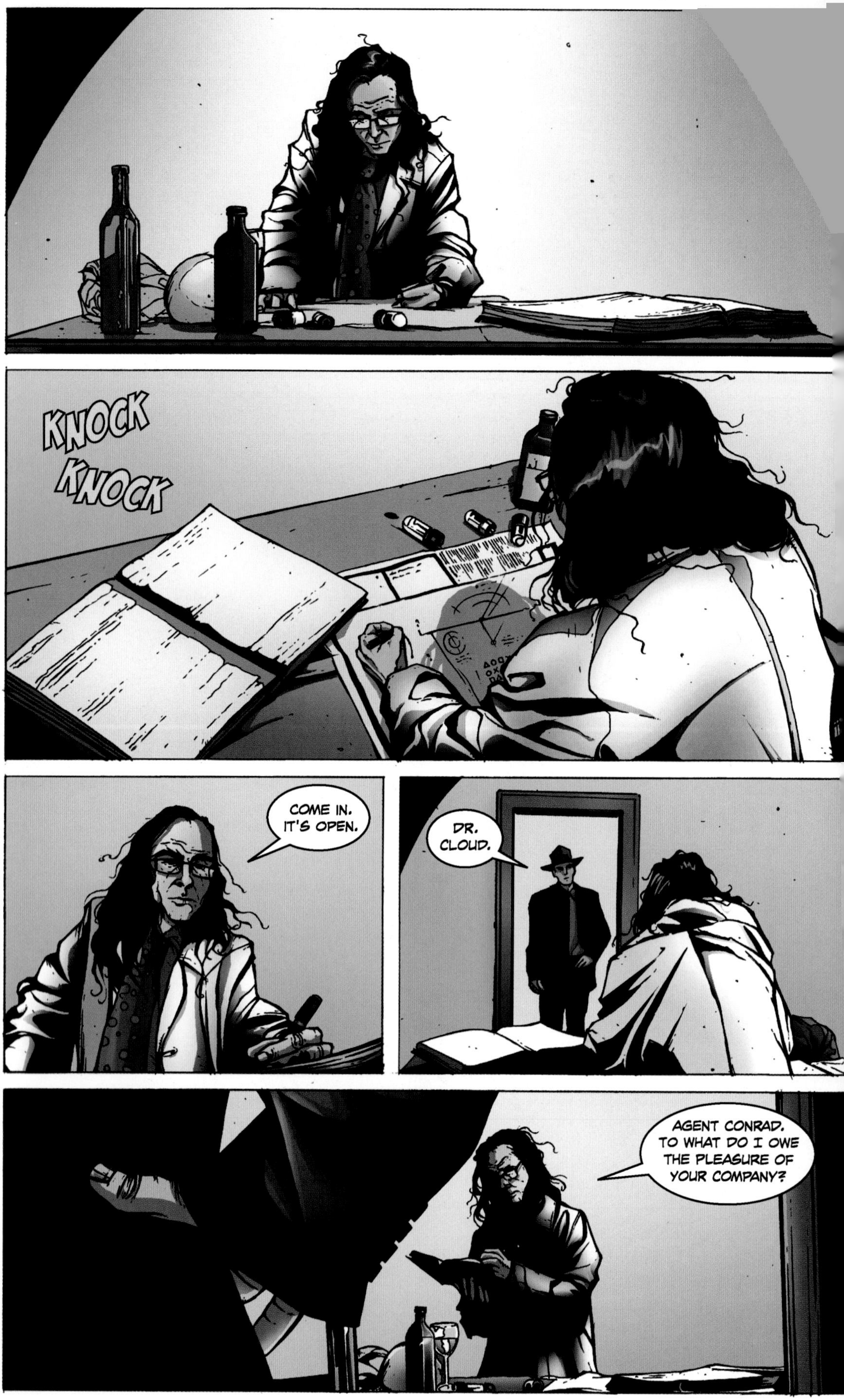
KNOCK
KNOCK
COME IN. IT'S OPEN.
DR. CLOUD.
AGENT CONRAD. TO WHAT DO I OWE THE PLEASURE OF YOUR COMPANY?

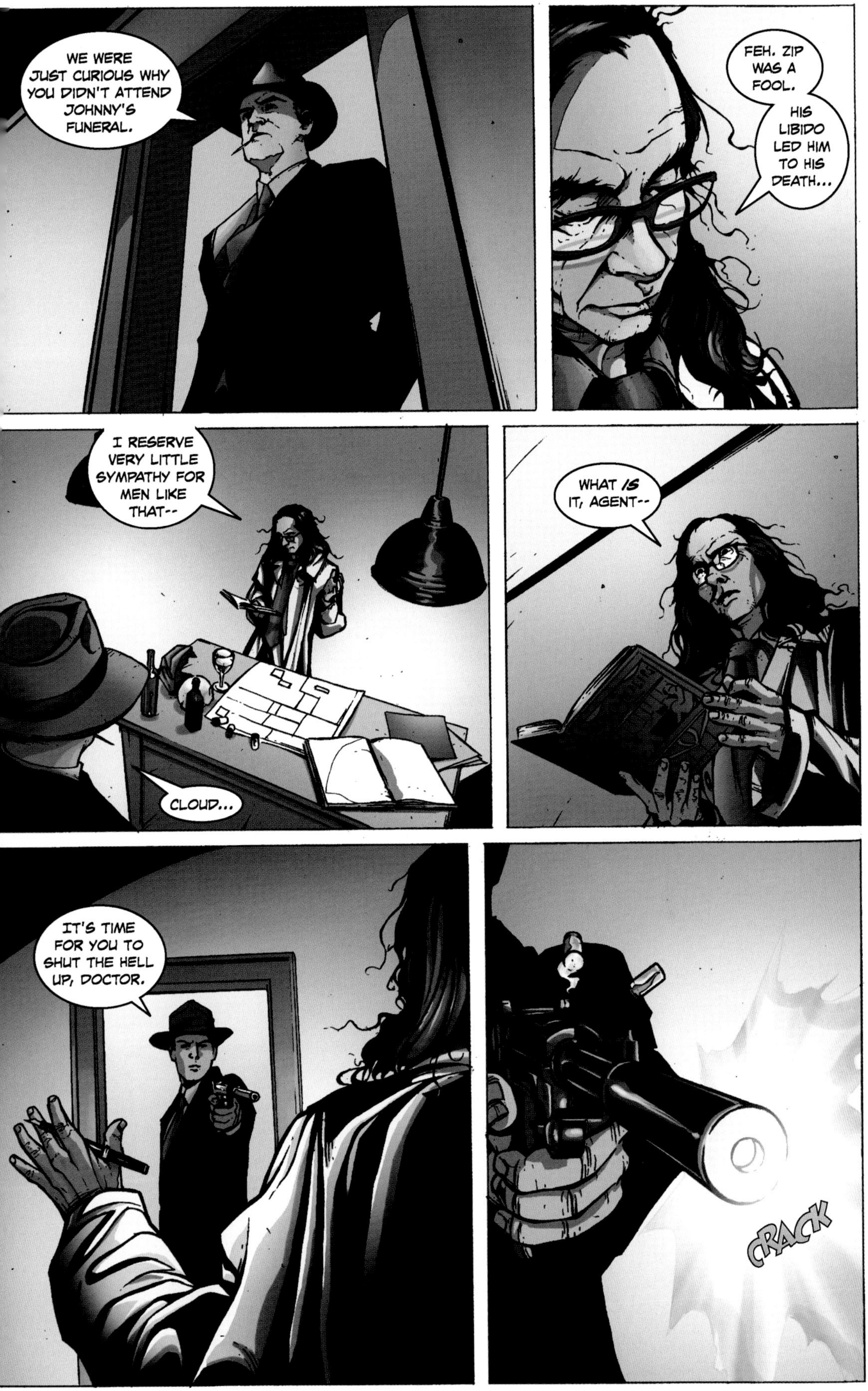
WE WERE JUST CURIOUS WHY YOU DIDN'T ATTEND JOHNNY'S FUNERAL.
FEH. ZIP WAS A FOOL.
HIS LIBIDO LED HIM TO HIS DEATH...
I RESERVE VERY LITTLE SYMPATHY FOR MEN LIKE THAT--
CLOUD...
WHAT IS IT, AGENT--
IT'S TIME FOR YOU TO SHUT THE HELL UP, DOCTOR.
CRACK

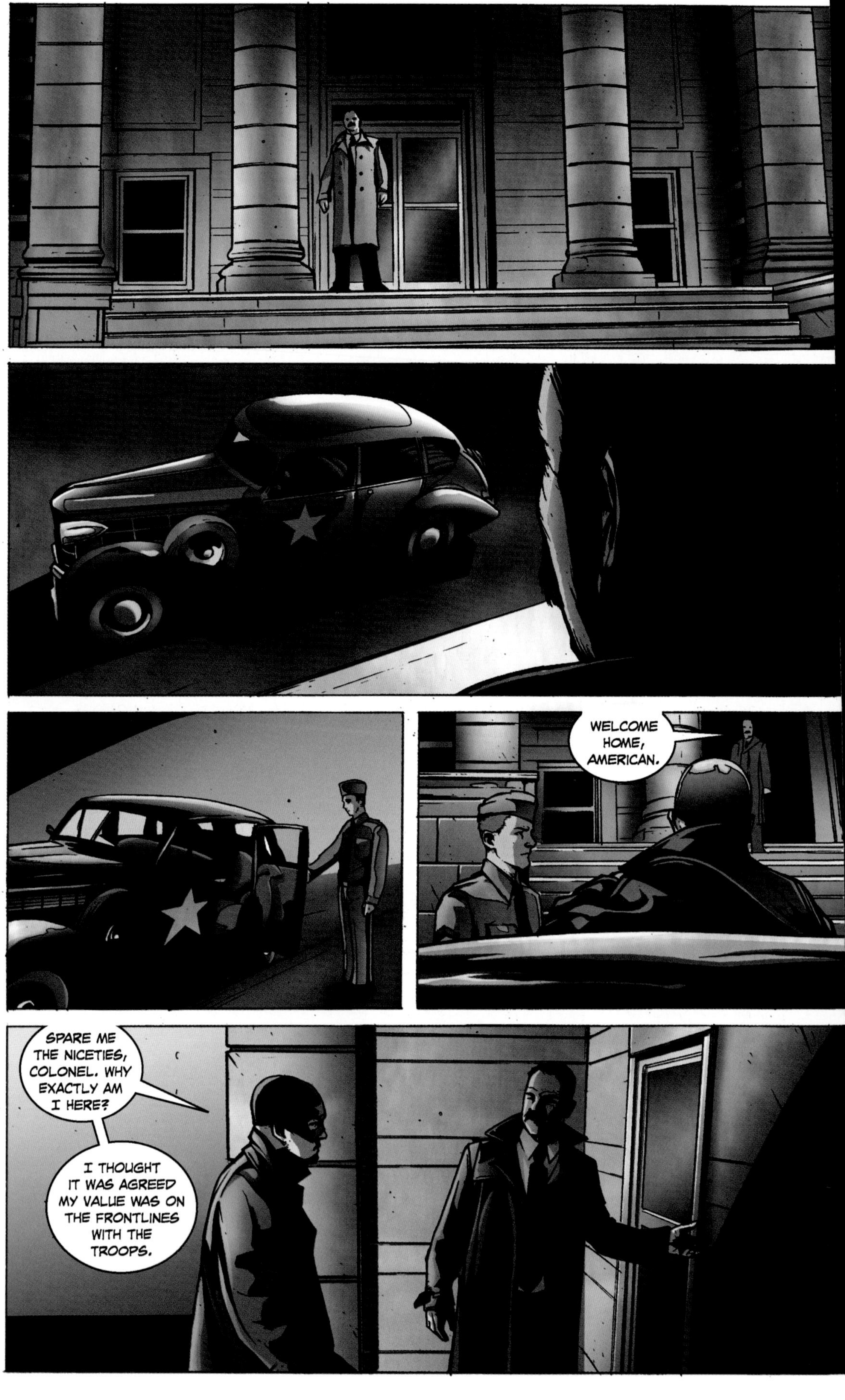
WELCOME HOME, AMERICAN.
SPARE ME THE NICETIES, COLONEL. WHY EXACTLY AM I HERE?
I THOUGHT IT WAS AGREED MY VALUE WAS ON THE FRONTLINES WITH THE TROOPS.

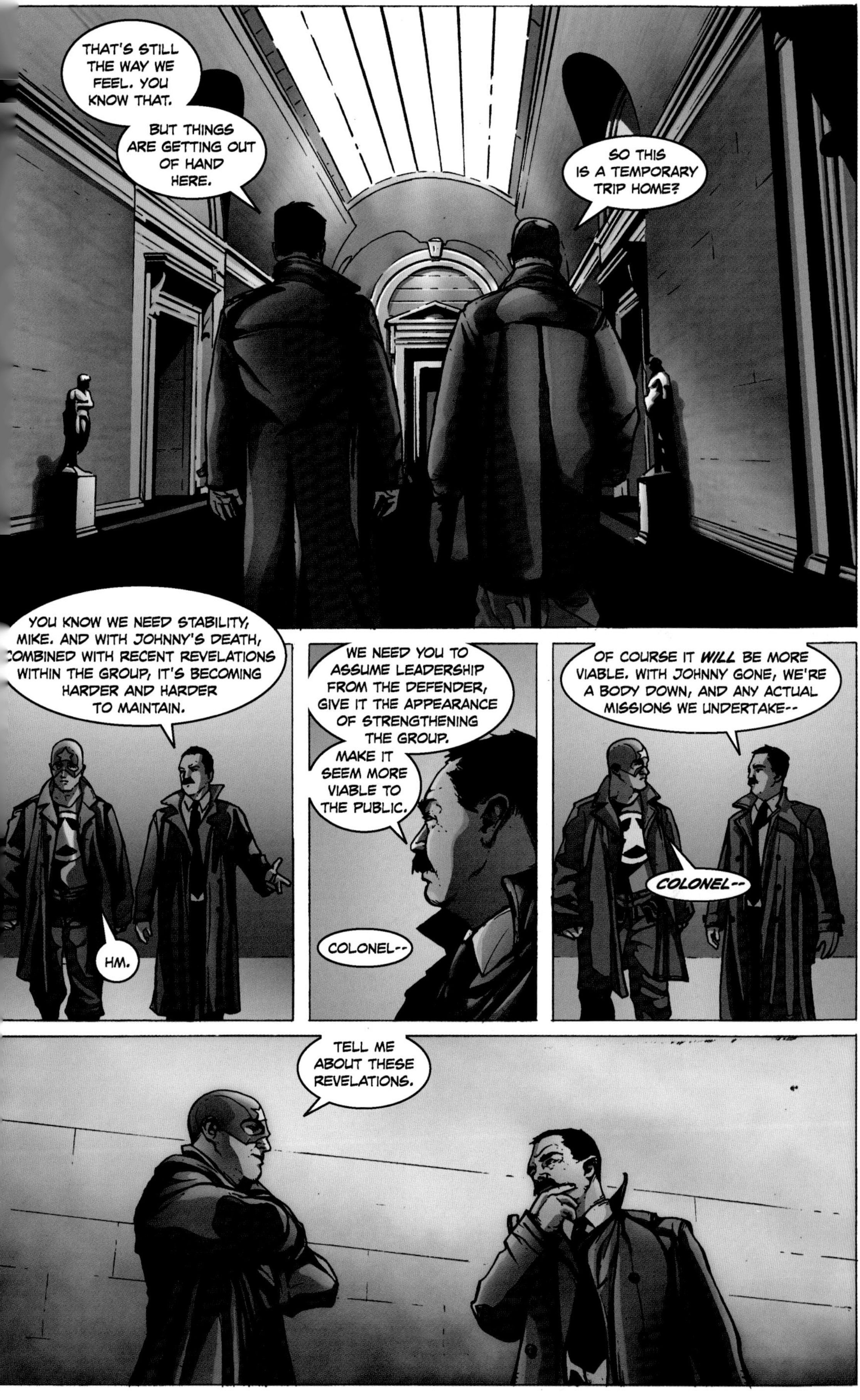
THAT'S STILL THE WAY WE FEEL. YOU KNOW THAT.
BUT THINGS ARE GETTING OUT OF HAND HERE.
SO THIS IS A TEMPORARY TRIP HOME?
YOU KNOW WE NEED STABILITY, MIKE. AND WITH JOHNNY'S DEATH, COMBINED WITH RECENT REVELATIONS WITHIN THE GROUP, IT'S BECOMING HARDER AND HARDER TO MAINTAIN.
HM.
WE NEED YOU TO ASSUME LEADERSHIP FROM THE DEFENDER, GIVE IT THE APPEARANCE OF STRENGTHENING THE GROUP.
MAKE IT SEEM MORE VIABLE TO THE PUBLIC.
COLONEL--
OF COURSE IT WILL BE MORE VIABLE. WITH JOHNNY GONE, WE'RE A BODY DOWN, AND ANY ACTUAL MISSIONS WE UNDERTAKE--
COLONEL--
TELL ME ABOUT THESE REVELATIONS.

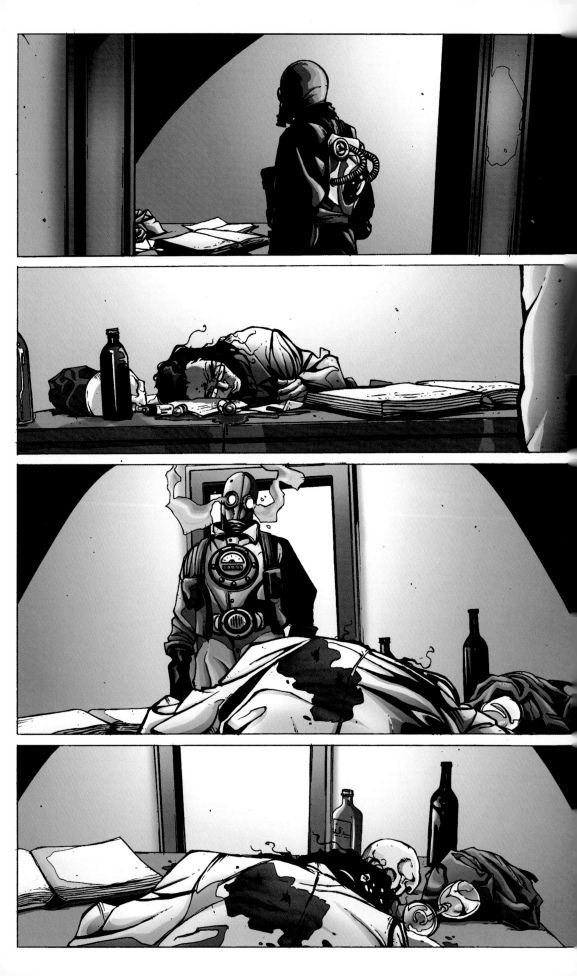

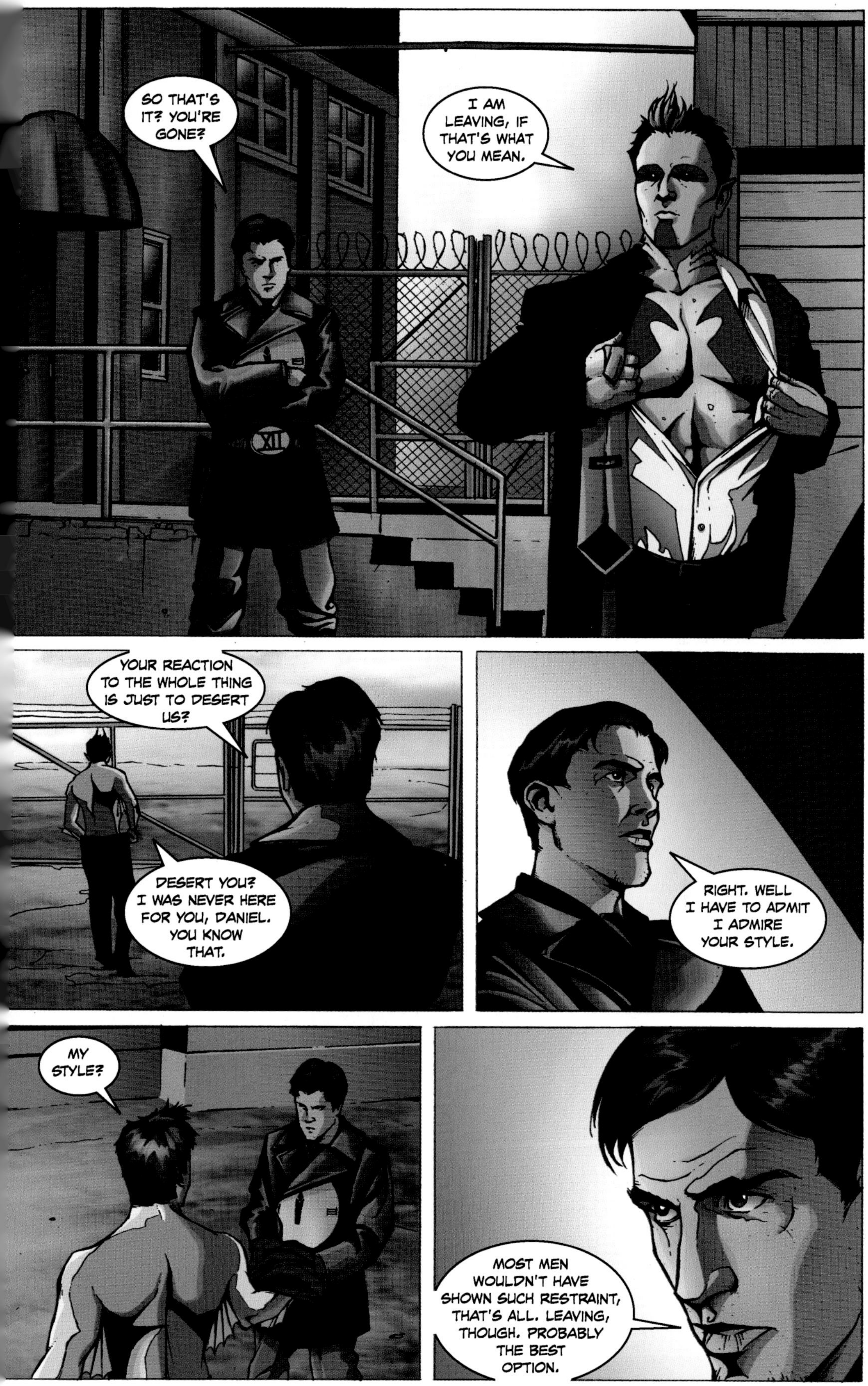
SO THAT'S IT? YOU'RE GONE?
I AM LEAVING, IF THAT'S WHAT YOU MEAN.
YOUR REACTION TO THE WHOLE THING IS JUST TO DESERT US?
DESERT YOU? I WAS NEVER HERE FOR YOU, DANIEL. YOU KNOW THAT.
RIGHT. WELL I HAVE TO ADMIT I ADMIRE YOUR STYLE.
MY STYLE?
MOST MEN WOULDN'T HAVE SHOWN SUCH RESTRAINT, THAT'S ALL. LEAVING, THOUGH. PROBABLY THE BEST OPTION.

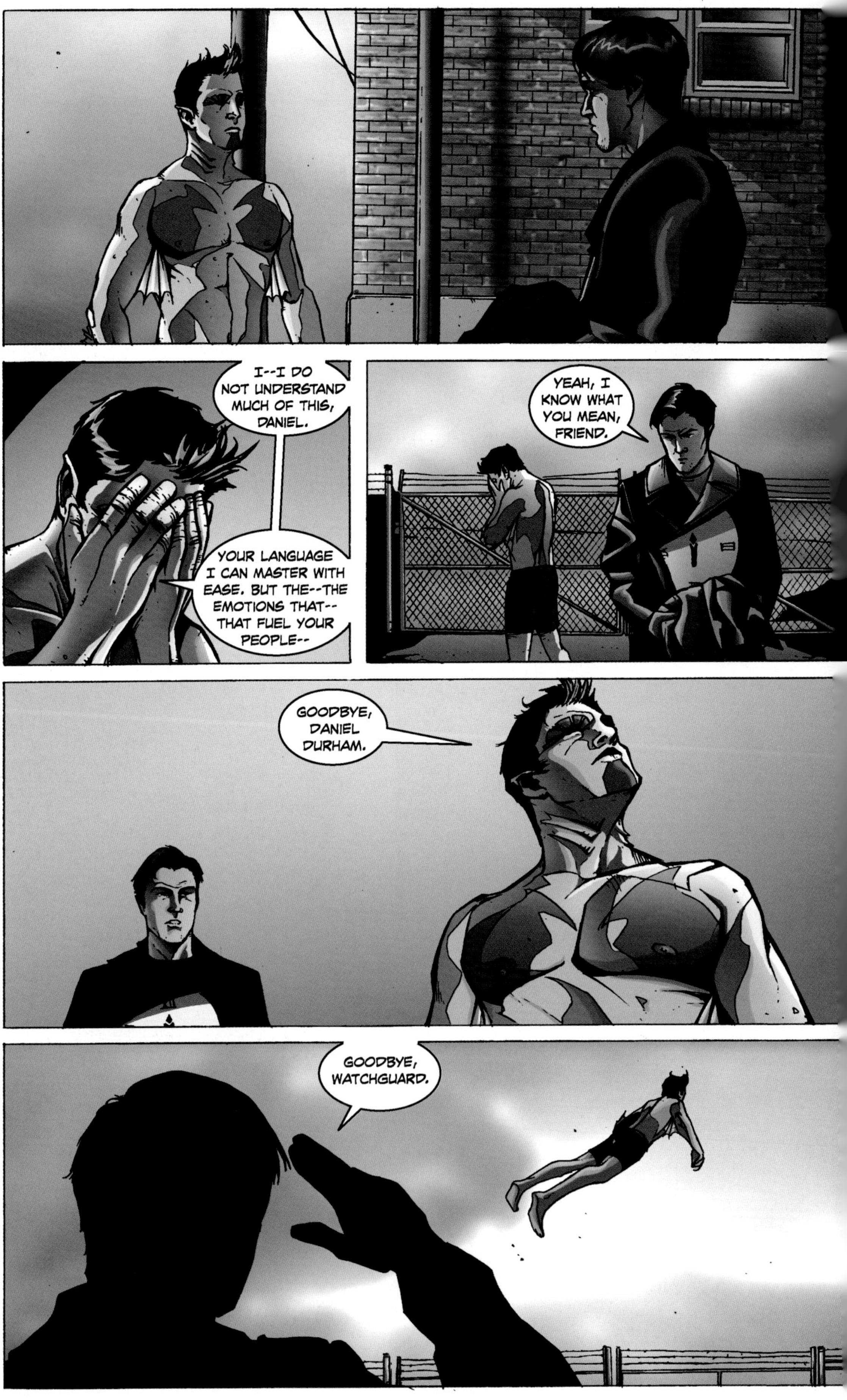
I--I DO NOT UNDERSTAND MUCH OF THIS, DANIEL.
YOUR LANGUAGE I CAN MASTER WITH EASE. BUT THE--THE EMOTIONS THAT--THAT FUEL YOUR PEOPLE--
YEAH, I KNOW WHAT YOU MEAN, FRIEND.
GOODBYE, DANIEL DURHAM.
GOODBYE, WATCHGUARD.

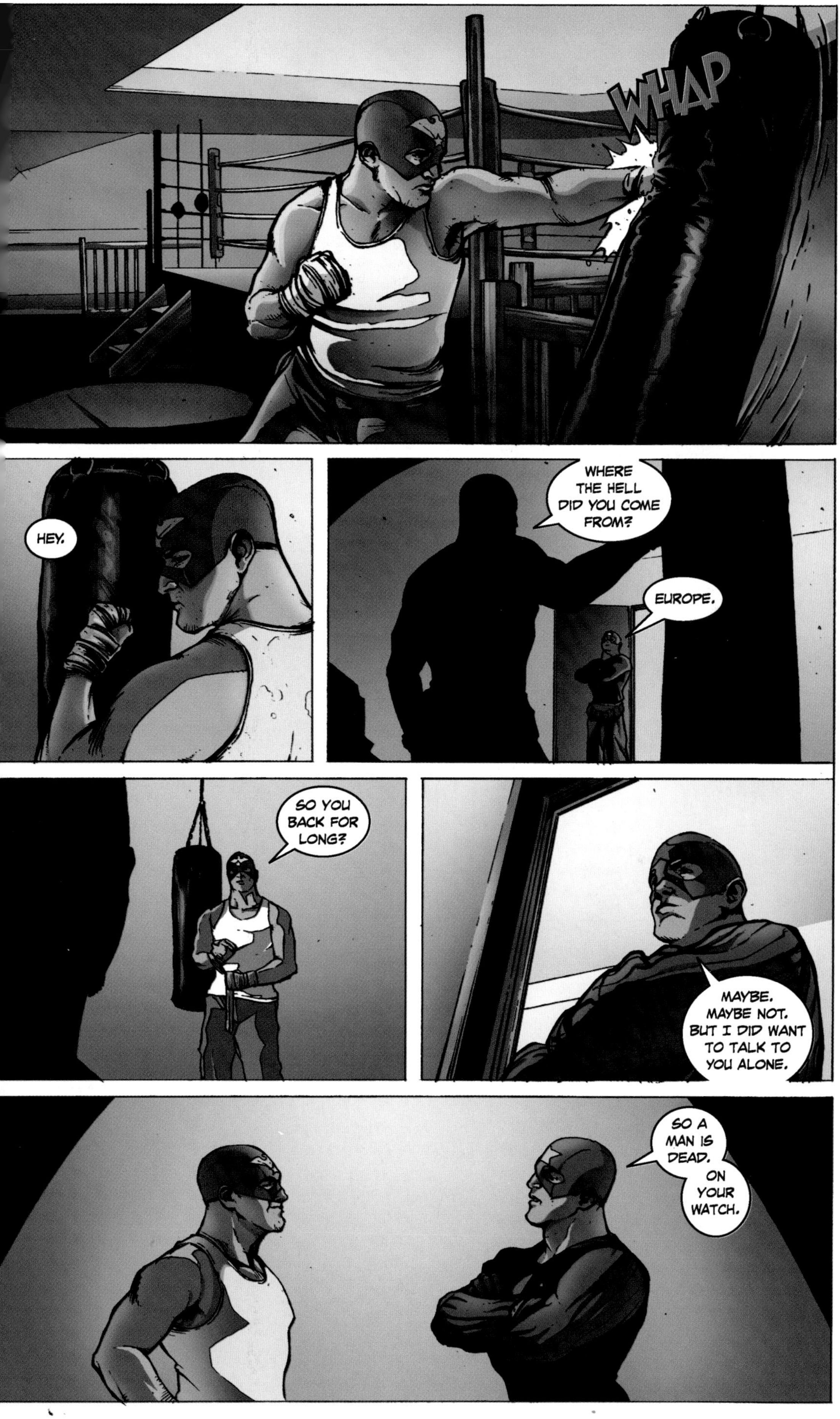
WHAP
HEY.
WHERE THE HELL DID YOU COME FROM?
EUROPE.
SO YOU BACK FOR LONG?
MAYBE. MAYBE NOT. BUT I DID WANT TO TALK TO YOU ALONE.
SO A MAN IS DEAD.
ON YOUR WATCH.

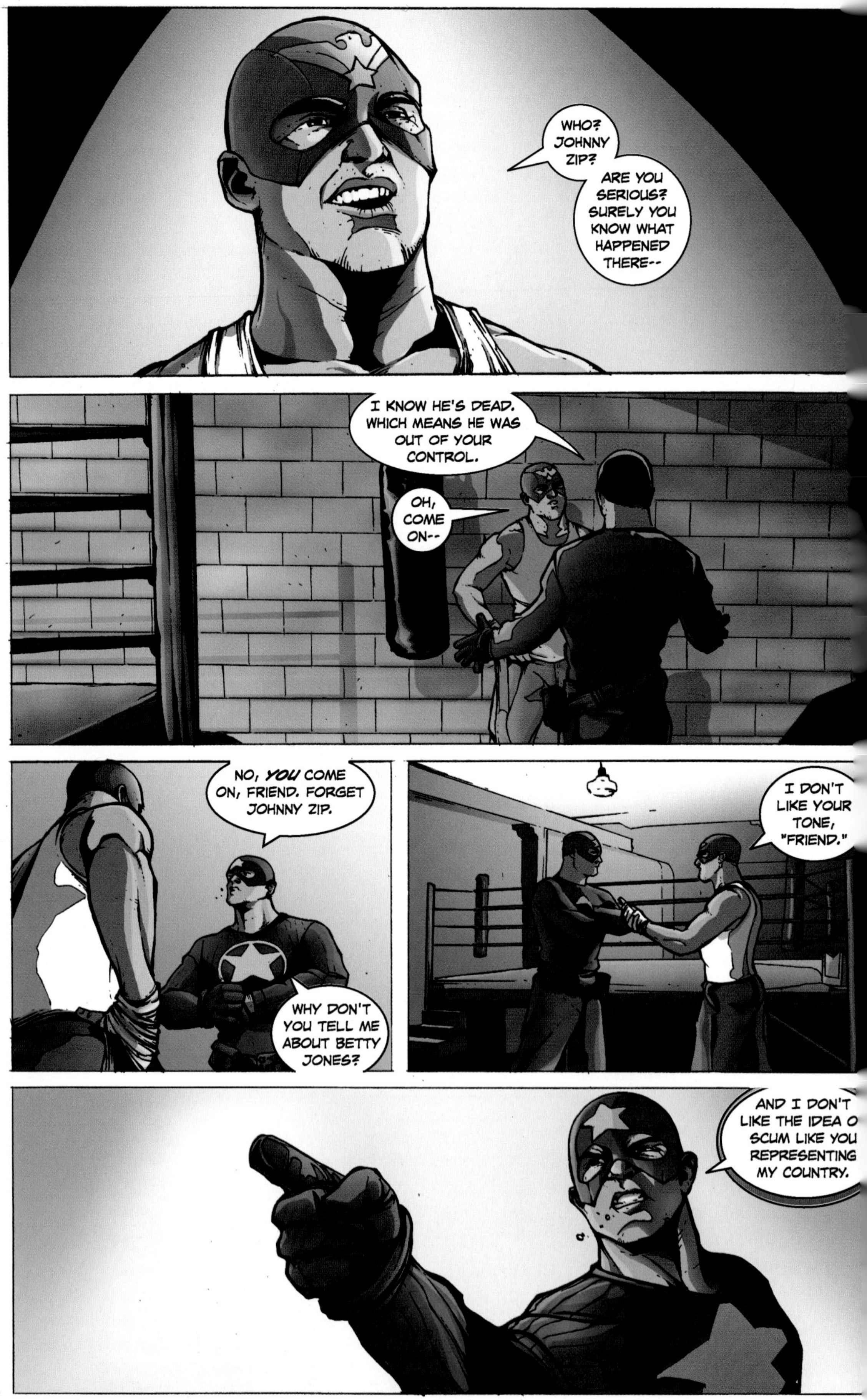
WHO? JOHNNY ZIP?
ARE YOU SERIOUS? SURELY YOU KNOW WHAT HAPPENED THERE--
I KNOW HE'S DEAD. WHICH MEANS HE WAS OUT OF YOUR CONTROL.
OH, COME ON--
NO, *YOU* COME ON, FRIEND. FORGET JOHNNY ZIP.
WHY DON'T YOU TELL ME ABOUT BETTY JONES?
I DON'T LIKE YOUR TONE, "FRIEND."
AND I DON'T LIKE THE IDEA O
SCUM LIKE YOU REPRESENTING MY COUNTRY.

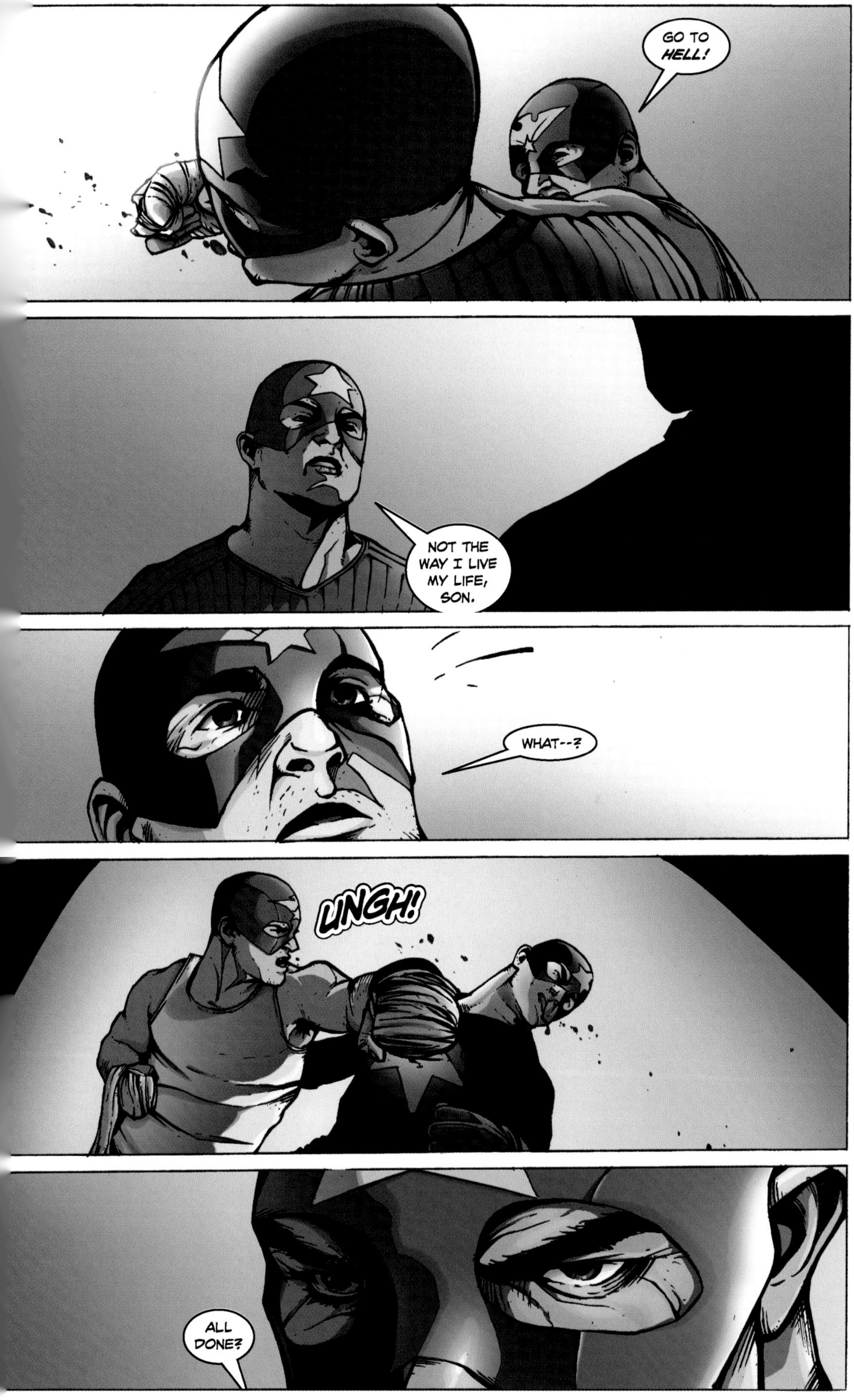
GO TO HELL!
NOT THE WAY I LIVE MY LIFE, SON.
WHAT--?
UNGH!
ALL DONE?

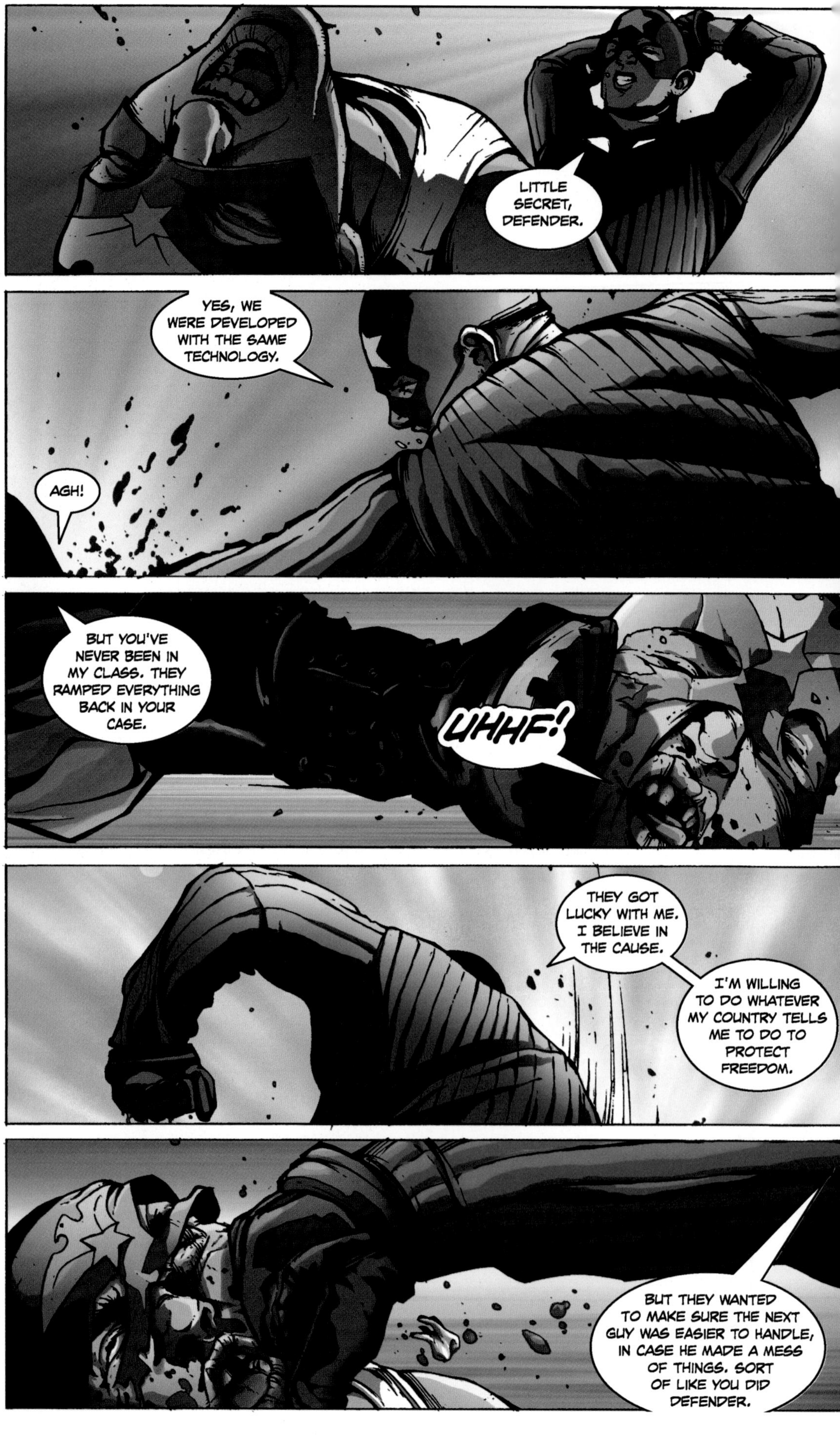
LITTLE SECRET, DEFENDER.
YES, WE WERE DEVELOPED WITH THE SAME TECHNOLOGY.
AGH!
BUT YOU'VE NEVER BEEN IN MY CLASS. THEY RAMPED EVERYTHING BACK IN YOUR CASE.
UHHF!
THEY GOT LUCKY WITH ME. I BELIEVE IN THE CAUSE.
I'M WILLING TO DO WHATEVER MY COUNTRY TELLS ME TO DO TO PROTECT FREEDOM.
BUT THEY WANTED TO MAKE SURE THE NEXT GUY WAS EASIER TO HANDLE, IN CASE HE MADE A MESS OF THINGS. SORT OF LIKE YOU DID DEFENDER.

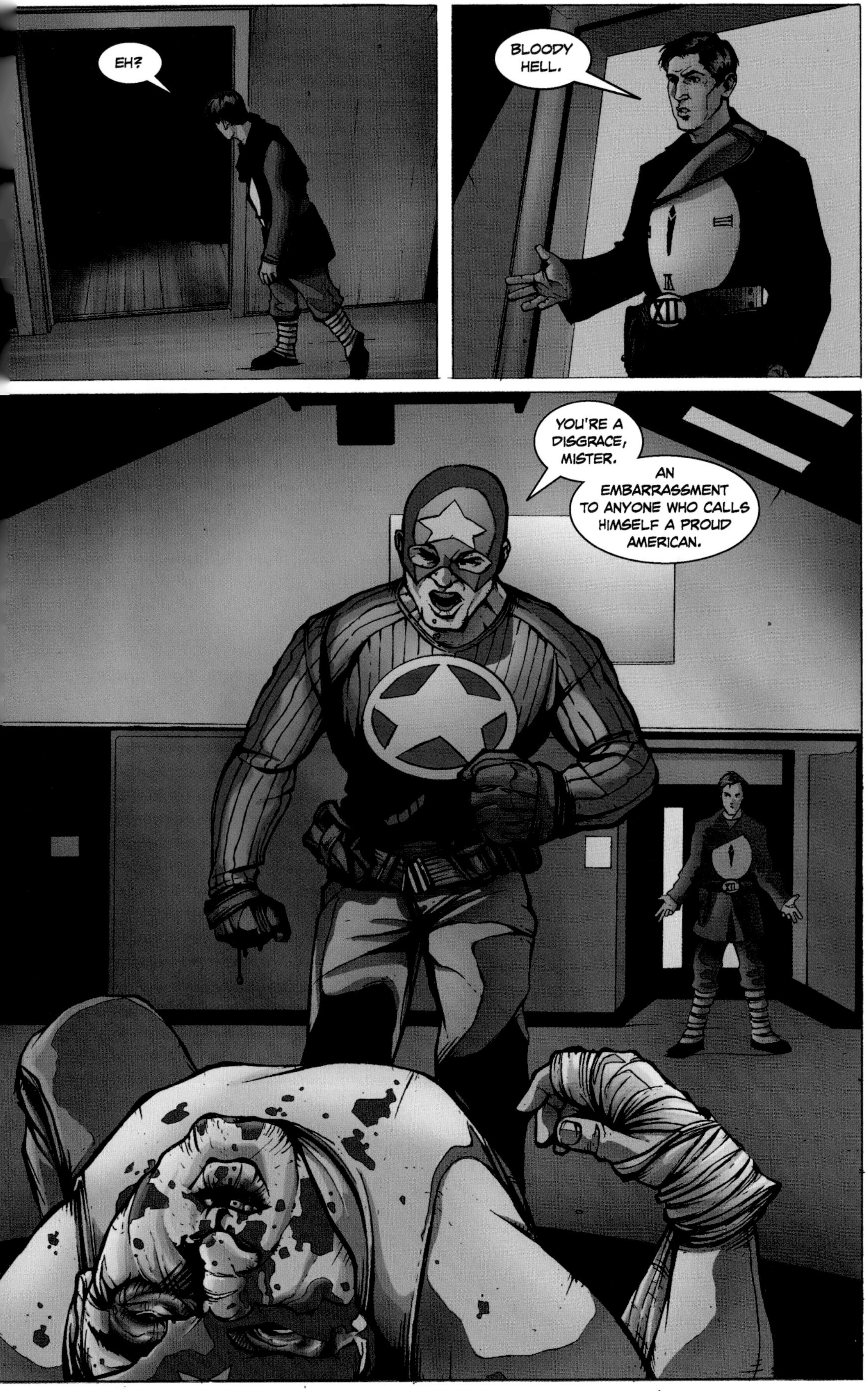
EH?
BLOODY HELL.
YOU'RE A DISGRACE, MISTER.
AN EMBARRASSMENT TO ANYONE WHO CALLS HIMSELF A PROUD AMERICAN.

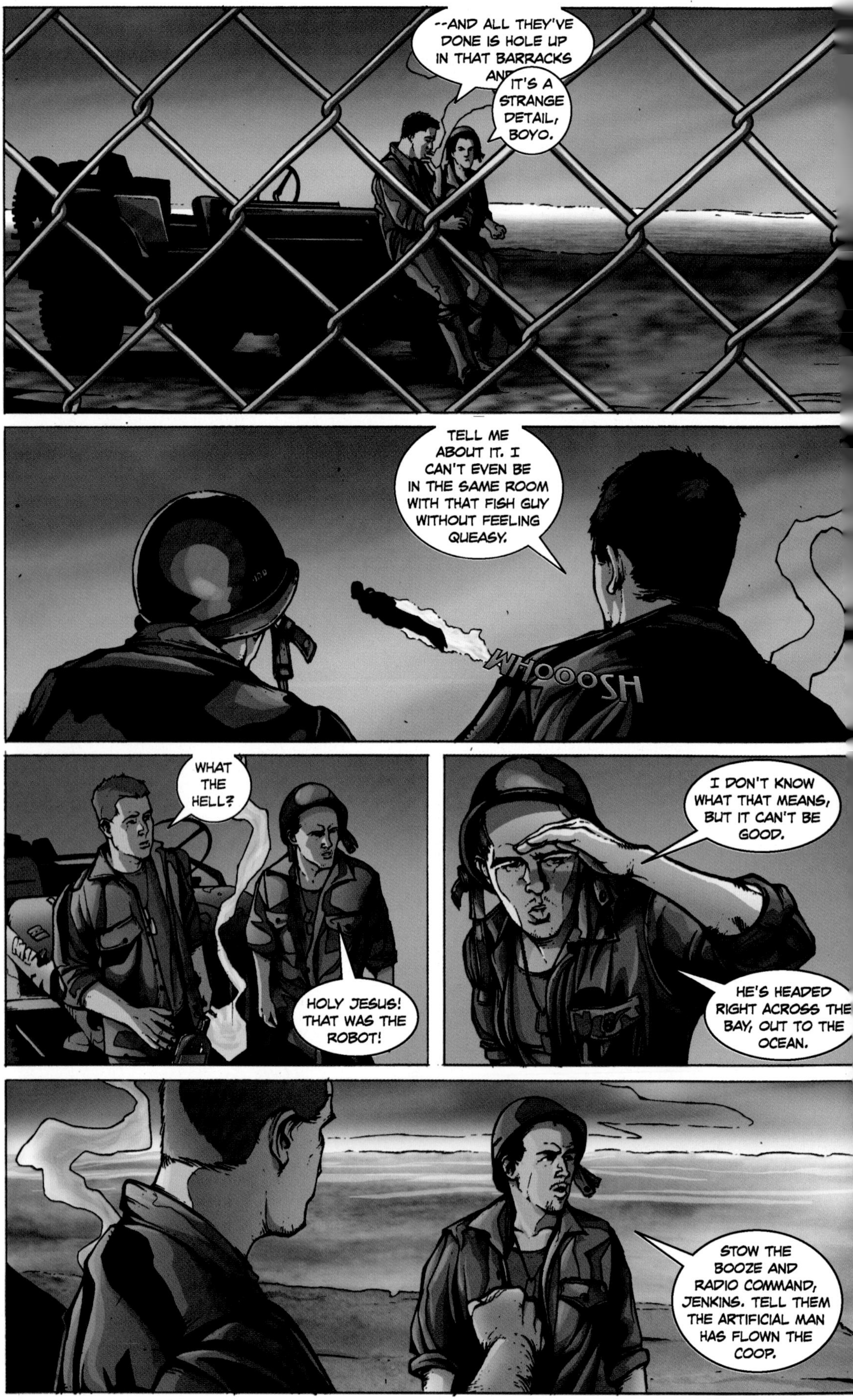
--AND ALL THEY'VE DONE IS HOLE UP IN THAT BARRACKS AND--
IT'S A STRANGE DETAIL, BOYO.
TELL ME ABOUT IT. I CAN'T EVEN BE IN THE SAME ROOM WITH THAT FISH GUY WITHOUT FEELING QUEASY.
WHOOOSH
WHAT THE HELL?
HOLY JESUS! THAT WAS THE ROBOT!
I DON'T KNOW WHAT THAT MEANS, BUT IT CAN'T BE GOOD.
HE'S HEADED RIGHT ACROSS THE BAY, OUT TO THE OCEAN.
STOW THE BOOZE AND RADIO COMMAND, JENKINS. TELL THEM THE ARTIFICIAL MAN HAS FLOWN THE COOP.

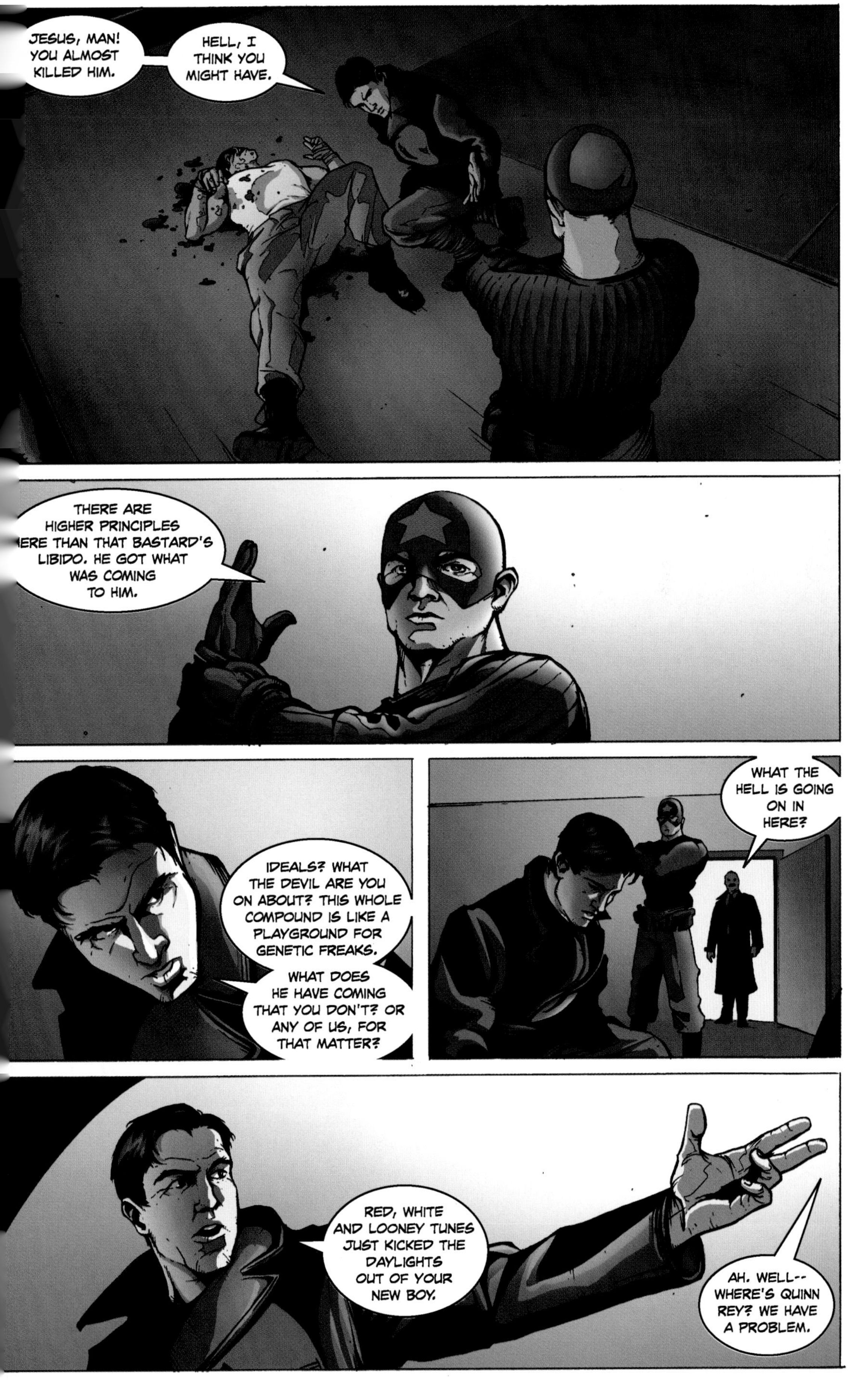

JESUS, MAN! YOU ALMOST KILLED HIM.
HELL, I THINK YOU MIGHT HAVE.
THERE ARE HIGHER PRINCIPLES HERE THAN THAT BASTARD'S LIBIDO. HE GOT WHAT WAS COMING TO HIM.
IDEALS? WHAT THE DEVIL ARE YOU ON ABOUT? THIS WHOLE COMPOUND IS LIKE A PLAYGROUND FOR GENETIC FREAKS.
WHAT DOES HE HAVE COMING THAT YOU DON'T? OR ANY OF US, FOR THAT MATTER?
WHAT THE HELL IS GOING ON IN HERE?
RED, WHITE AND LOONEY TUNES JUST KICKED THE DAYLIGHTS OUT OF YOUR NEW BOY.
AH. WELL-- WHERE'S QUINN REY? WE HAVE A PROBLEM.

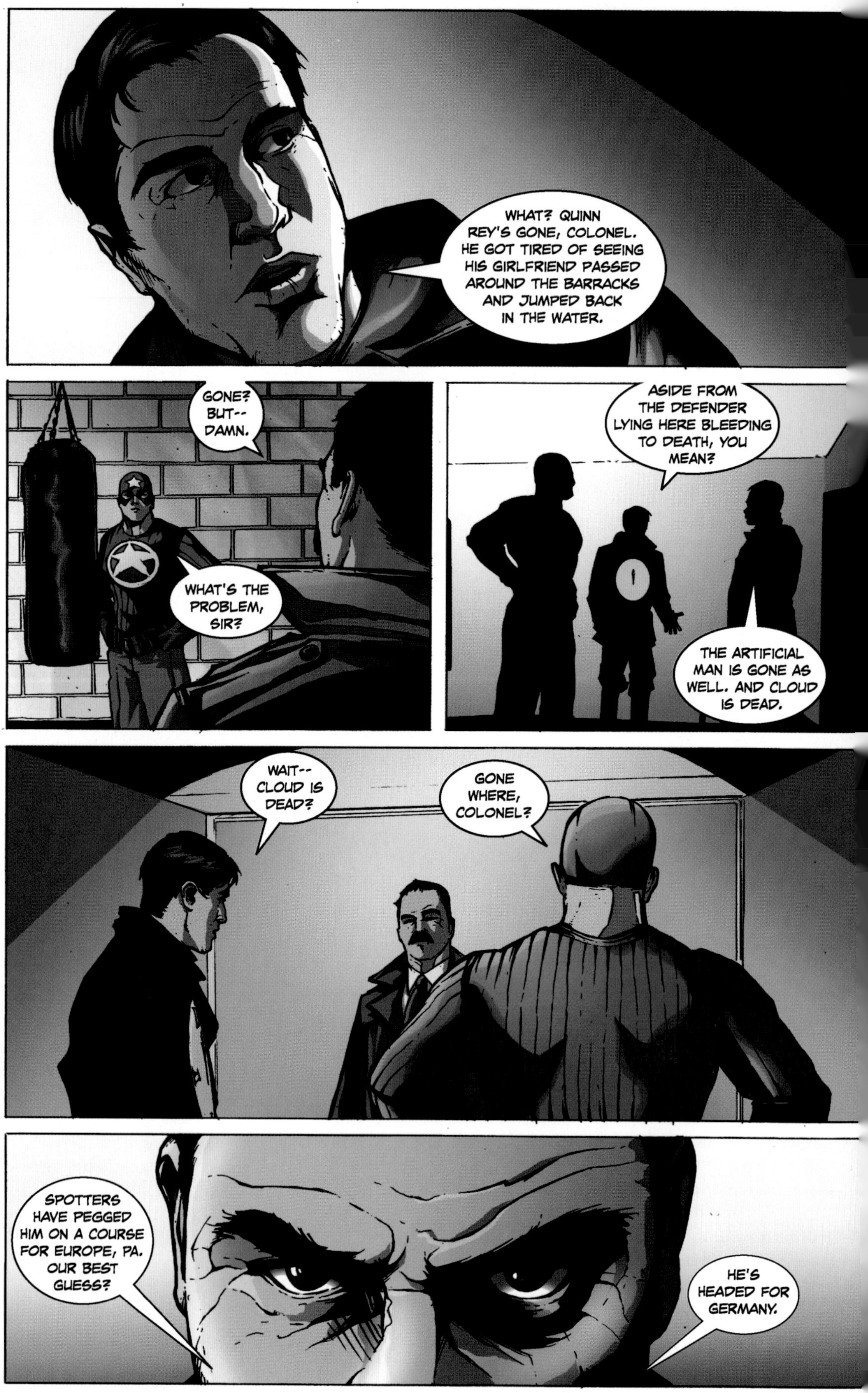
WHAT? QUINN REY'S GONE, COLONEL. HE GOT TIRED OF SEEING HIS GIRLFRIEND PASSED AROUND THE BARRACKS AND JUMPED BACK IN THE WATER.
GONE? BUT-- DAMN.
WHAT'S THE PROBLEM, SIR?
ASIDE FROM THE DEFENDER LYING HERE BLEEDING TO DEATH, YOU MEAN?
THE ARTIFICIAL MAN IS GONE AS WELL. AND CLOUD IS DEAD.
WAIT-- CLOUD IS DEAD?
GONE WHERE, COLONEL?
SPOTTERS HAVE PEGGED HIM ON A COURSE FOR EUROPE, PA. OUR BEST GUESS?
HE'S HEADED FOR GERMANY.

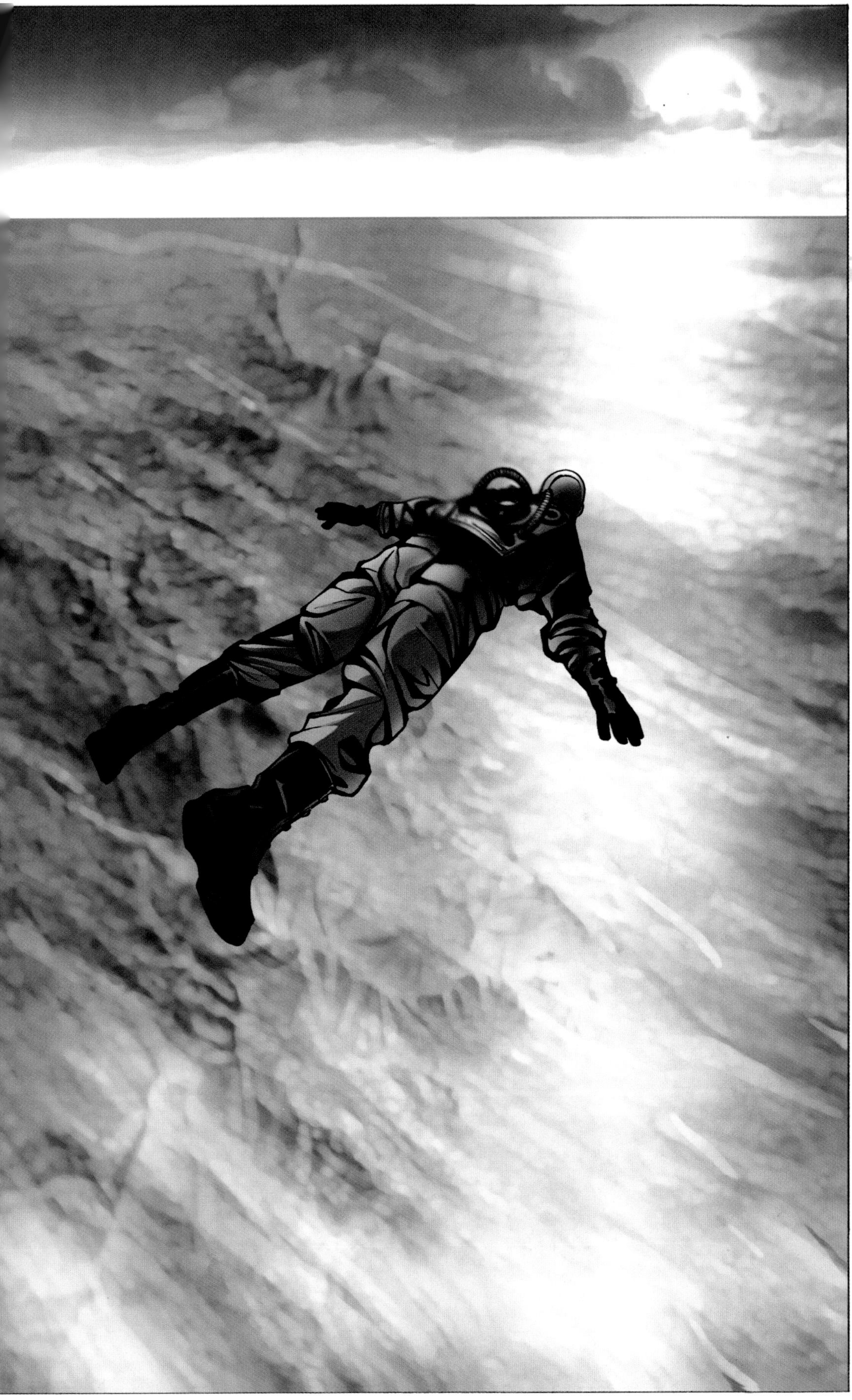

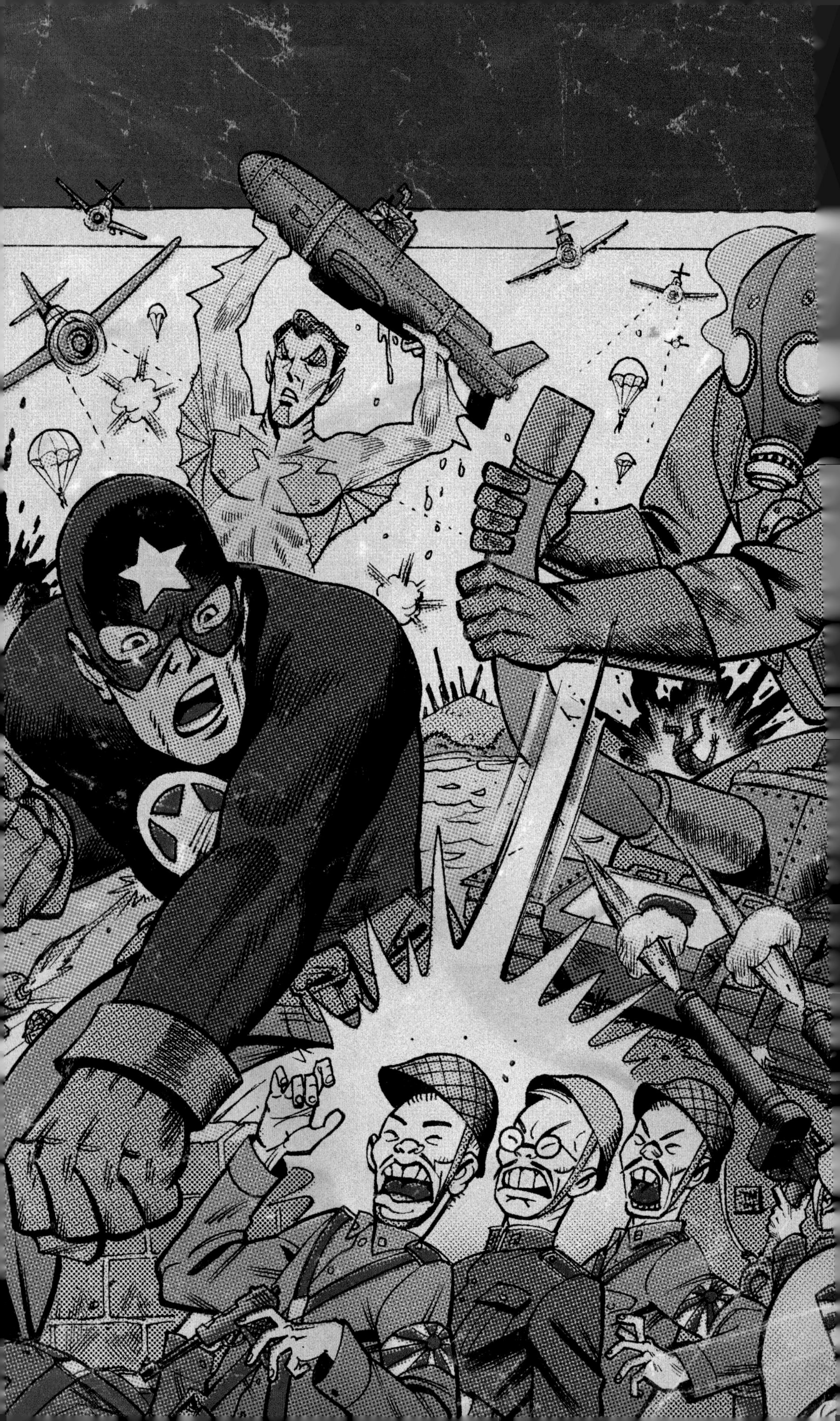

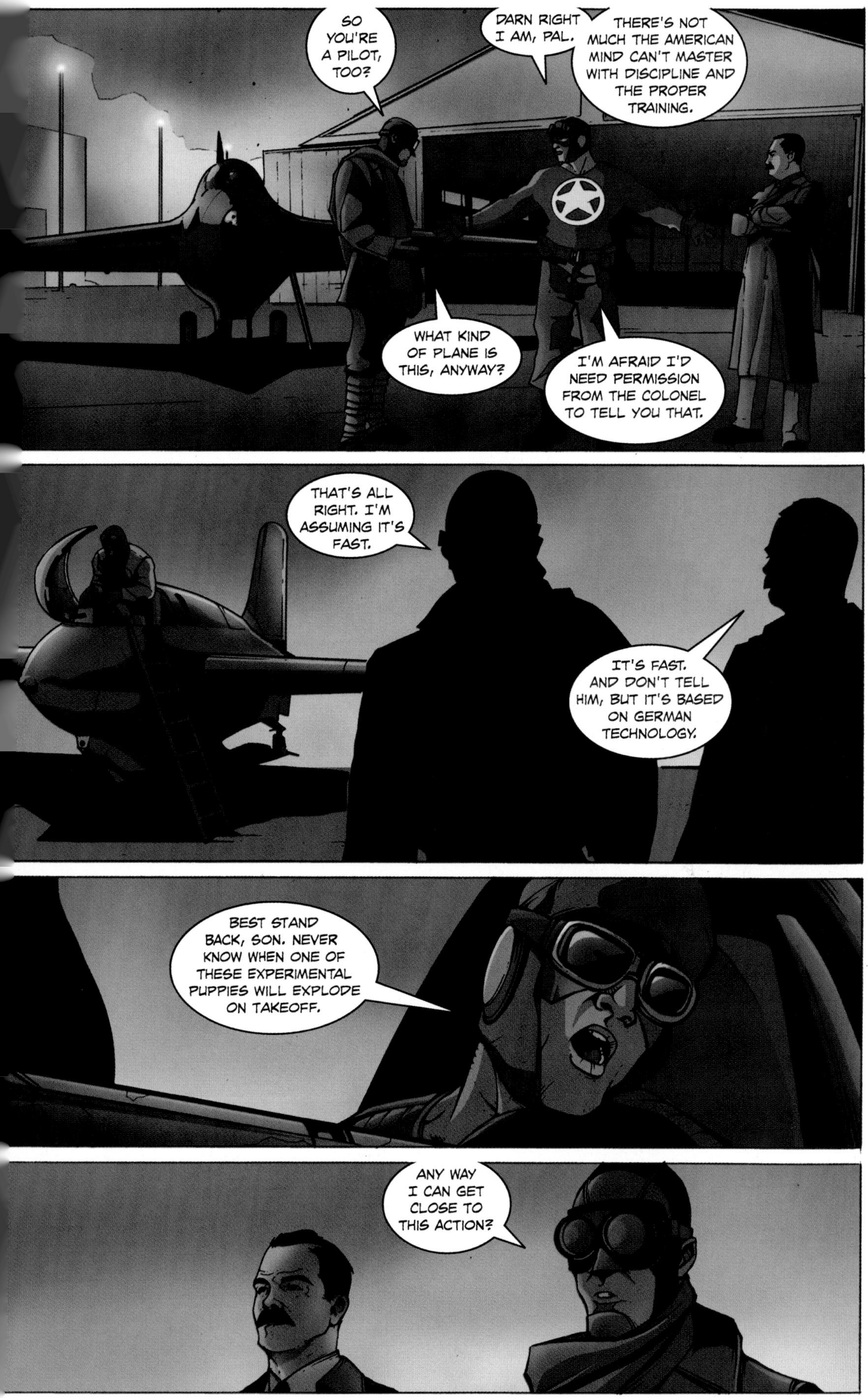
SO YOU'RE A PILOT, TOO?
DARN RIGHT I AM, PAL.
THERE'S NOT MUCH THE AMERICAN MIND CAN'T MASTER WITH DISCIPLINE AND THE PROPER TRAINING.
WHAT KIND OF PLANE IS THIS, ANYWAY?
I'M AFRAID I'D NEED PERMISSION FROM THE COLONEL TO TELL YOU THAT.
THAT'S ALL RIGHT. I'M ASSUMING IT'S FAST.
IT'S FAST. AND DON'T TELL HIM, BUT IT'S BASED ON GERMAN TECHNOLOGY.
BEST STAND BACK, SON. NEVER KNOW WHEN ONE OF THESE EXPERIMENTAL PUPPIES WILL EXPLODE ON TAKEOFF.
ANY WAY I CAN GET CLOSE TO THIS ACTION?

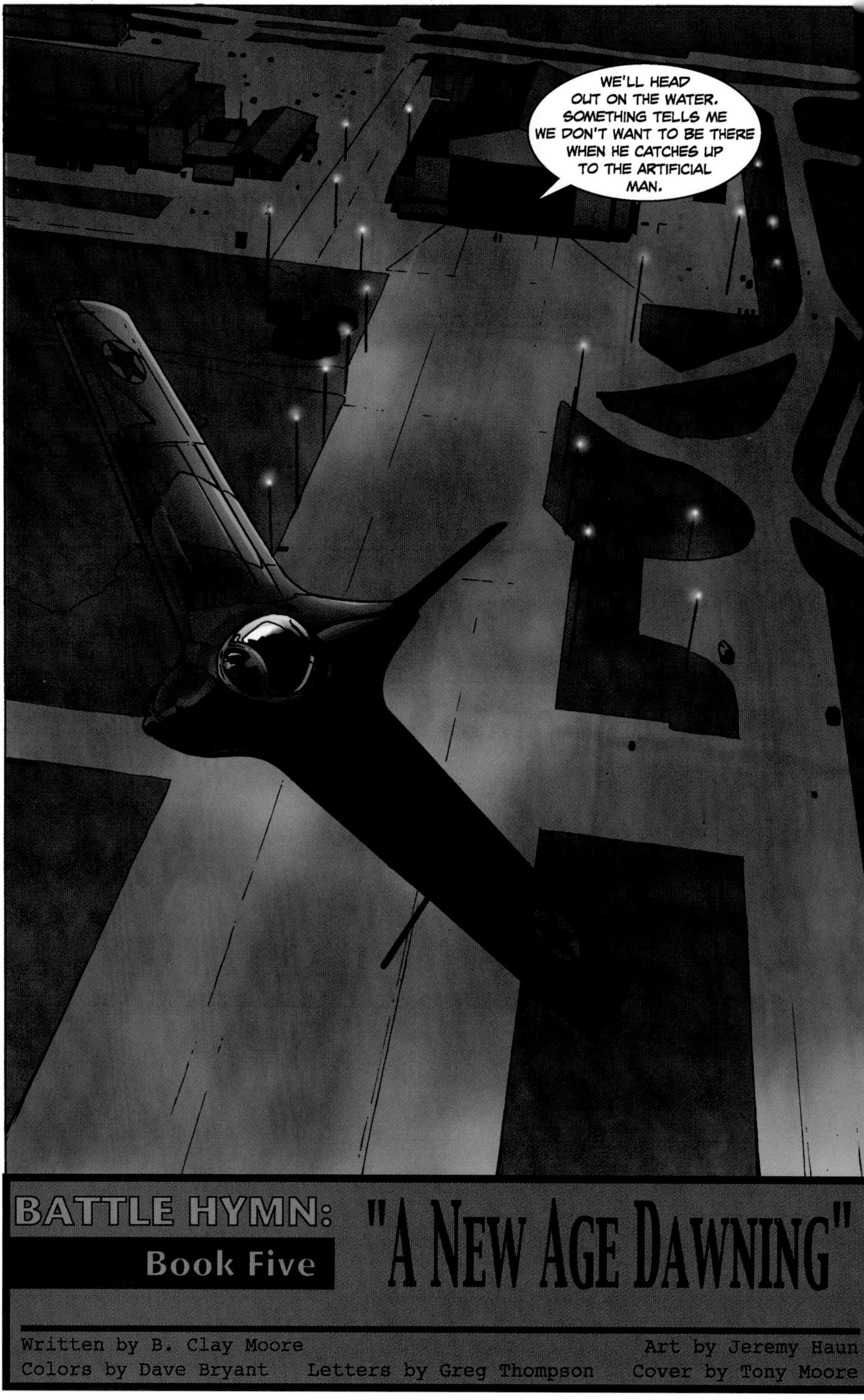
WE'LL HEAD OUT ON THE WATER. SOMETHING TELLS ME WE DON'T WANT TO BE THERE WHEN HE CATCHES UP TO THE ARTIFICIAL MAN.

BATTLE HYMN: "A NEW AGE DAWNING"

Book Five

Written by B. Clay Moore
Art by Jeremy Haun
Colors by Dave Bryant
Letters by Greg Thompson
Cover by Tony Moore

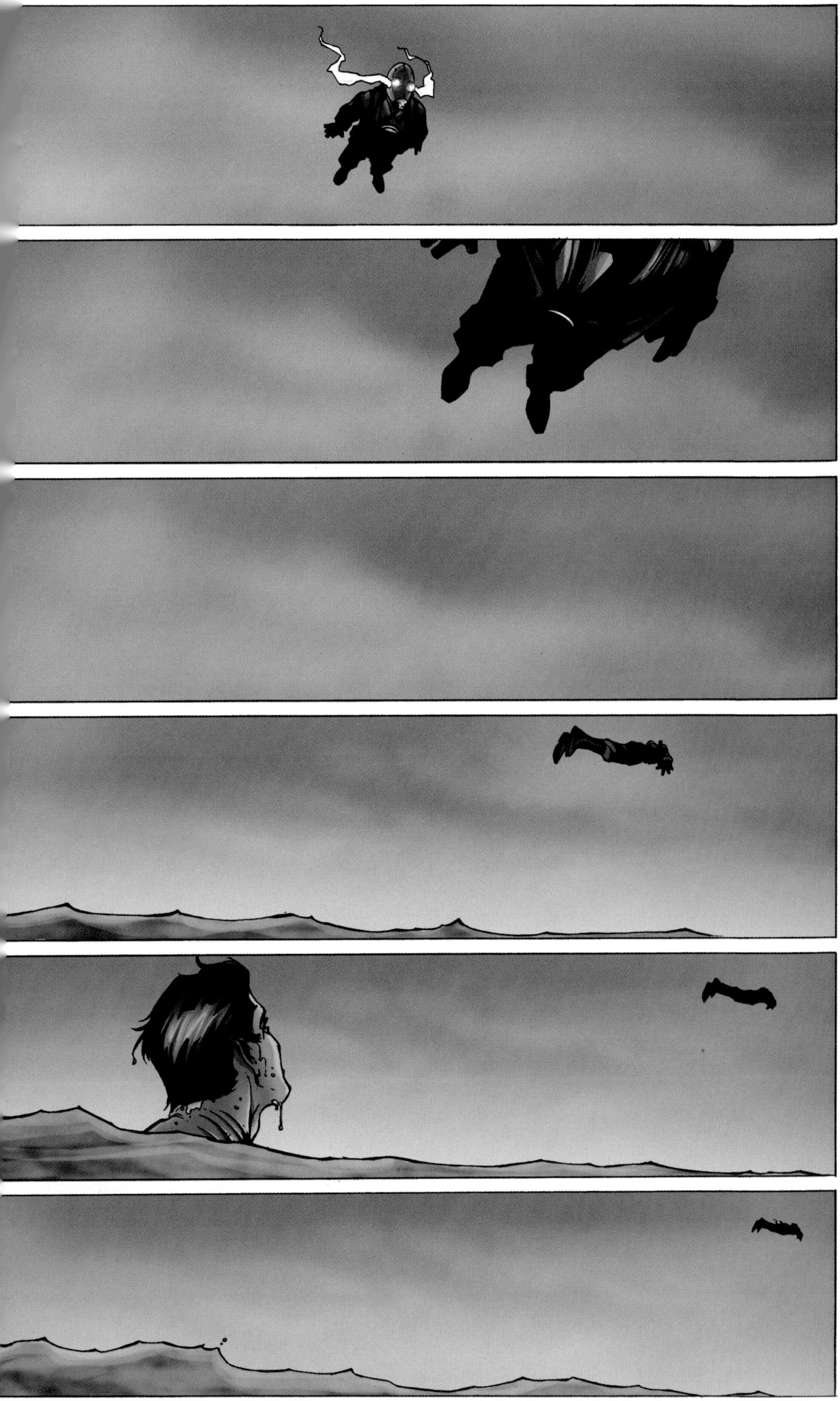

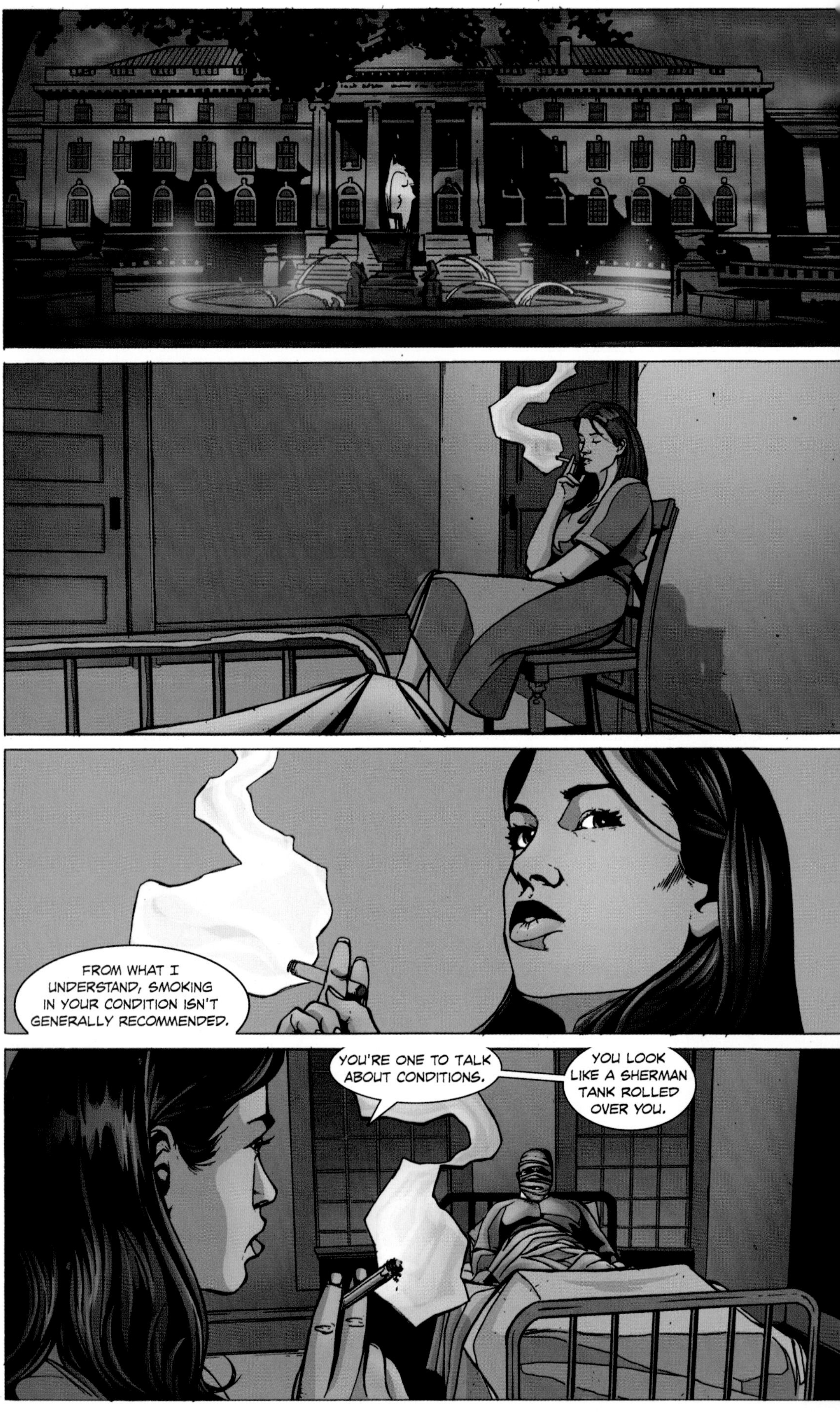
FROM WHAT I UNDERSTAND, SMOKING IN YOUR CONDITION ISN'T GENERALLY RECOMMENDED.
YOU'RE ONE TO TALK ABOUT CONDITIONS.
YOU LOOK LIKE A SHERMAN TANK ROLLED OVER YOU.

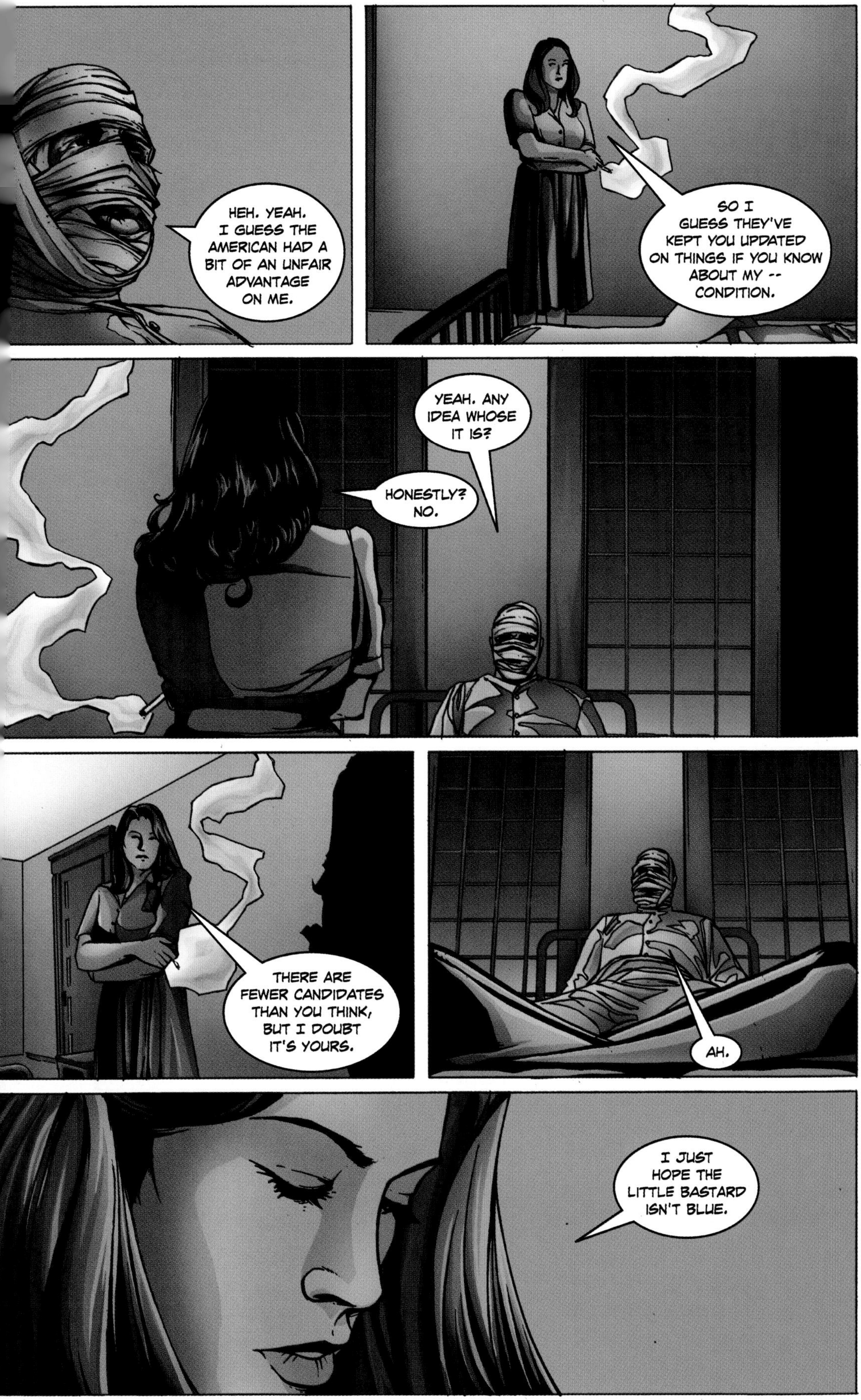
HEH. YEAH. I GUESS THE AMERICAN HAD A BIT OF AN UNFAIR ADVANTAGE ON ME.
SO I GUESS THEY'VE KEPT YOU UPDATED ON THINGS IF YOU KNOW ABOUT MY -- CONDITION.
YEAH. ANY IDEA WHOSE IT IS?
HONESTLY? NO.
THERE ARE FEWER CANDIDATES THAN YOU THINK, BUT I DOUBT IT'S YOURS.
AH.
I JUST HOPE THE LITTLE BASTARD ISN'T BLUE.

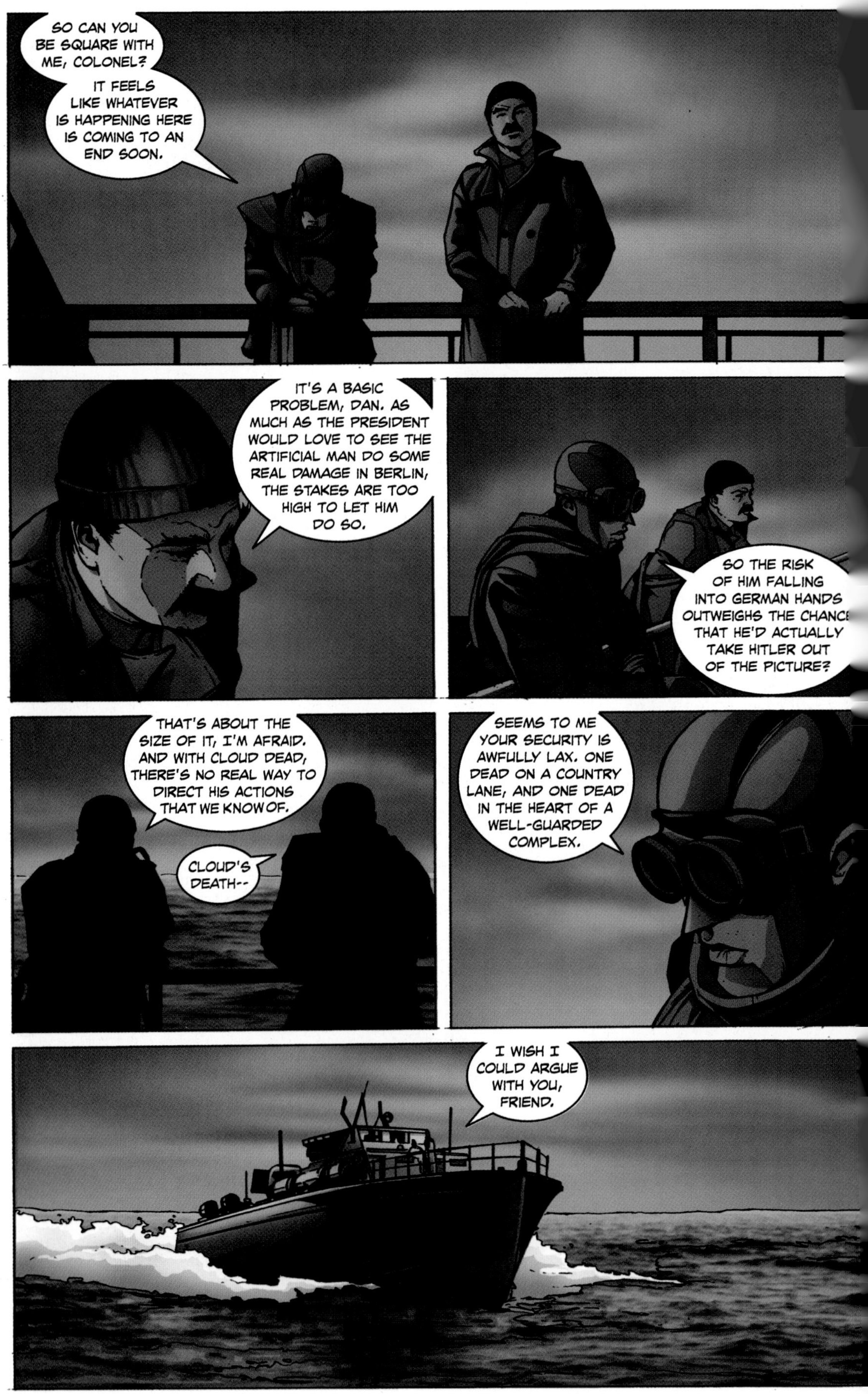
SO CAN YOU BE SQUARE WITH ME, COLONEL?
IT FEELS LIKE WHATEVER IS HAPPENING HERE IS COMING TO AN END SOON.
IT'S A BASIC PROBLEM, DAN. AS MUCH AS THE PRESIDENT WOULD LOVE TO SEE THE ARTIFICIAL MAN DO SOME REAL DAMAGE IN BERLIN, THE STAKES ARE TOO HIGH TO LET HIM DO SO.
SO THE RISK OF HIM FALLING INTO GERMAN HANDS OUTWEIGHS THE CHANCE THAT HE'D ACTUALLY TAKE HITLER OUT OF THE PICTURE?
THAT'S ABOUT THE SIZE OF IT, I'M AFRAID. AND WITH CLOUD DEAD, THERE'S NO REAL WAY TO DIRECT HIS ACTIONS THAT WE KNOW OF.
CLOUD'S DEATH--
SEEMS TO ME YOUR SECURITY IS AWFULLY LAX. ONE DEAD ON A COUNTRY LANE, AND ONE DEAD IN THE HEART OF A WELL-GUARDED COMPLEX.
I WISH I COULD ARGUE WITH YOU, FRIEND.

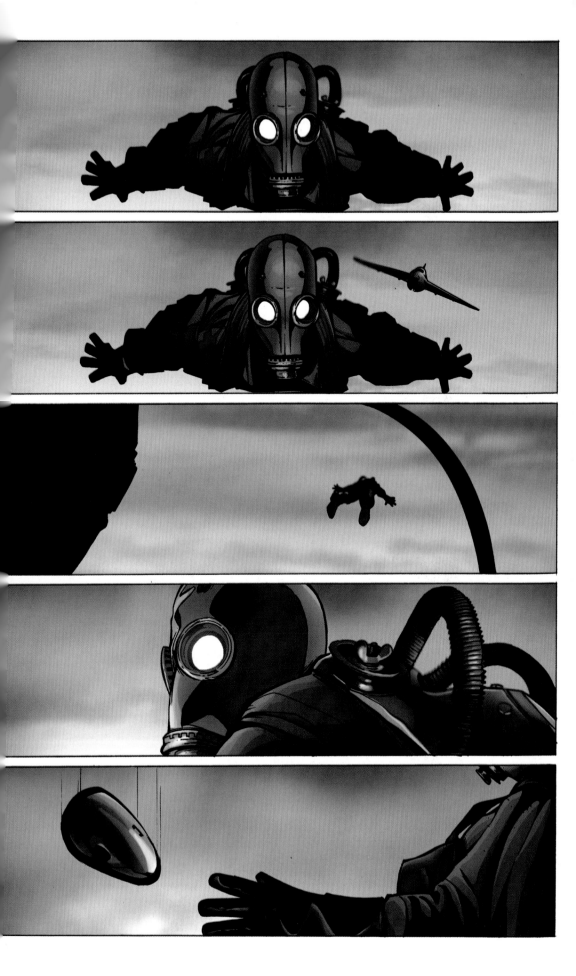

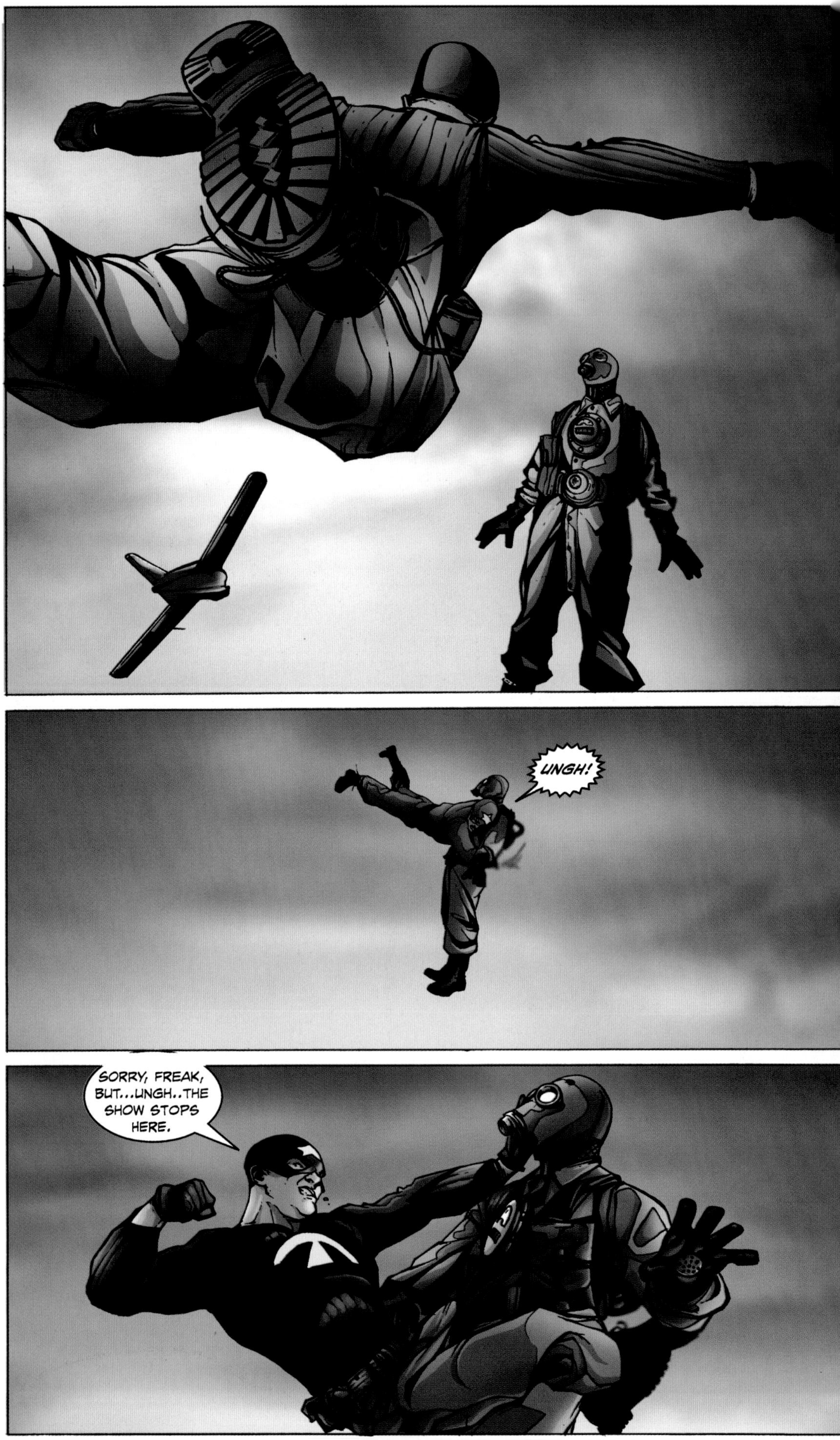
UNGH!
SORRY, FREAK, BUT...UNGH..THE SHOW STOPS HERE.

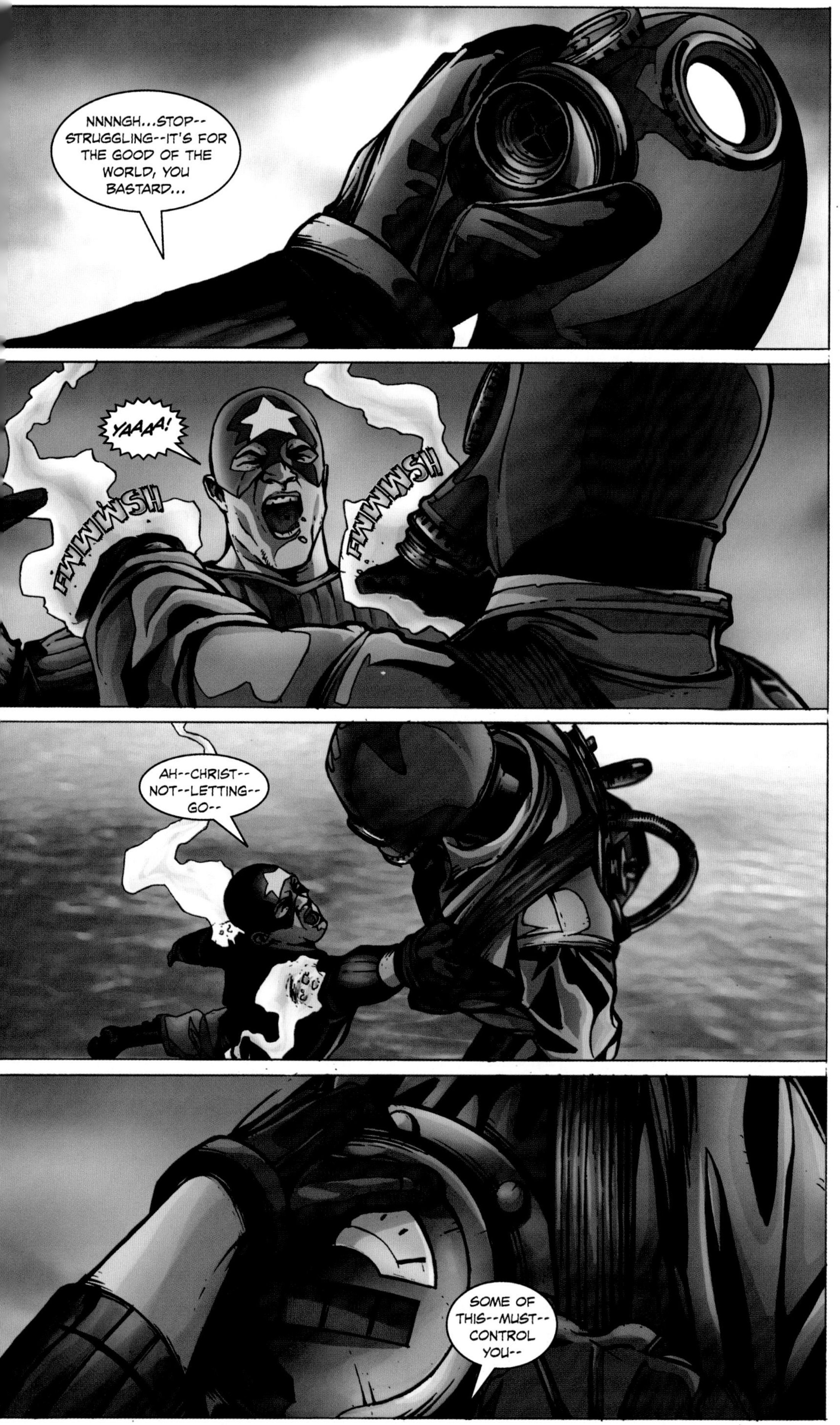
NNNNGH...STOP--STRUGGLING--IT'S FOR THE GOOD OF THE WORLD, YOU BASTARD...
YAAAA!
FWWWSH
FWWWSH
AH--CHRIST--NOT--LETTING--GO--
SOME OF THIS--MUST--CONTROL YOU--

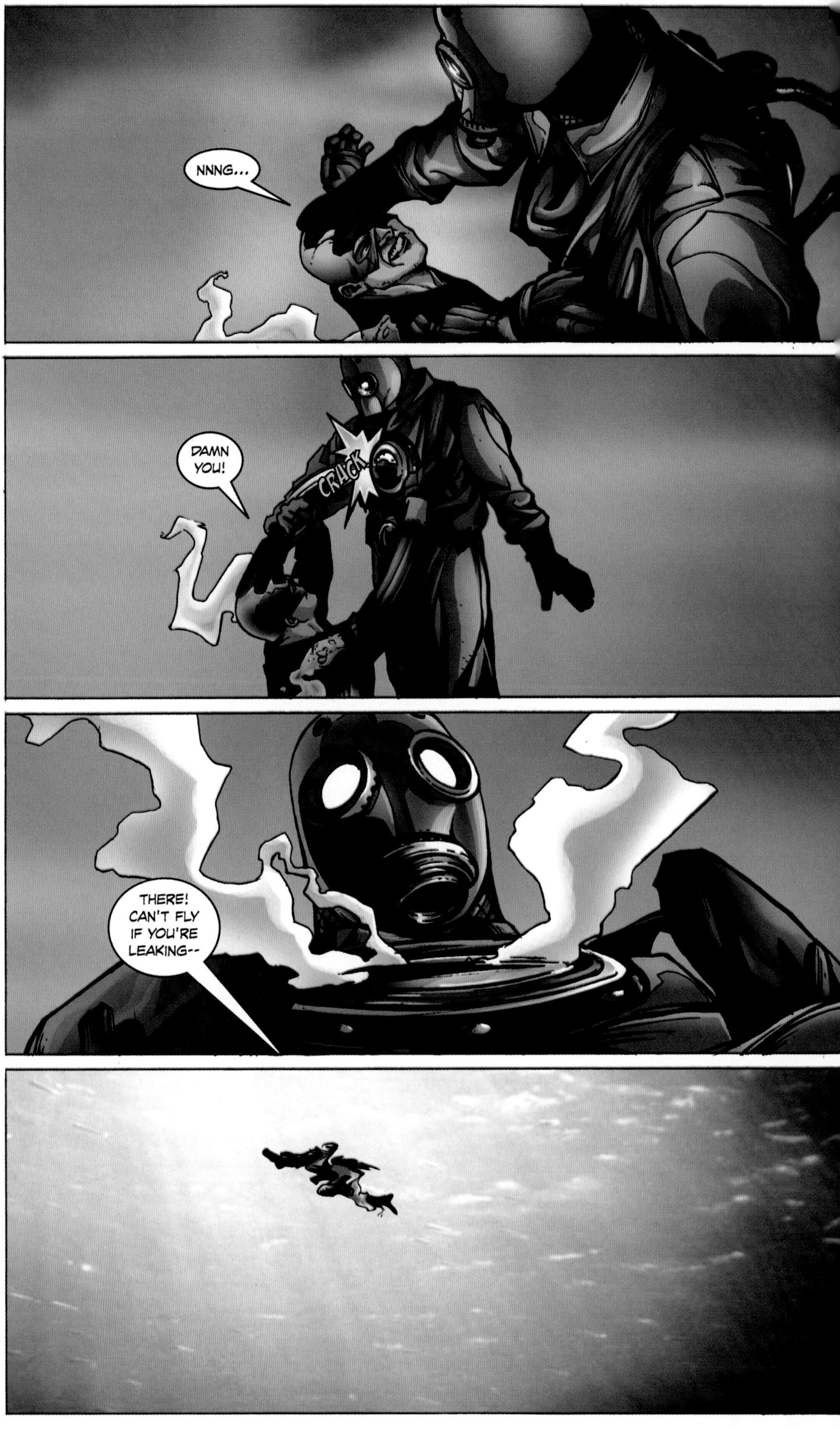
NNNG...
DAMN YOU!
CRACK
THERE! CAN'T FLY IF YOU'RE LEAKING--

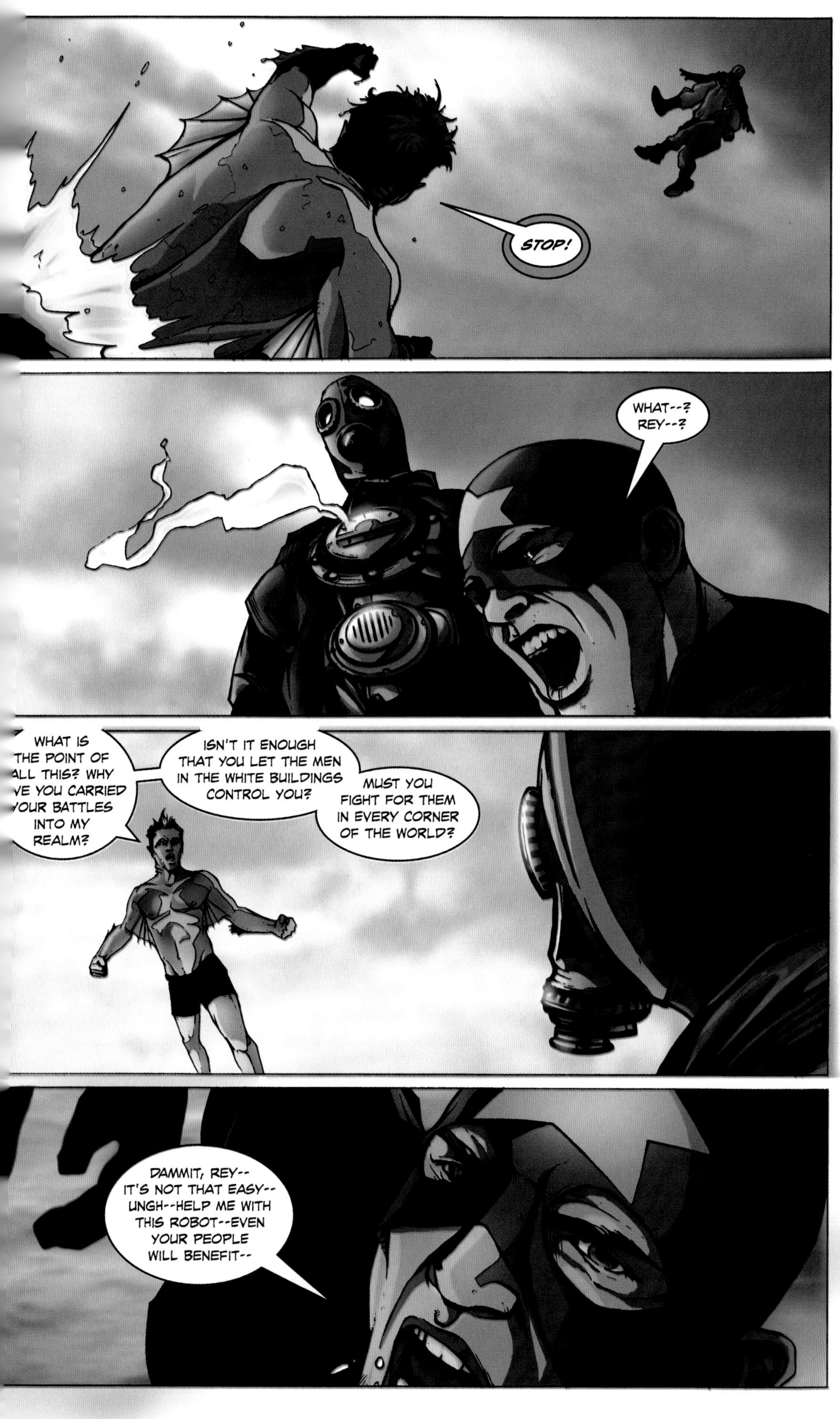
STOP!
WHAT--?
REY--?
WHAT IS
THE POINT OF
ALL THIS? WHY
VE YOU CARRIED
YOUR BATTLES
INTO MY
REALM?
ISN'T IT ENOUGH
THAT YOU LET THE MEN
IN THE WHITE BUILDINGS
CONTROL YOU?
MUST YOU
FIGHT FOR THEM
IN EVERY CORNER
OF THE WORLD?
DAMMIT, REY--
IT'S NOT THAT EASY--
UNGH--HELP ME WITH
THIS ROBOT--EVEN
YOUR PEOPLE
WILL BENEFIT--

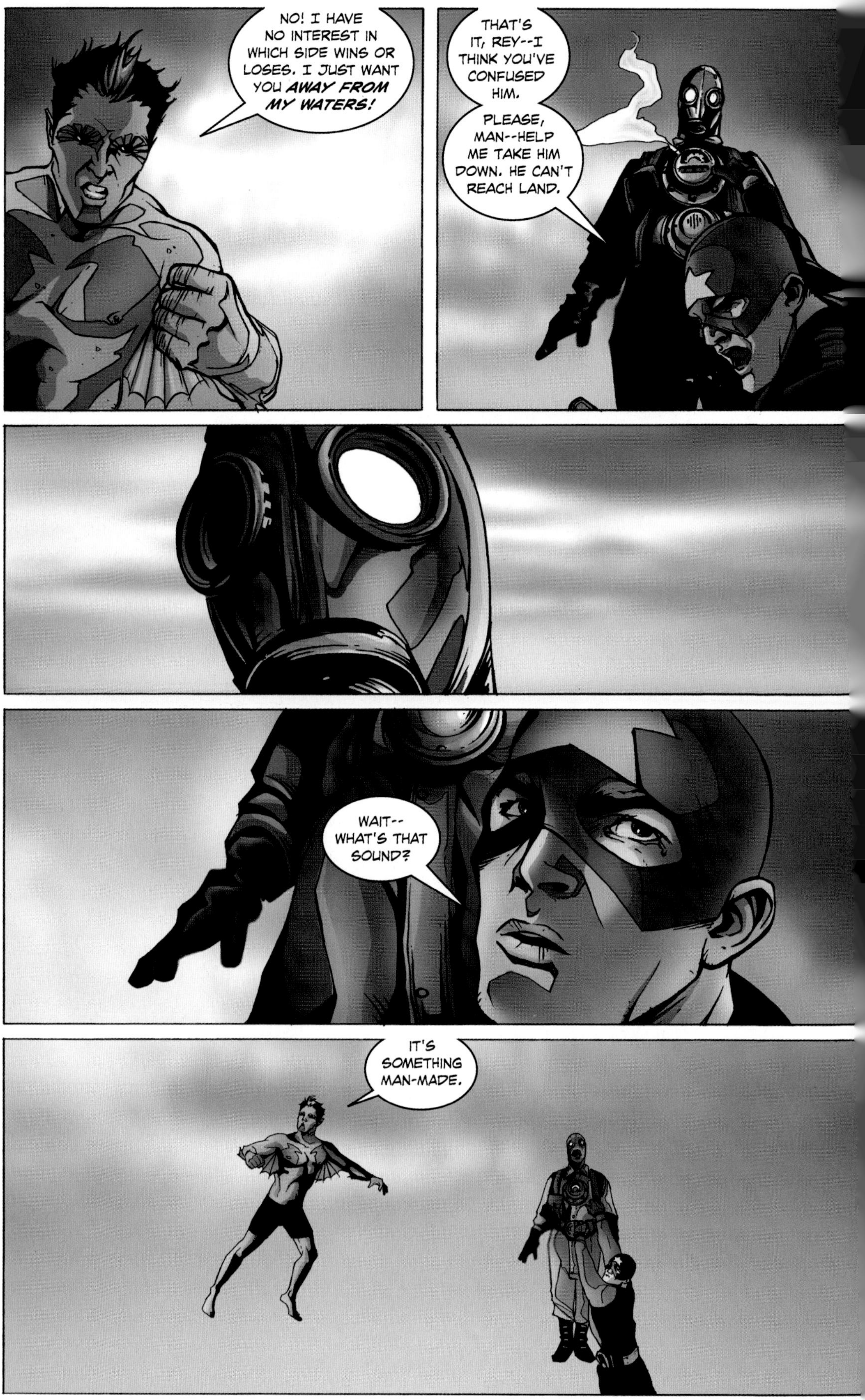
NO! I HAVE NO INTEREST IN WHICH SIDE WINS OR LOSES. I JUST WANT YOU **AWAY FROM MY WATERS!**
THAT'S IT, REY--I THINK YOU'VE CONFUSED HIM.
PLEASE, MAN--HELP ME TAKE HIM DOWN. HE CAN'T REACH LAND.
WAIT-- WHAT'S THAT SOUND?
IT'S SOMETHING MAN-MADE.

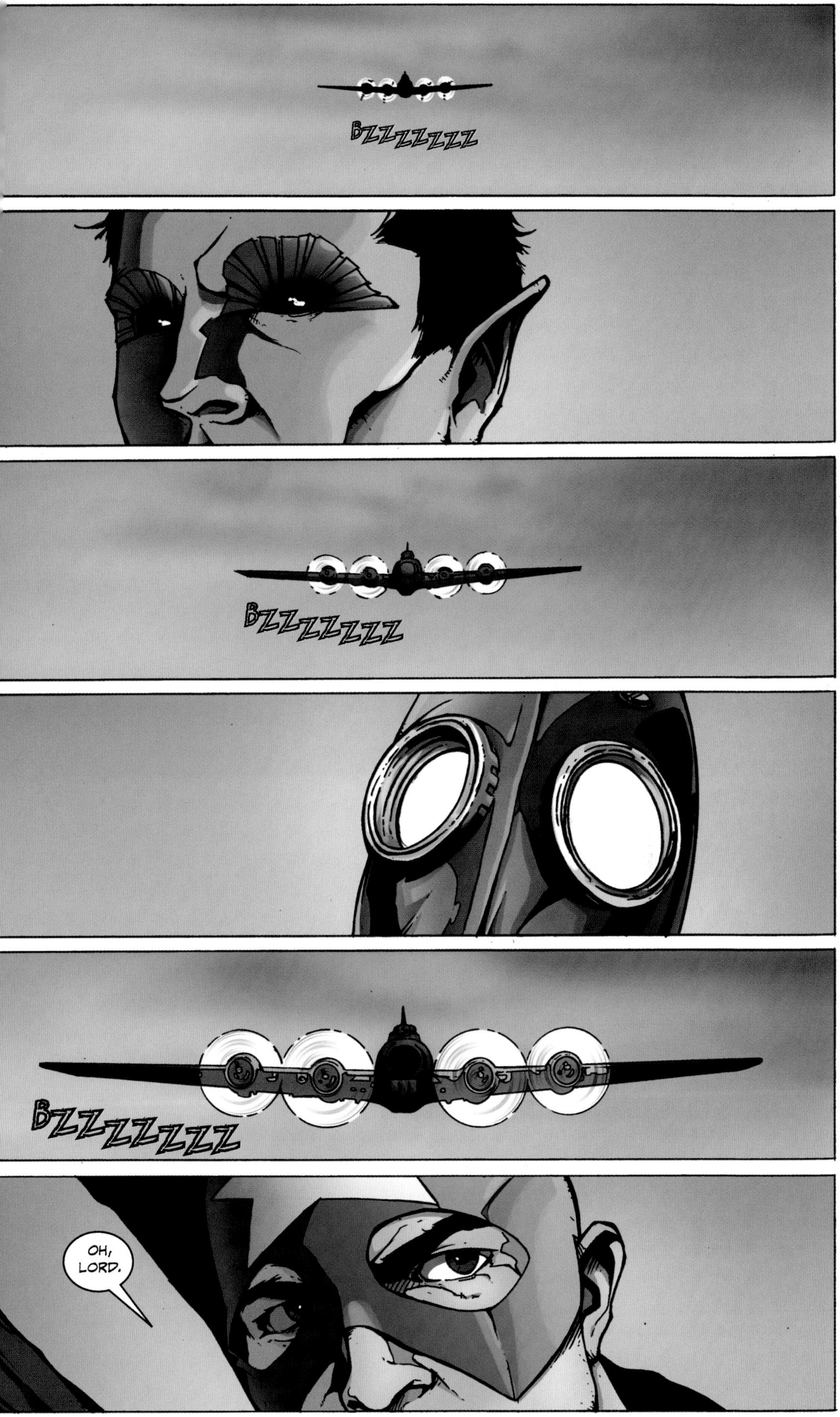
BZZZZZZZ
BZZZZZZZZ
BZZZZZZZZ
OH, LORD.

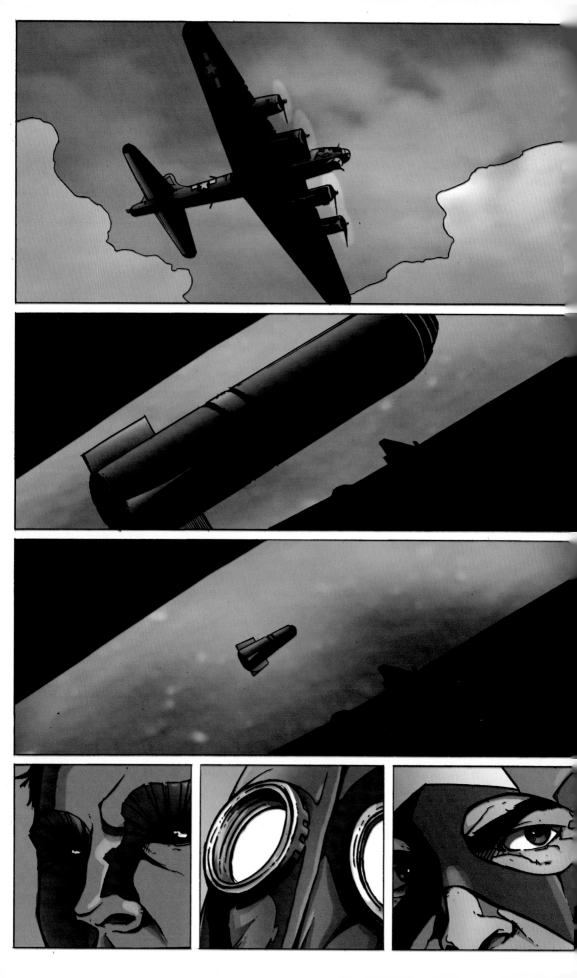

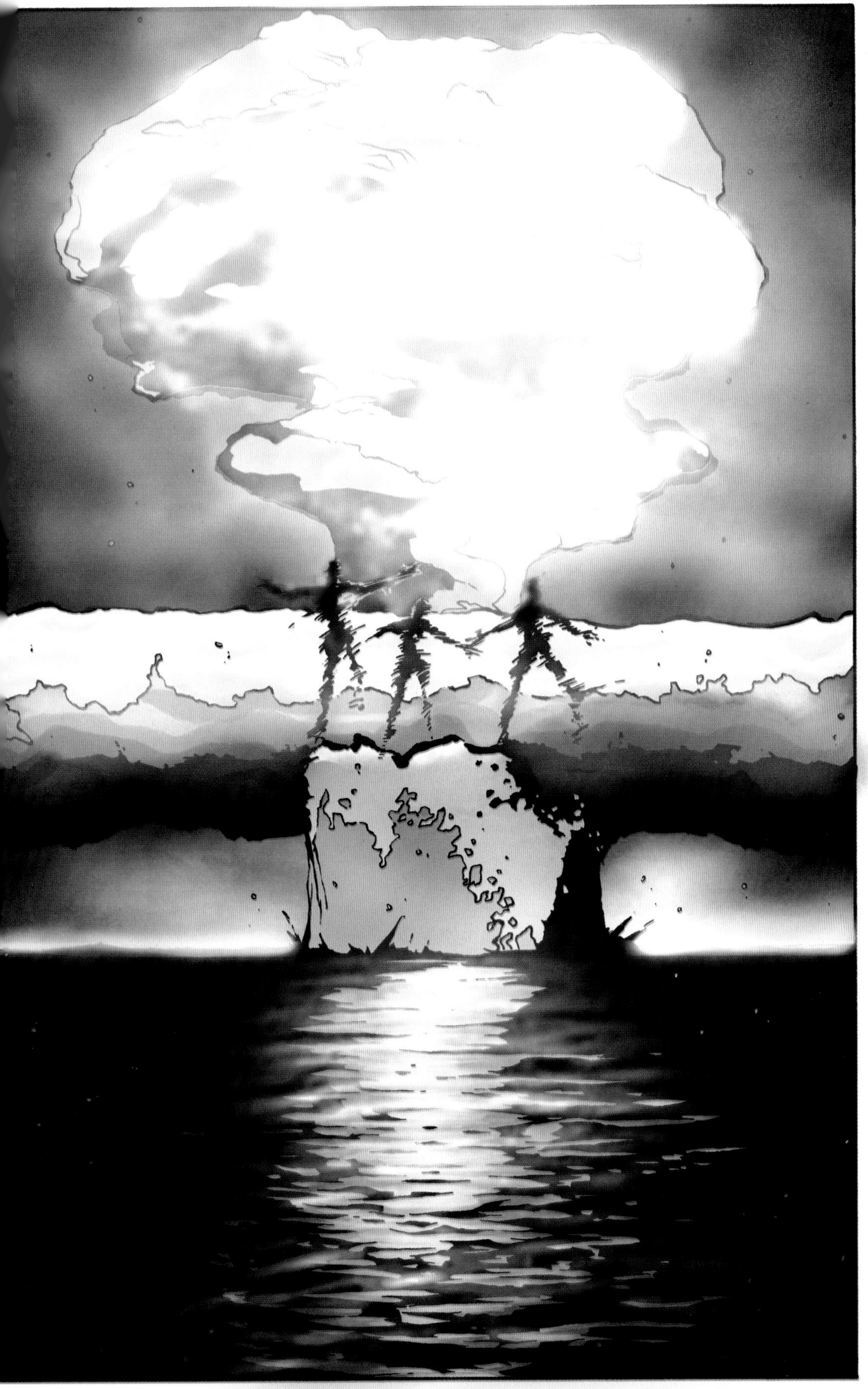

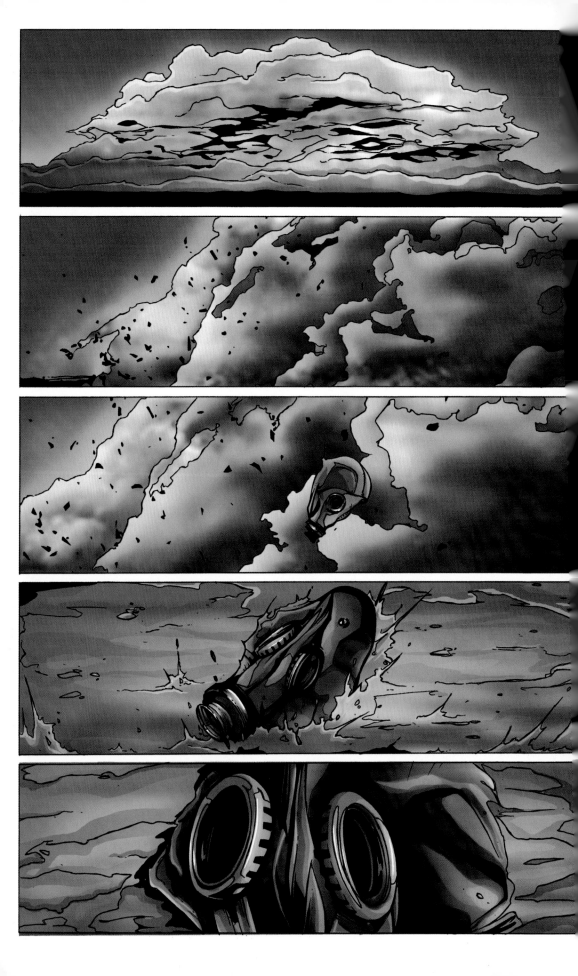

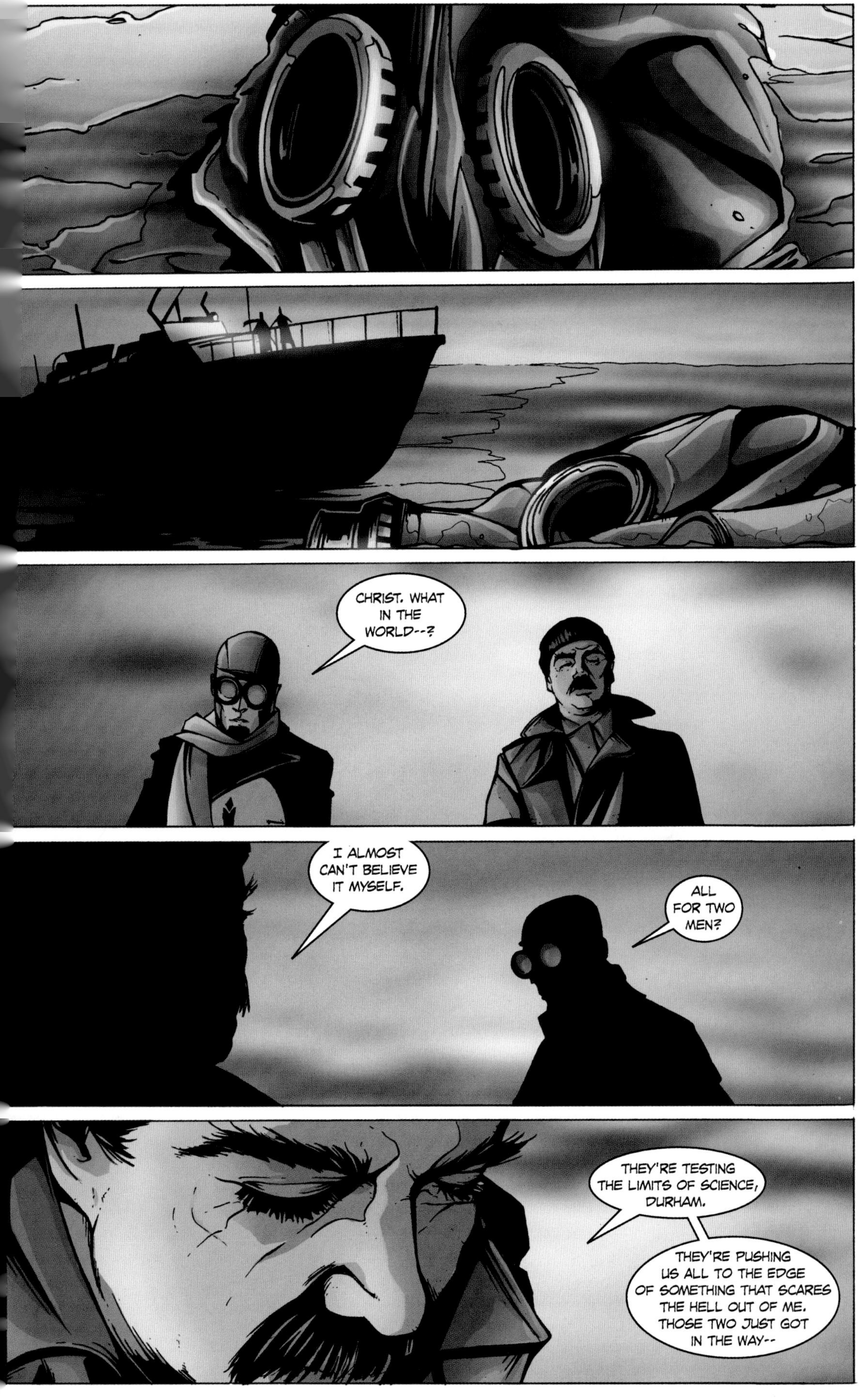
CHRIST. WHAT IN THE WORLD--?
I ALMOST CAN'T BELIEVE IT MYSELF.
ALL FOR TWO MEN?
THEY'RE TESTING THE LIMITS OF SCIENCE, DURHAM.
THEY'RE PUSHING US ALL TO THE EDGE OF SOMETHING THAT SCARES THE HELL OUT OF ME. THOSE TWO JUST GOT IN THE WAY--

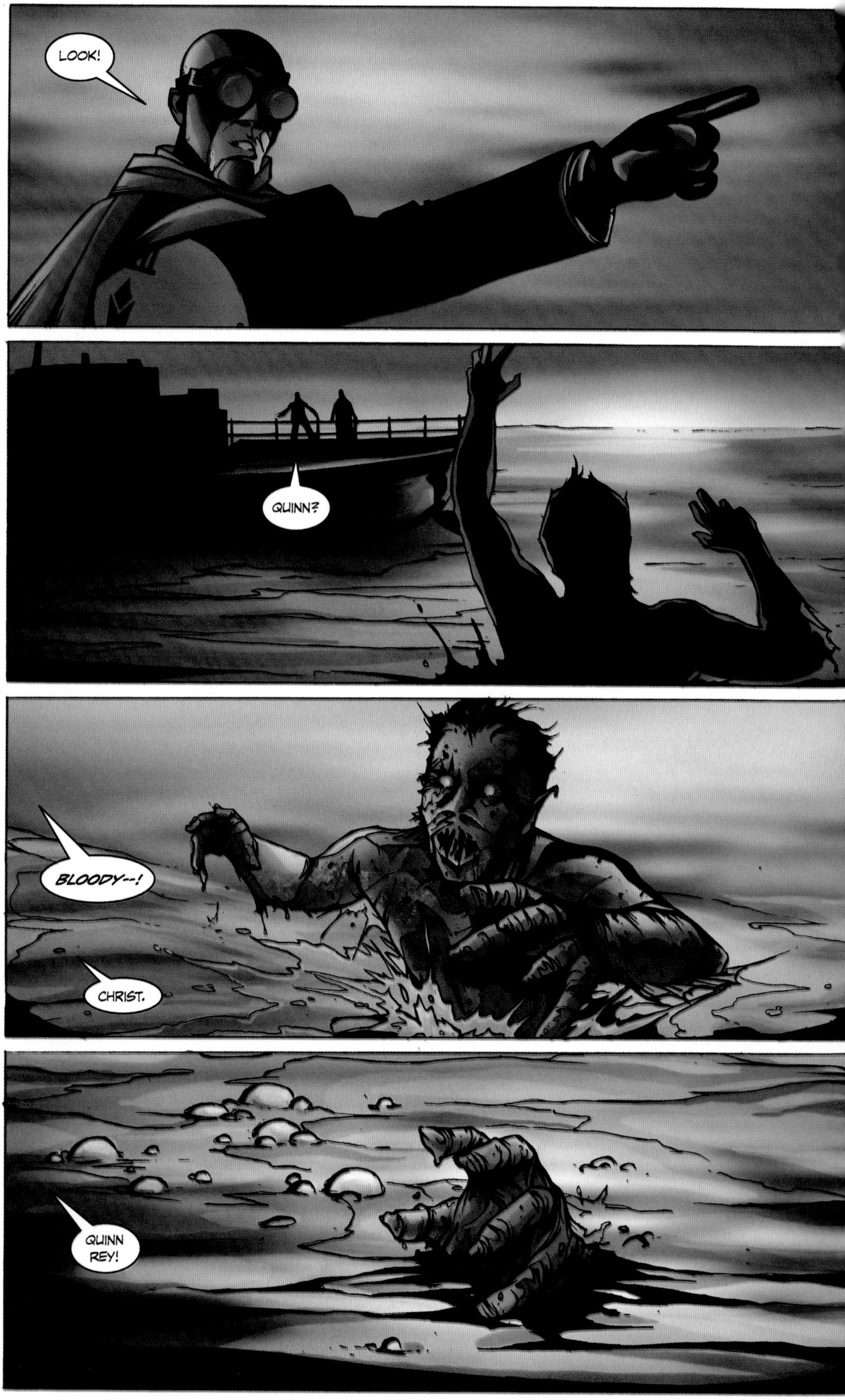
LOOK!
QUINN?
BLOODY--!
CHRIST.
QUINN REY!

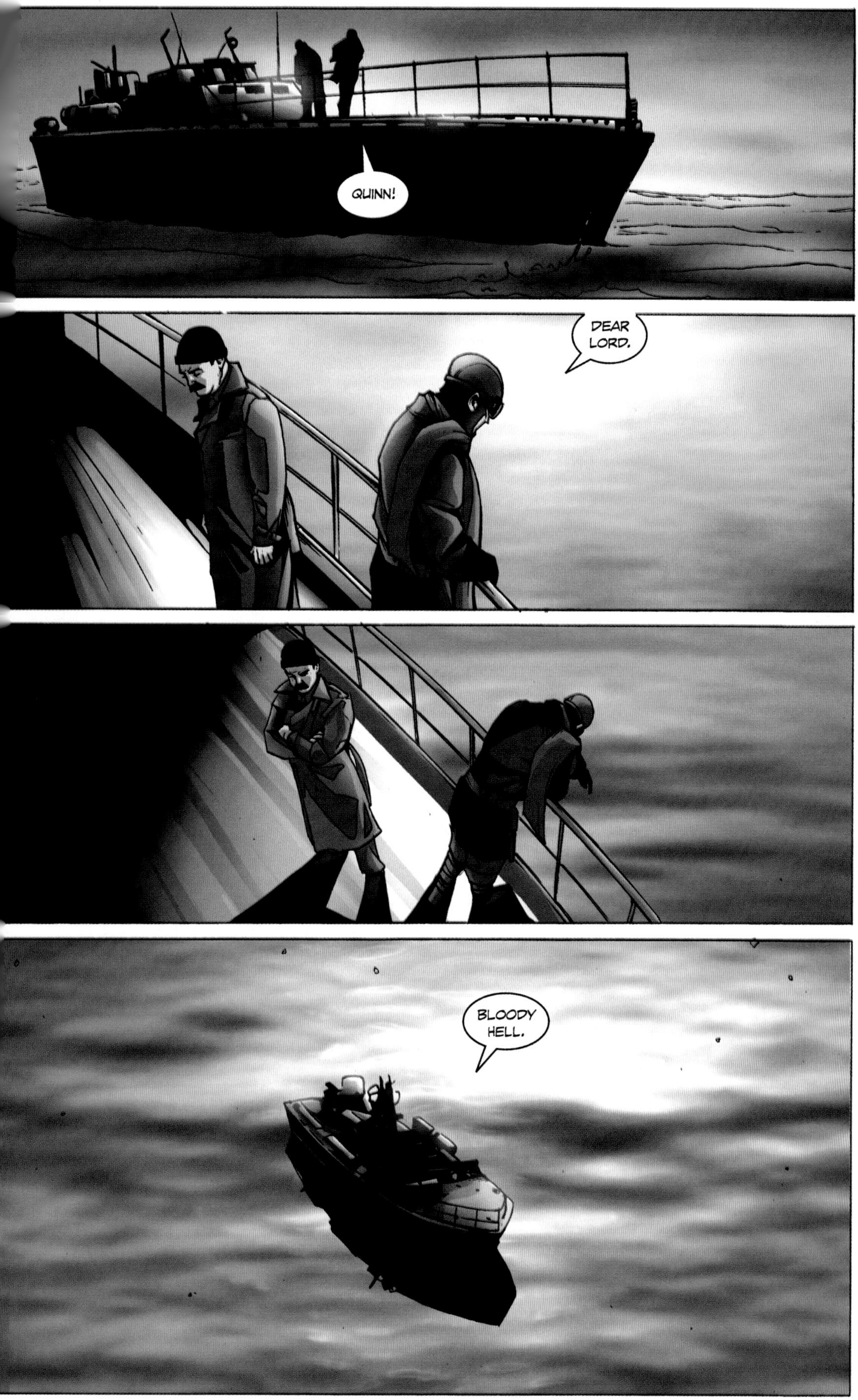
QUINN!
DEAR LORD.
BLOODY HELL.

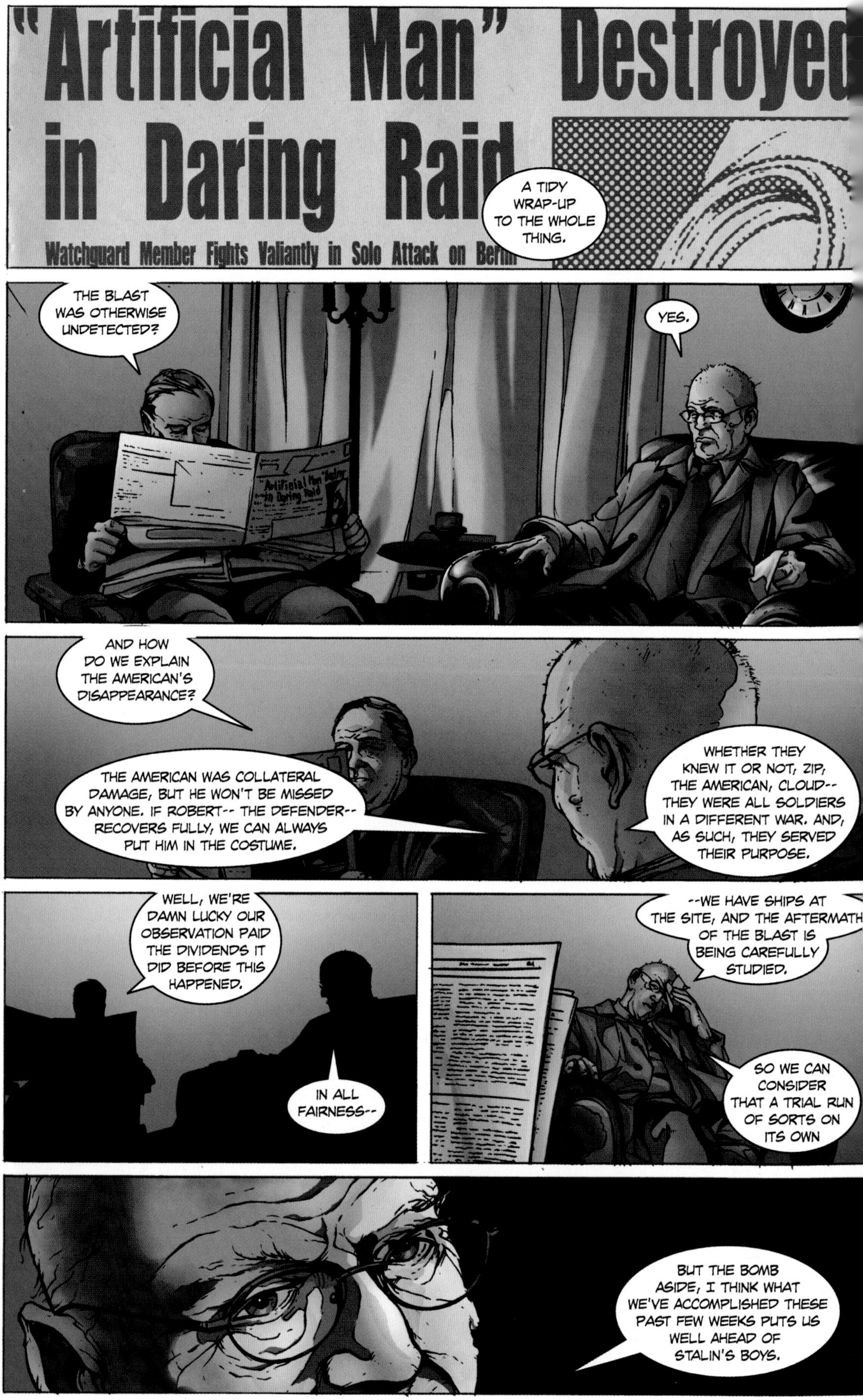
"Artificial Man" Destroyed in Daring Raid
Watchguard Member Fights Valiantly in Solo Attack on Berlin
A TIDY WRAP-UP TO THE WHOLE THING.
THE BLAST WAS OTHERWISE UNDETECTED?
YES.
"Artificial Man" Destroyed in Daring Raid
AND HOW DO WE EXPLAIN THE AMERICAN'S DISAPPEARANCE?
THE AMERICAN WAS COLLATERAL DAMAGE, BUT HE WON'T BE MISSED BY ANYONE. IF ROBERT-- THE DEFENDER-- RECOVERS FULLY, WE CAN ALWAYS PUT HIM IN THE COSTUME.
WHETHER THEY KNEW IT OR NOT, ZIP, THE AMERICAN, CLOUD-- THEY WERE ALL SOLDIERS IN A DIFFERENT WAR. AND, AS SUCH, THEY SERVED THEIR PURPOSE.
WELL, WE'RE DAMN LUCKY OUR OBSERVATION PAID THE DIVIDENDS IT DID BEFORE THIS HAPPENED.
IN ALL FAIRNESS--
--WE HAVE SHIPS AT THE SITE, AND THE AFTERMATH OF THE BLAST IS BEING CAREFULLY STUDIED.
SO WE CAN CONSIDER THAT A TRIAL RUN OF SORTS ON ITS OWN
BUT THE BOMB ASIDE, I THINK WHAT WE'VE ACCOMPLISHED THESE PAST FEW WEEKS PUTS US WELL AHEAD OF STALIN'S BOYS.

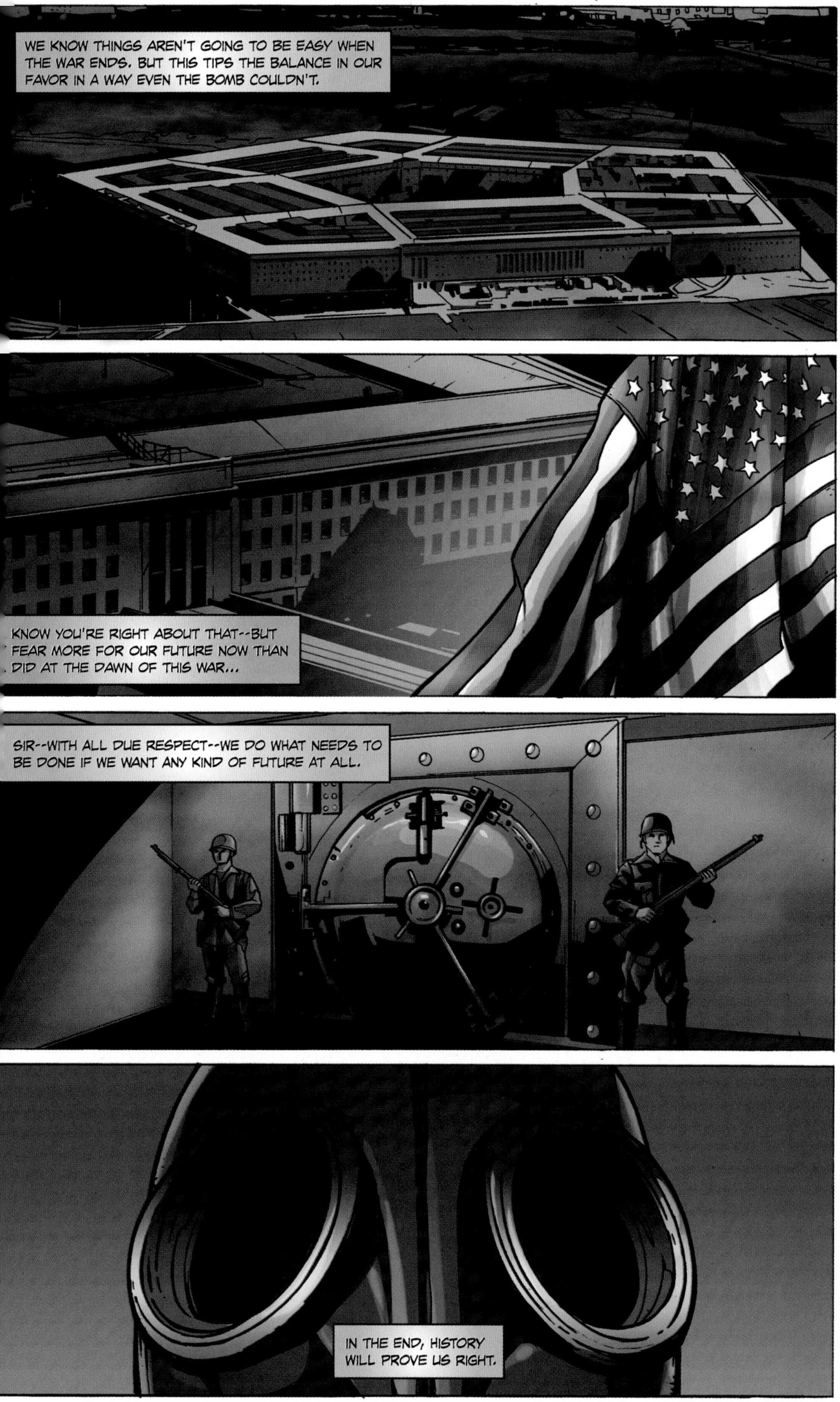
WE KNOW THINGS AREN'T GOING TO BE EASY WHEN THE WAR ENDS. BUT THIS TIPS THE BALANCE IN OUR FAVOR IN A WAY EVEN THE BOMB COULDN'T.
KNOW YOU'RE RIGHT ABOUT THAT--BUT FEAR MORE FOR OUR FUTURE NOW THAN DID AT THE DAWN OF THIS WAR...
SIR--WITH ALL DUE RESPECT--WE DO WHAT NEEDS TO BE DONE IF WE WANT ANY KIND OF FUTURE AT ALL.
IN THE END, HISTORY WILL PROVE US RIGHT.

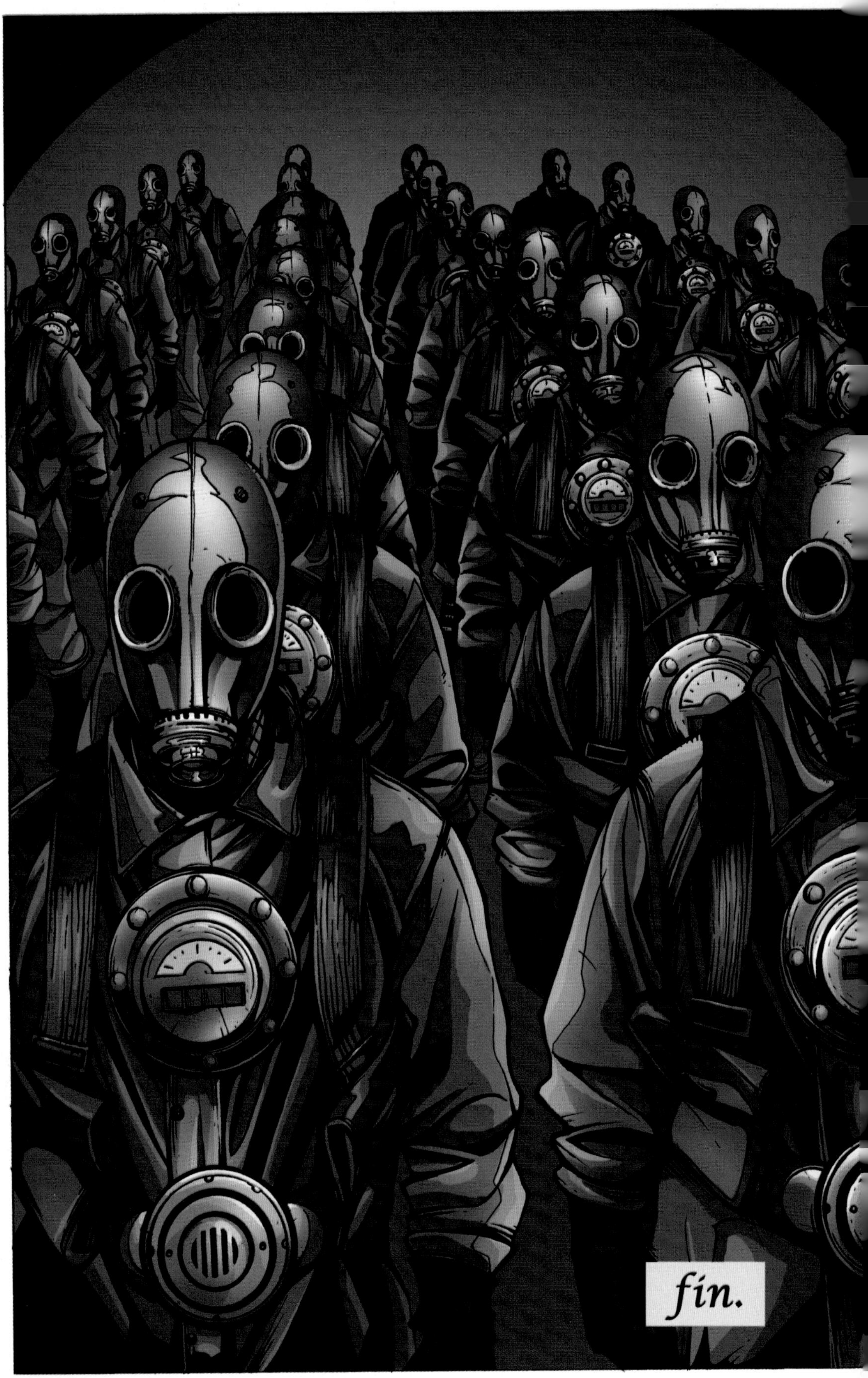
fin.

A Brief History of the Mid-Nite Hour (and his Mid-Nite Hourmen)

...r about ten years, I was a member of an APA (amatuer Press Alliance) called LEGENDS. ...sically, An APA is a place for fans to gather and produce individual fanzines, which are ...en sent out (stapled together) to the membership. It was in LEGENDS that I first met ...iter J. Torres, who eventually led me into comics, as well as a number of other good ...ends, some involved in the industry on a professional level, some not. As coincidence ...uld have it, a few years after I left, Jeremy and (PARADIGM writer)Matt Cashel joined ...GENDS.

...was within the pages of LEGENDS that I first created the Mid-Nite Hour. He would run ...roughout my zines, and the other members of the APA seemed to take to him. Eventually, ...ould create a group for the Hour to lead (the Mid-Nite Hourmen), and several other ...roes for him to pal around with, including an early version of Johnny Zip. While it was all ...fun, other members of the APA eventually tried their hand at drawing him, and APA ...ember and artist Toby Mays and I even put together a minicomic starring the Hourmen ...d his creation, the Quantum Mechanics.

...1998, J. Torres and I were co-editing a book called LOVE IN TIGHTS, which was a ...perhero-meets-romance comics anthology published by Slave Labor Graphics. While ...sting about for story ideas, I decided to bring the Hour into "real" comics, and wrote a ...tle story about the Hour, post-war, and his girlfriend. I asked friend and mega-talent ...alman Androsofzky (who went on to draw iCANDY for DC) to handle the artwork, and the ...st thing he did was redesign the Hour's costume. Whereas the costume had originally ...en loosely based on a combination of Captain America's and Dr. Mid-Nite's, Kalman ...anted to place it more in the Golden Age era. After tweaks and suggestions from me, he ...me up with a design based on aviation outfits of the day. I urged him toward the original ...ackhawks' design, and eventually we ended up with a costume we both really dug. And ...o, the Hour made his first "official" appearance in the pages of LOVE IN TIGHTS #5.

...hen I started putting together ANTHEM (which eventually became BATTLE HYMN, after ...oy Thomas revealed his plans for a book using the name ANTHEM), I knew I wanted the ...our to be involved. Original artist Toby Cypress's sample pages used Kalman's costume ...esign, but when Toby dropped out and Jeremy climbed on board, Jeremy did a slight ...edesign (again, with intrusive input from yours truly). One of the problems with Kalman's ...esign is that Mike Mignola's design for Lobster Johnson from HELLBOY ended up ...oking a lot like our Mid-Nite Hour (Lobster Johnson first appeared on the stands at ...lmost the exact same time as the Hour's LOVE IN TIGHTS debut). We also added Johnny ...ip to the cast, and he underwent a fairly extreme makeover. Jeremy took Toby's designs ...nd added his own flair for Johnny.

...Quinn Rey appeared first in a LOVE IN TIGHTS story, as well, but we almost completely re-...vented the character for BATTLE HYMN. At one point artist J. Bone and I had plotted and ...umbnailed a second Mid-Nite Hour story for LOVE IN TIGHTS, but we never got around to ...nishing it. I do still have J's thumbs, though, and they're a ton of fun.

...n any event, what follows are some early images of the Mid-Nite Hour and his pals.

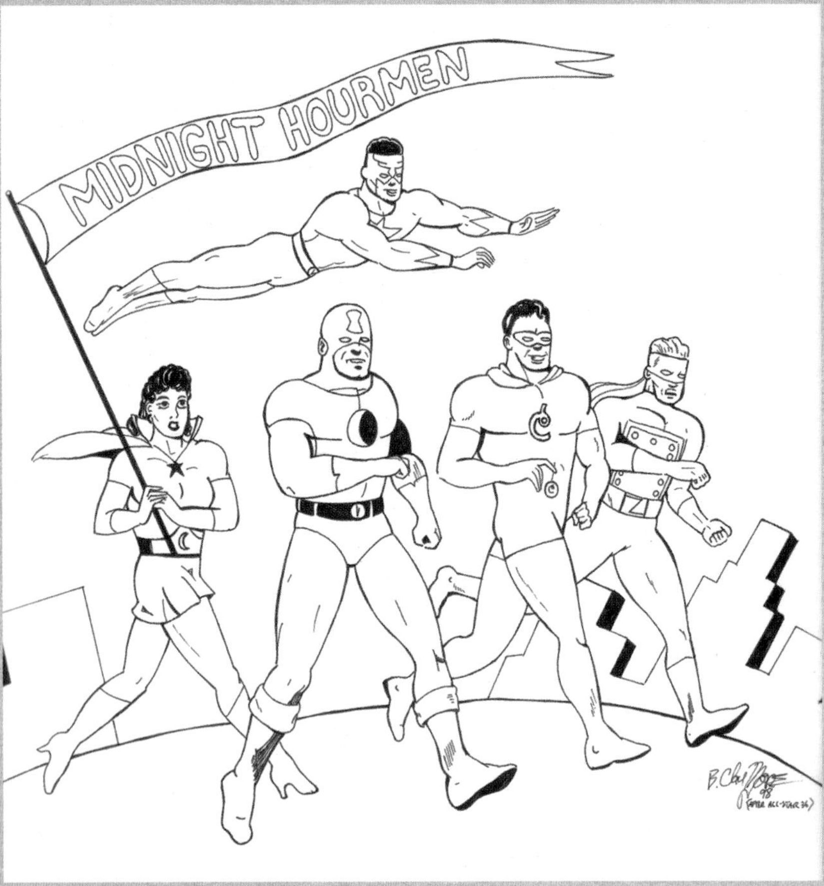
MIDNIGHT HOURMEN

This is a 'zine drawi
I did riffing on an ol
ALL-STAR COMICS
cover from the 40s.

The Mid-Nite Hour is
front and center, an
the early version of
Johnny Zip is behin
the dude with the "C
on his chest.

None of the others
had anything to do
with BATTLE HYMN.

Actually, Betty was
initially going to be
the heroine pictured
here, but I decided it
was unlikely the U.S
government would p
a woman on the tea
in 1944.

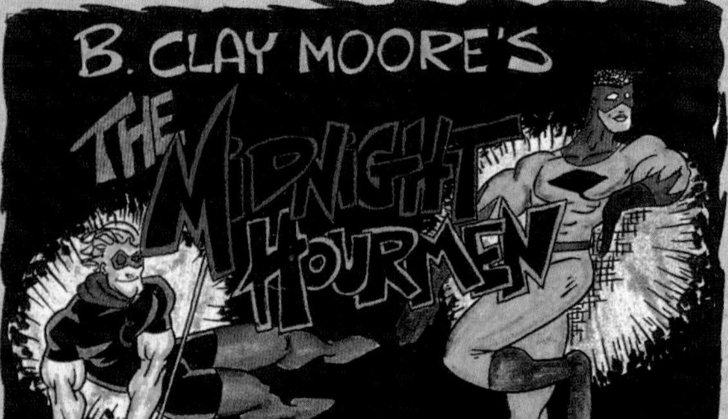
B. CLAY MOORE'S
THE MIDNIGHT HOURMEN
TOBY MAYS '95

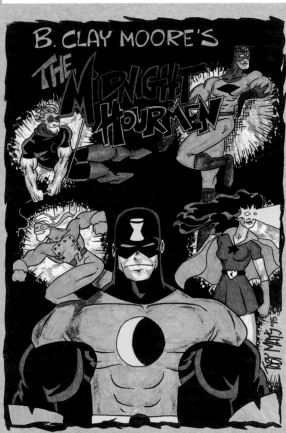

Toby Mays was a prolific minicomics creator whose imagination was captured by the Hourmen. Here's a piece he did years ago.

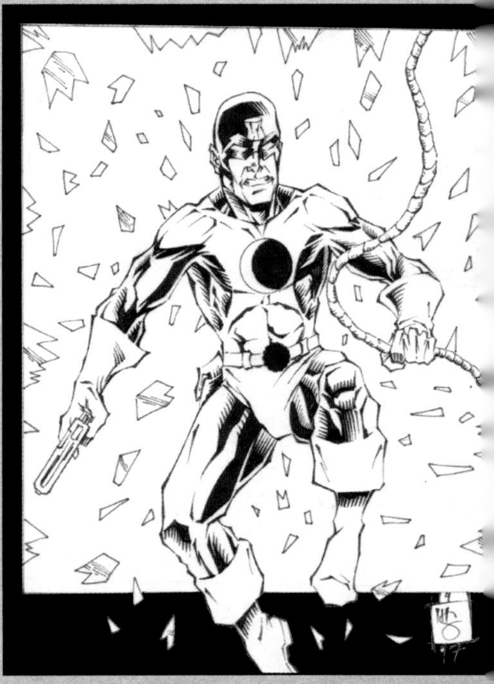

Mark Stegbauer is an accomplished inker, having worked for Marvel, DC, Image, and any number of other companies. In 1997 he took a stab at the original Mid-Nite Hour.

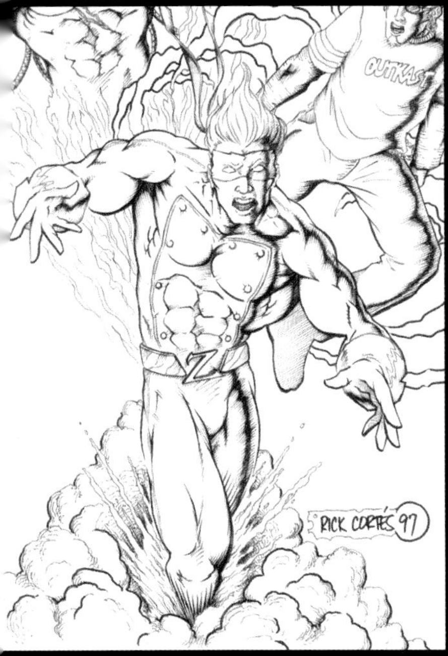
OUTKAST
RICK CORTÉS 97

To the left is another shot of the original design for Johnny Zip, as drawn by digital effects wiz Rick Cortes, a longtime friend. At the time Rick didn't even know what the character's name was, but had seen him in my zines. Note his character, G-Dogg, in an "Outkast" T-shirt. Clearly not a Golden Age portrait here. Hell, even in 1997, Outkast was a few years away from superstardom. Kudos to Rick for being ahead of the game.

Below is another piece by Rick. A beautiful pencil portrait of the Hour and assorted invented characters. Rick based this on Kalman's initial designs for the Mid-Nite Hour's "official" LOVE IN TIGHTS debutin 2000.

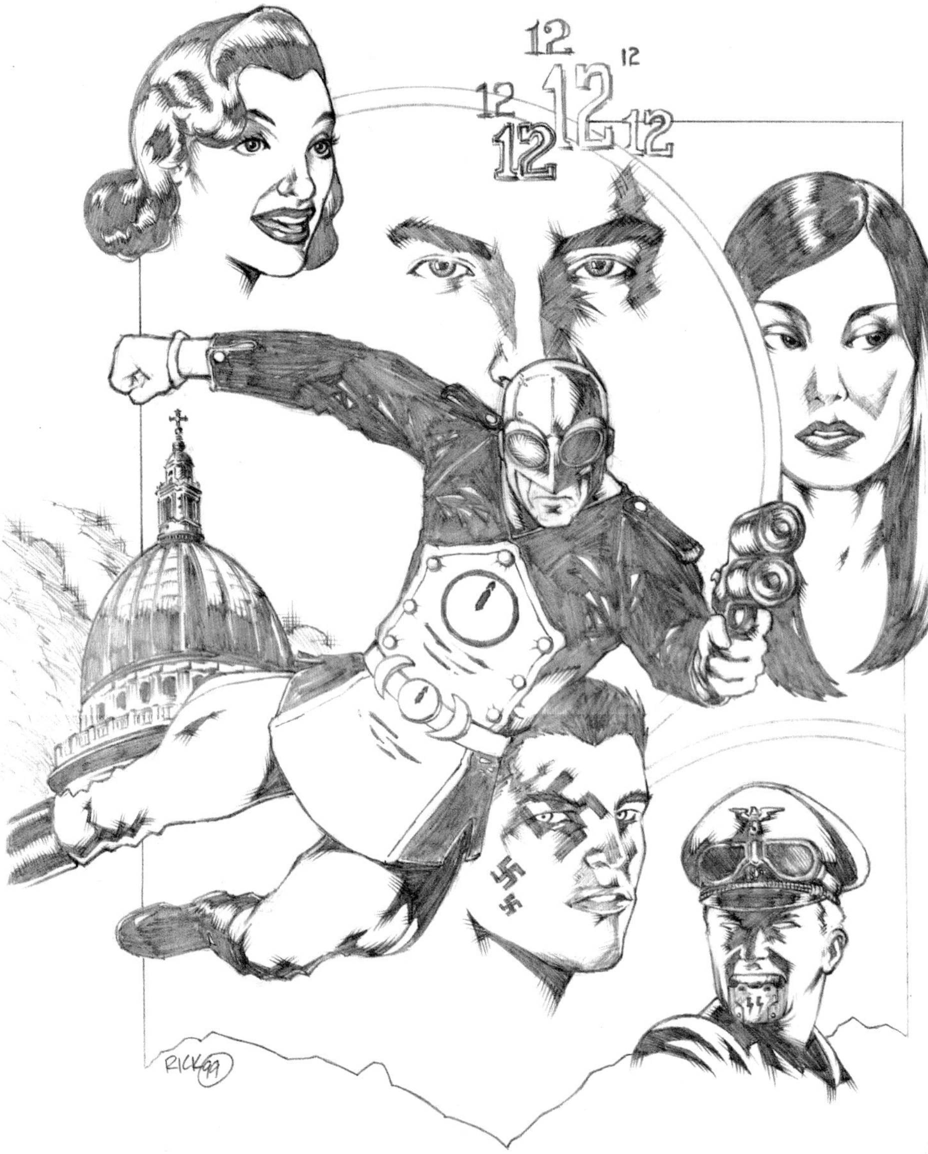
12
12
12
12
12
12
RICK 97

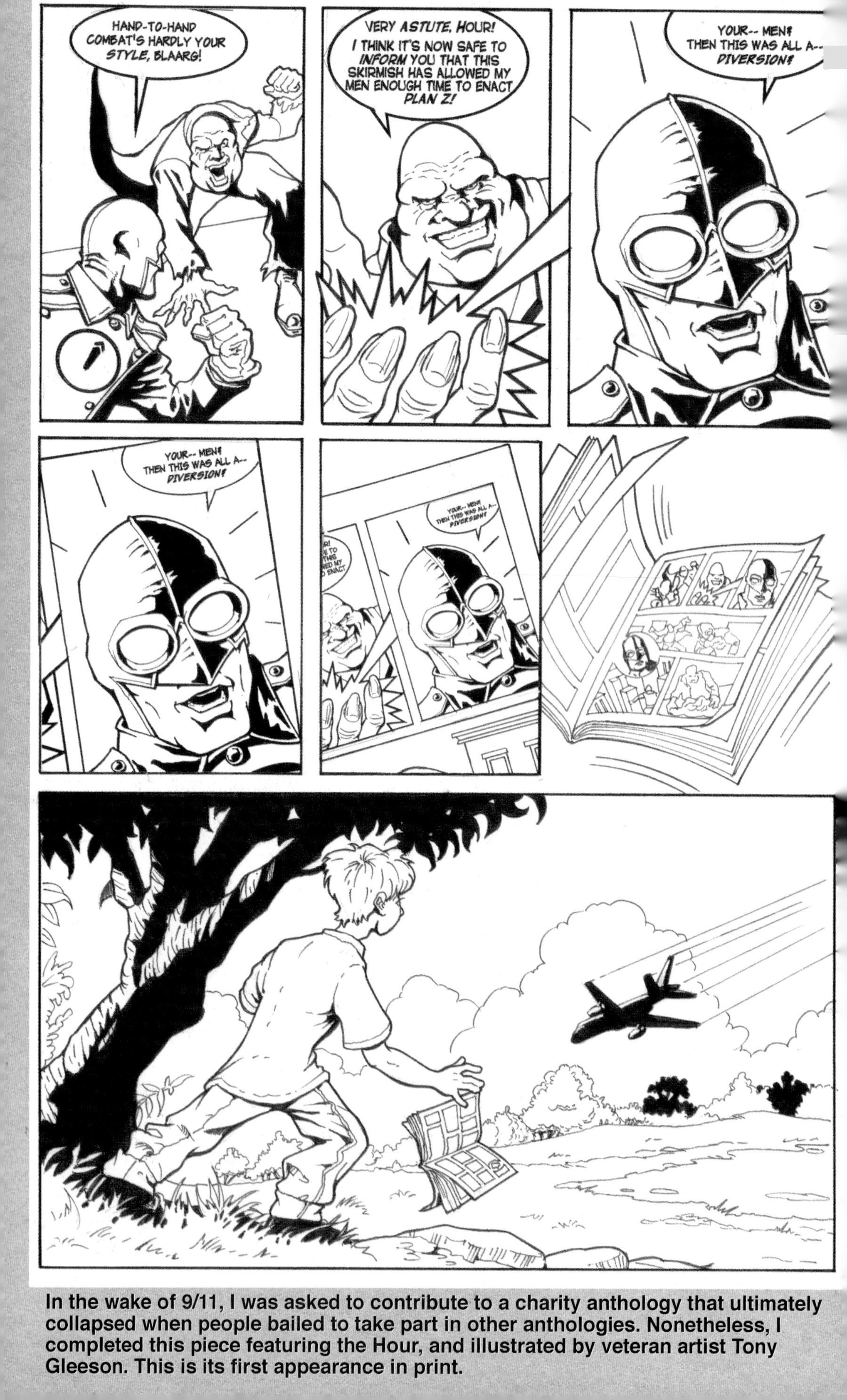

HAND-TO-HAND COMBAT'S HARDLY YOUR STYLE, BLAARG!
VERY ASTUTE, HOUR! I THINK IT'S NOW SAFE TO INFORM YOU THAT THIS SKIRMISH HAS ALLOWED MY MEN ENOUGH TIME TO ENACT PLAN Z!
YOUR-- MEN? THEN THIS WAS ALL A-- DIVERSION?
YOUR-- MEN? THEN THIS WAS ALL A-- DIVERSION?
YOUR-- MEN? THEN THIS WAS ALL A-- DIVERSION?

In the wake of 9/11, I was asked to contribute to a charity anthology that ultimately collapsed when people bailed to take part in other anthologies. Nonetheless, I completed this piece featuring the Hour, and illustrated by veteran artist Tony Gleeson. This is its first appearance in print.

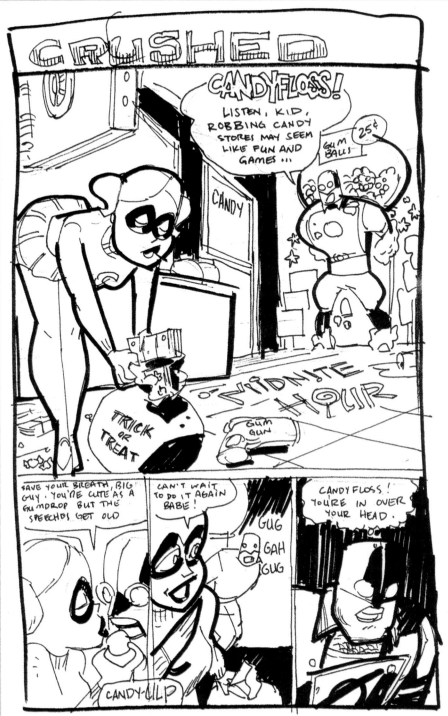

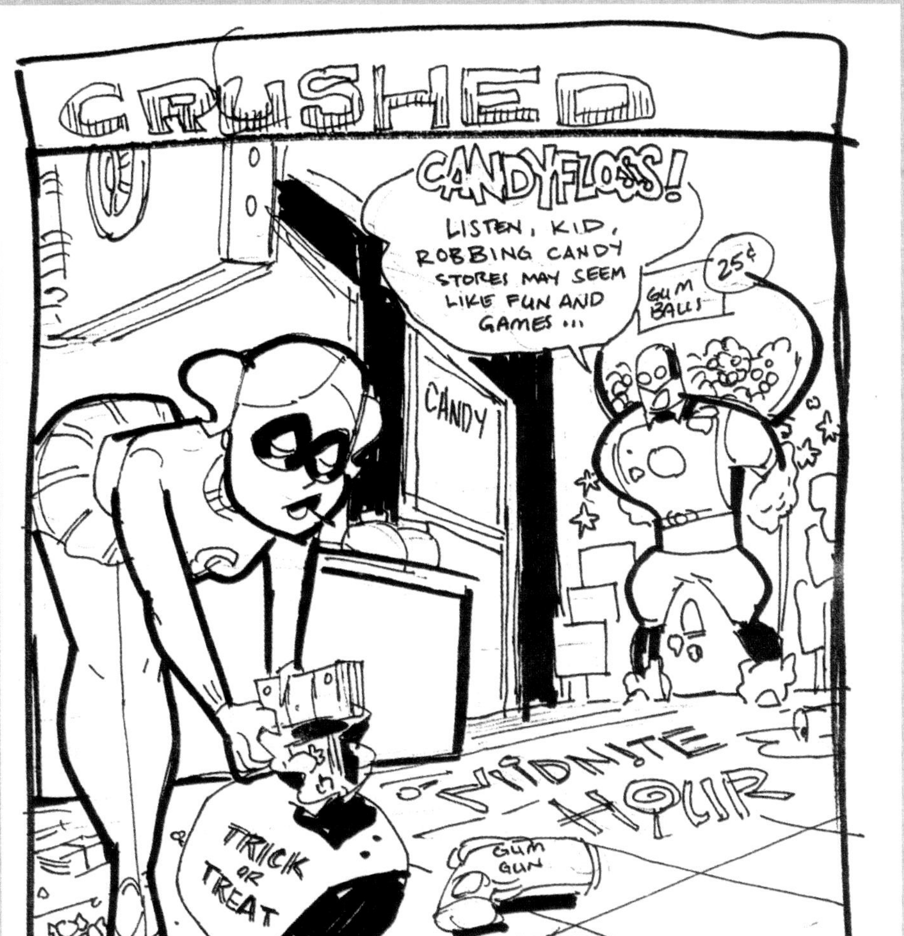
CRUSHED
CANDYFLOSS!
LISTEN, KID, ROBBING CANDY STORES MAY SEEM LIKE FUN AND GAMES...
GUM BALLS
25¢
CANDY
MIDNITE HOUR
TRICK OR TREAT
GUM GUN
SAVE YOUR BREATH, BIG GUY. YOU'RE CUTE AS A GUMDROP BUT THE SPEECHES GET OLD
CAN'T WAIT TO DO IT AGAIN BABE!
GUG
GAH
GUG
CANDY FLOSS! YOU'RE IN OVER YOUR HEAD.
CANDY-ULP
P. 1

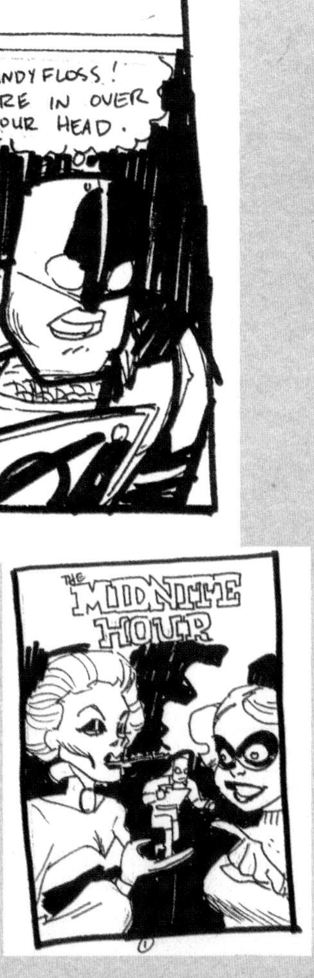
THE MIDNITE HOUR

One Hour story that never came together was also intended for LOVE IN TIGHTS. Artist J. Bone never got past the thumbnail stage, but even those are a lot of fun to see. The story took place in the fifties, and featured the Hour battling a nymphette named Candyfloss, as well as an older villainess modeled after Gloria Swanson, from Sunset Boulevard. Here Candy has gummed the Hour to a giant gumball machine before choking him with a giant jawbreaker. J. also did a few cover designs, one of which he intended to use to open the story. We pulled the plug on LOVE IN TIGHTS before the story was finished, and J. moved on to bigger and better things.

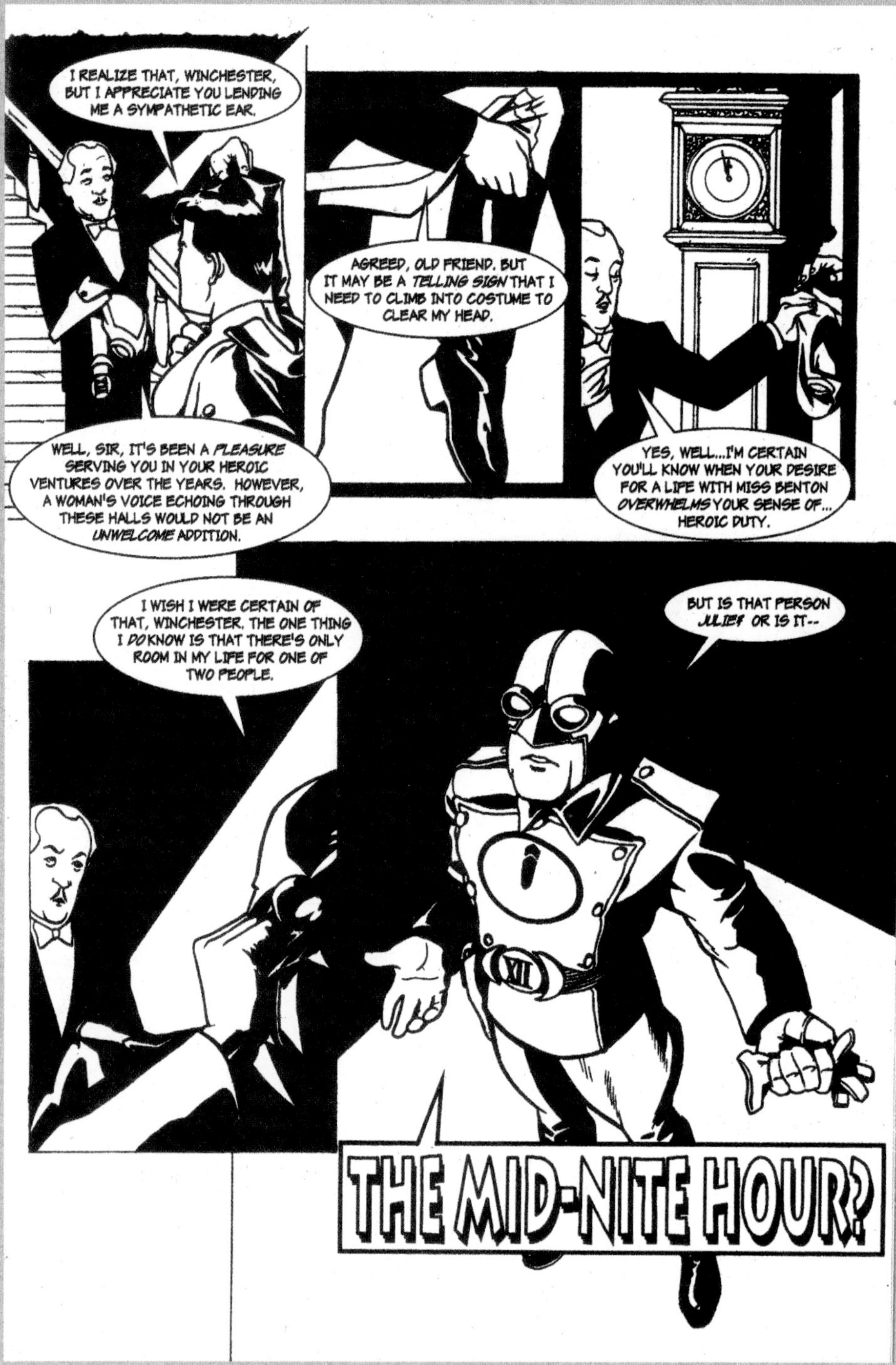
I REALIZE THAT, WINCHESTER, BUT I APPRECIATE YOU LENDING ME A SYMPATHETIC EAR.
AGREED, OLD FRIEND. BUT IT MAY BE A TELLING SIGN THAT I NEED TO CLIMB INTO COSTUME TO CLEAR MY HEAD.
WELL, SIR, IT'S BEEN A PLEASURE SERVING YOU IN YOUR HEROIC VENTURES OVER THE YEARS. HOWEVER, A WOMAN'S VOICE ECHOING THROUGH THESE HALLS WOULD NOT BE AN UNWELCOME ADDITION.
YES, WELL...I'M CERTAIN YOU'LL KNOW WHEN YOUR DESIRE FOR A LIFE WITH MISS BENTON OVERWHELMS YOUR SENSE OF... HEROIC DUTY.
I WISH I WERE CERTAIN OF THAT, WINCHESTER. THE ONE THING I DO KNOW IS THAT THERE'S ONLY ROOM IN MY LIFE FOR ONE OF TWO PEOPLE.
BUT IS THAT PERSON JULIE? OR IS IT--
THE MID-NITE HOUR?

From LOVE IN TIGHTS #5, 2000. The first "official" appearance of the Mid-Nite Hour. The story, called "Triangle," was written by myself, and drawn by Kalman Andrasofsz Kalman received inking assistance from J. Bone and Cameron Stewart (both were uncredited when the story was first published).

I always loved the design that Kalman and I (mainly Kalman) came up with here. But i order tosteer cleer of Lobster Johnson comparisons, Jeremy and I decided to rework the costume a bit for BATTLE HYMN.

The story was set in 1948, and was a tad on the melodramatic side. The Hour was an American, stressed out over having to choose between his true love, Julie Benton, an his costumed identity.

THE BATTLE HYMN

FLIP COVER GALLERY

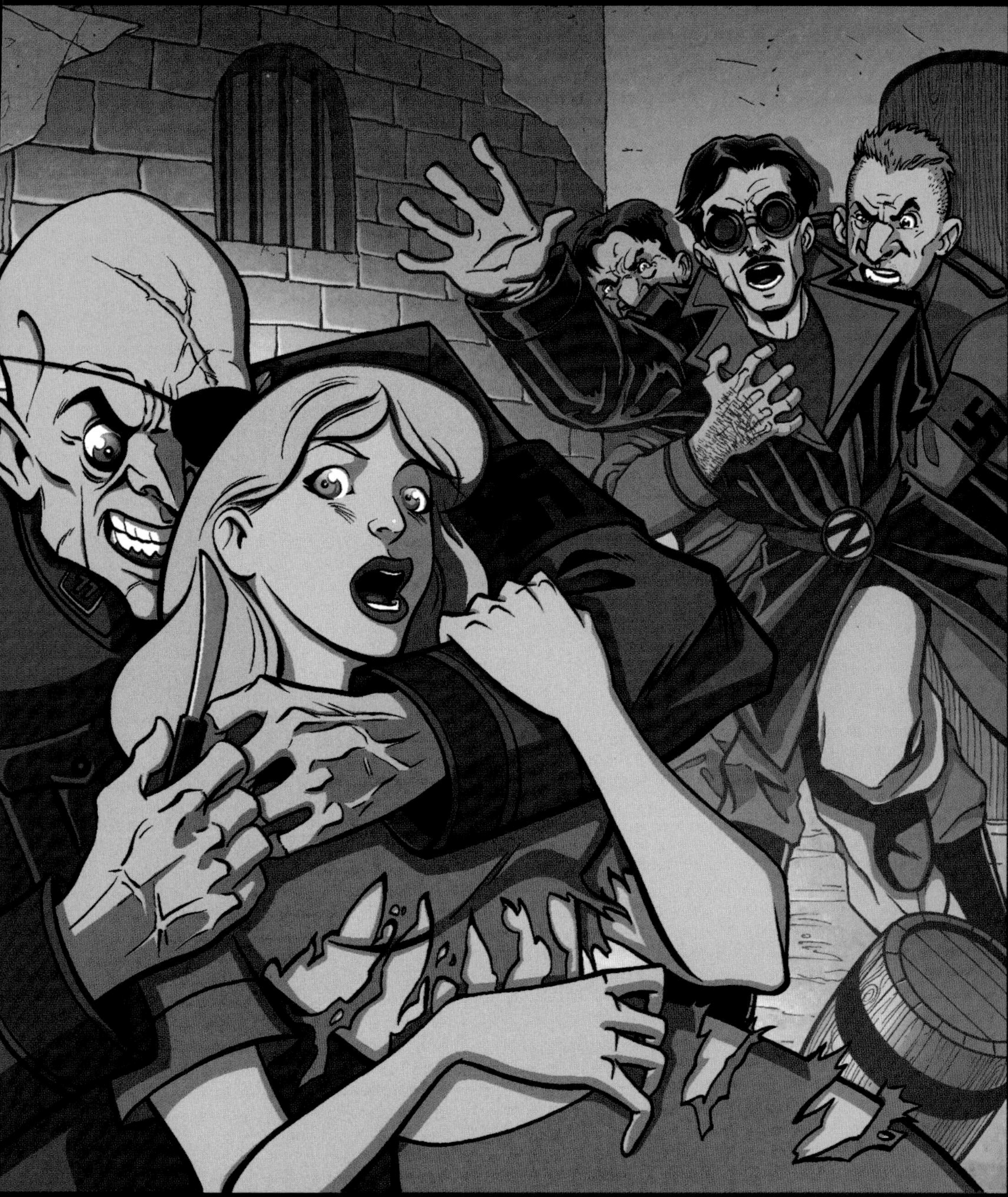

by MIKE NORTON

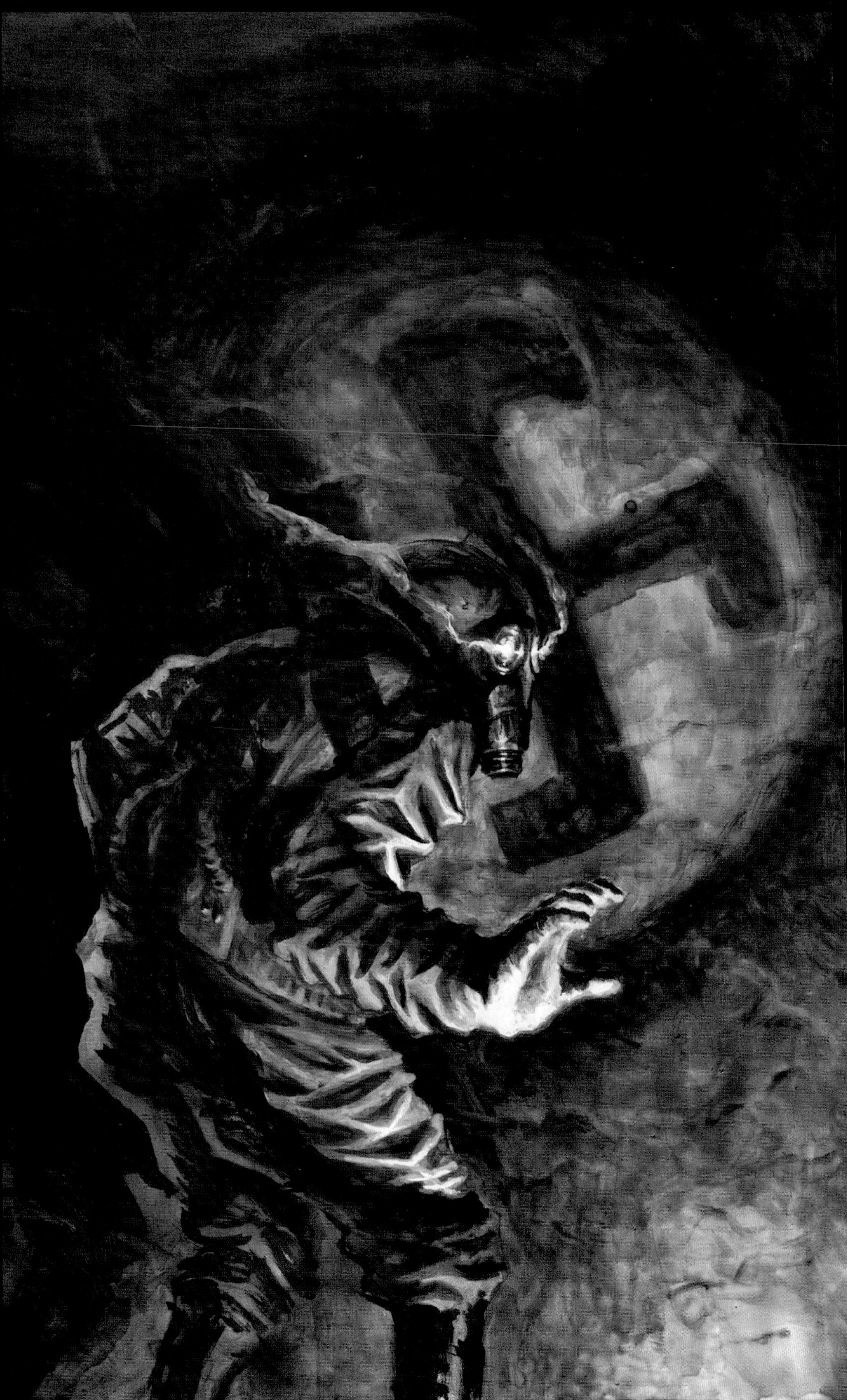

by ELIO GUEVAR

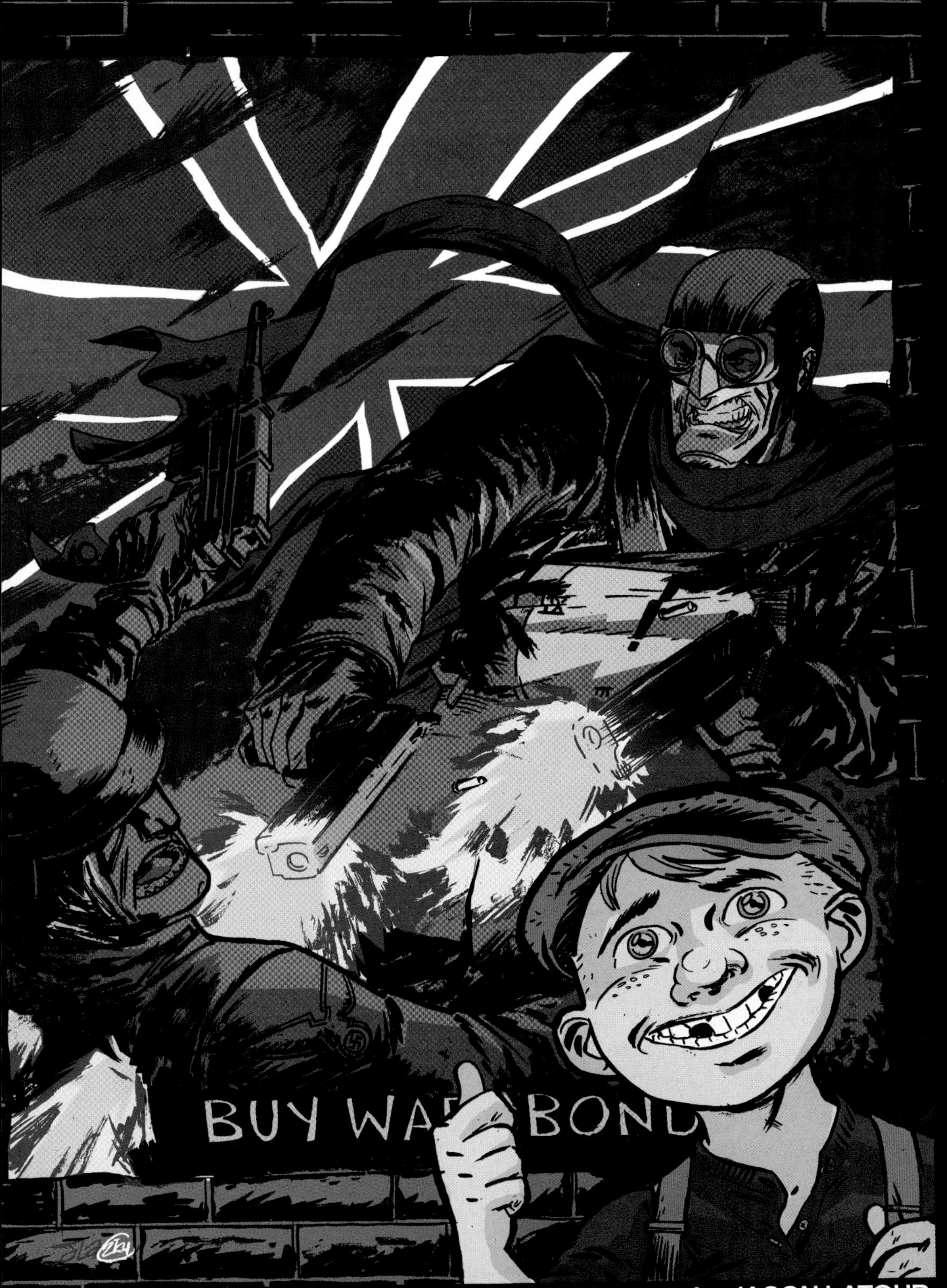
BUY WA BOND

by JASON LATOUR

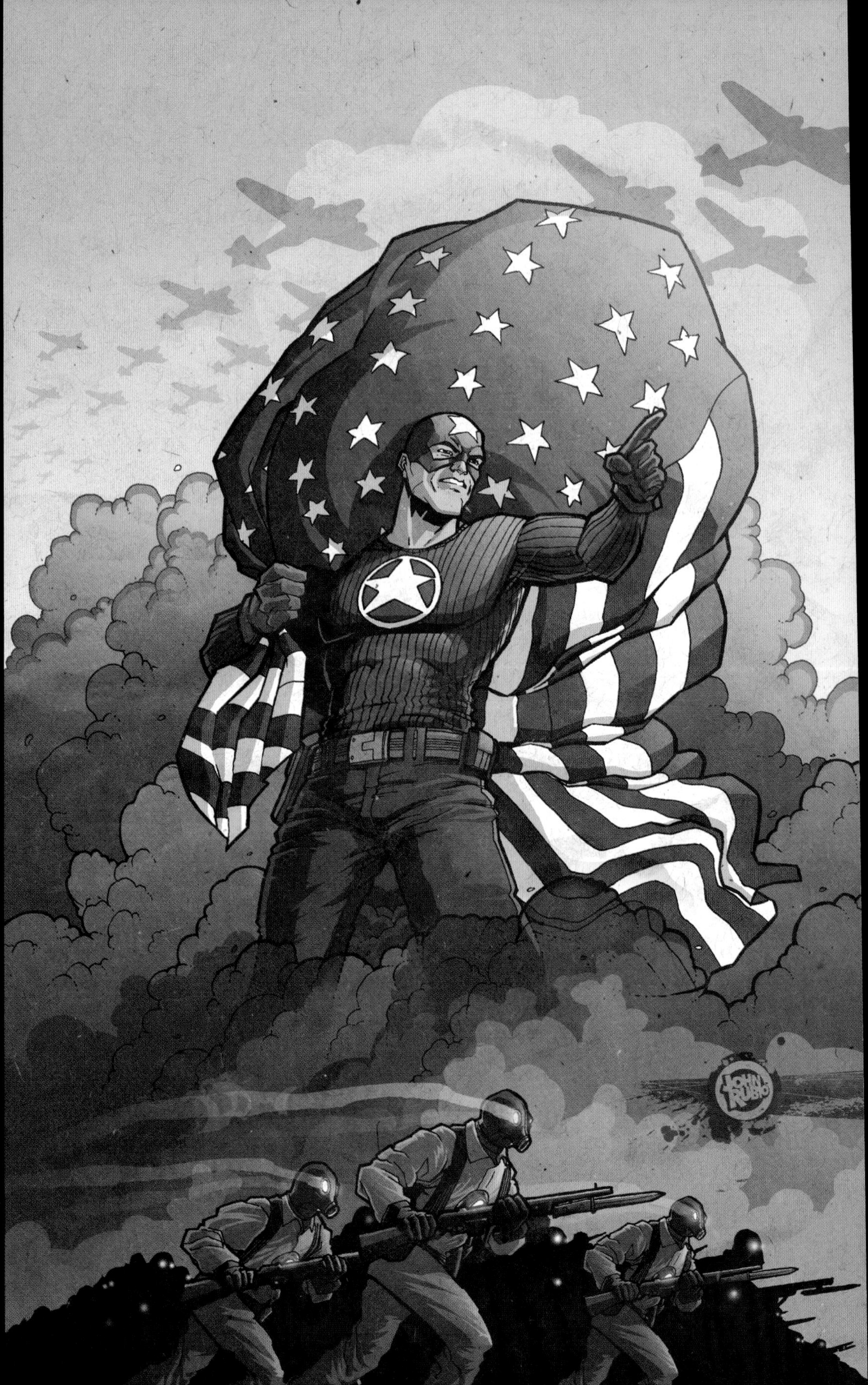
JOHN RUBIO

by JOHN RUBIO

BATTLE HYMN SKETCHBOOK

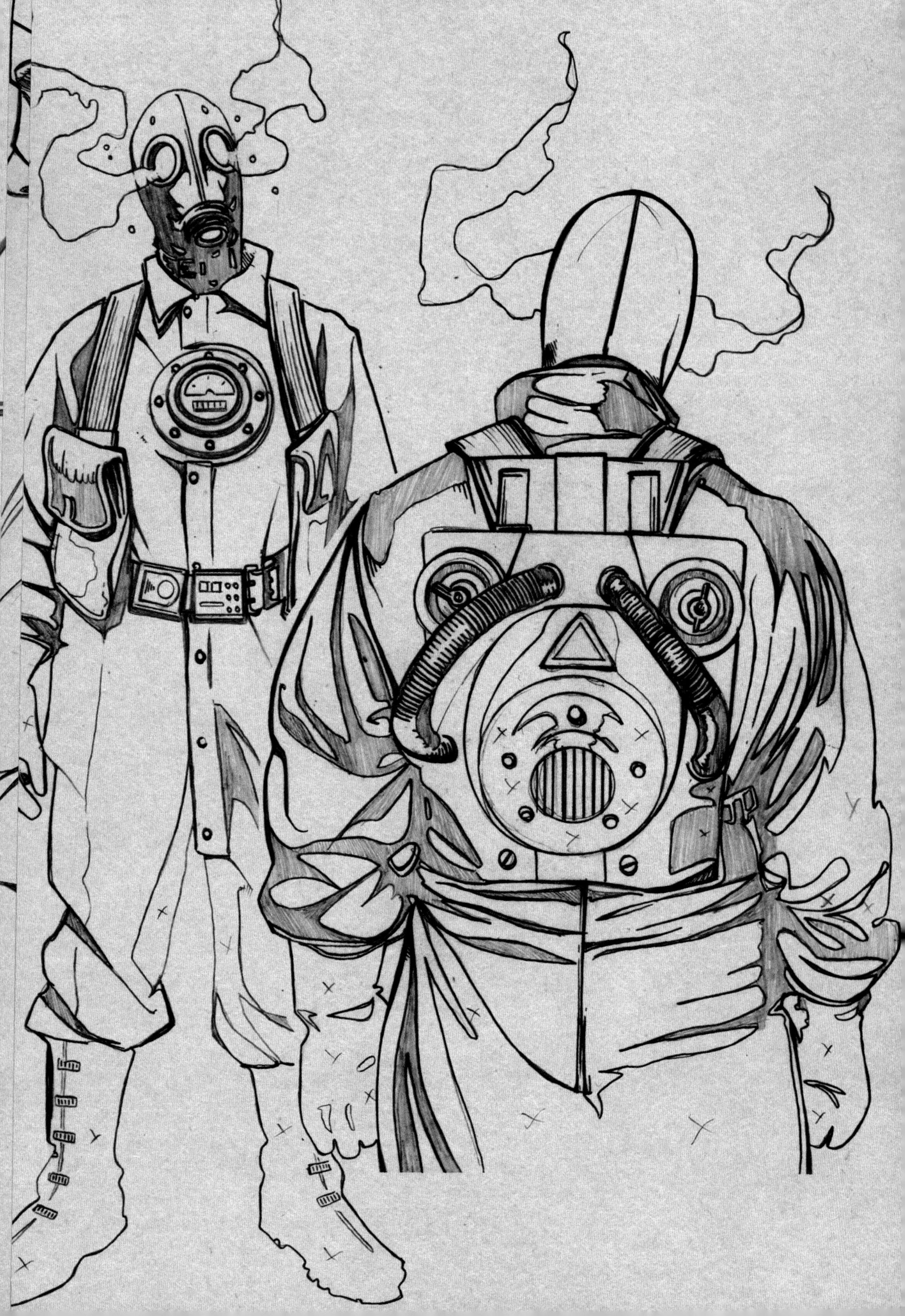

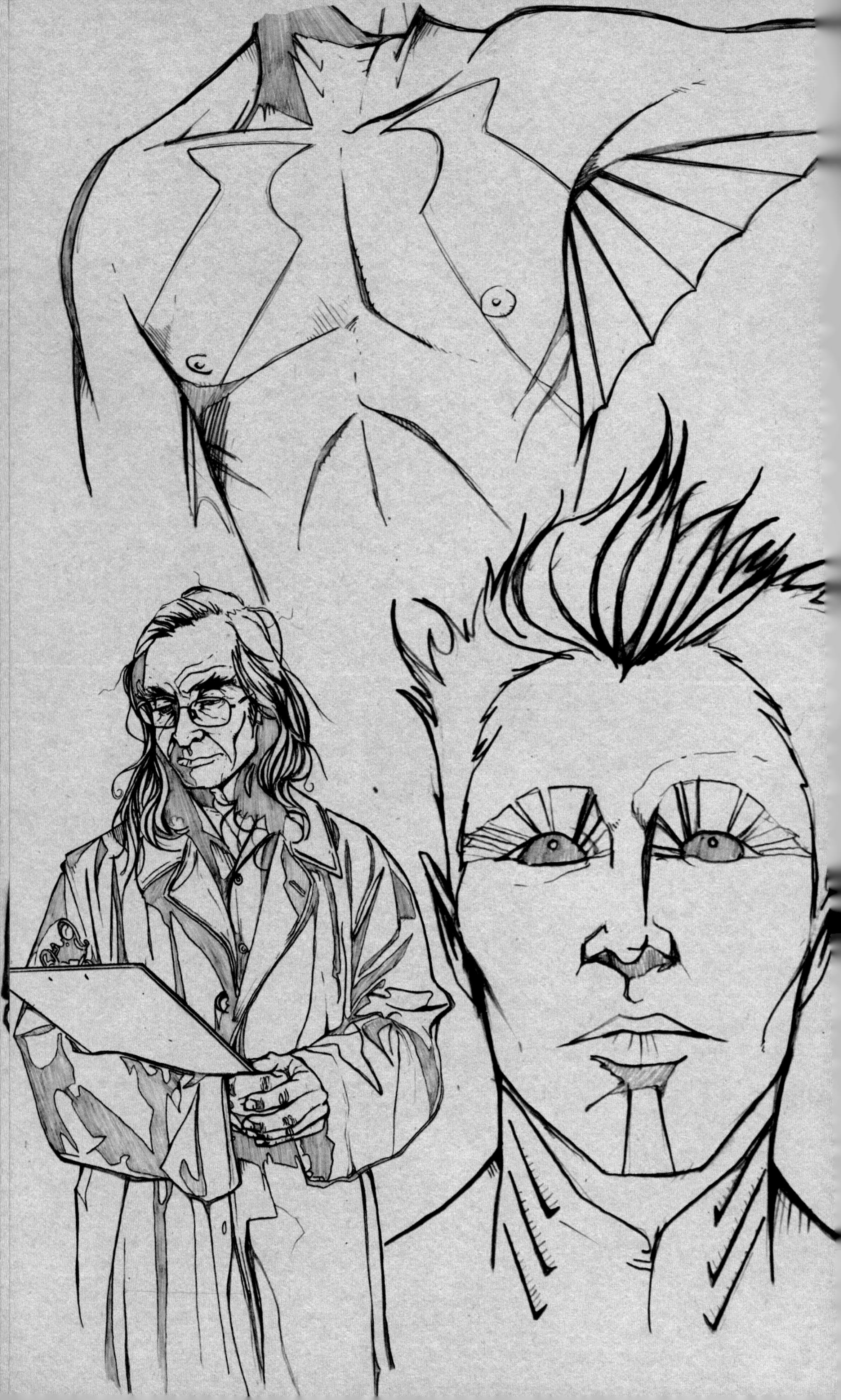

THE BATTLE HYMN

GALLERY

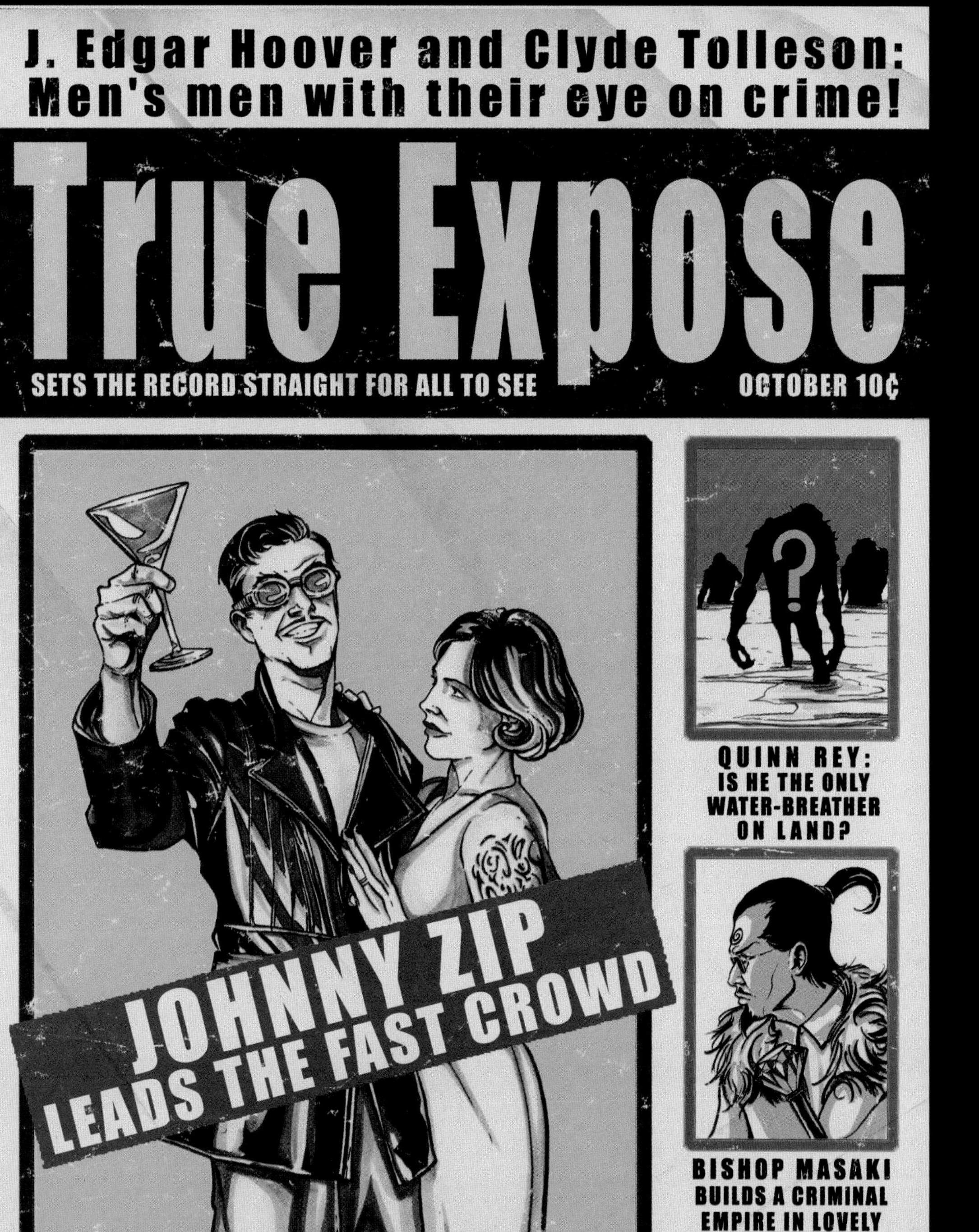

J. Edgar Hoover and Clyde Tolleson:
Men's men with their eye on crime!
True Expose
SETS THE RECORD STRAIGHT FOR ALL TO SEE
OCTOBER 10¢
JOHNNY ZIP
LEADS THE FAST CROWD
QUINN REY:
IS HE THE ONLY
WATER-BREATHER
ON LAND?
BISHOP MASAKI
BUILDS A CRIMINAL
EMPIRE IN LOVELY
HAWAII

by JEREMY HAUN

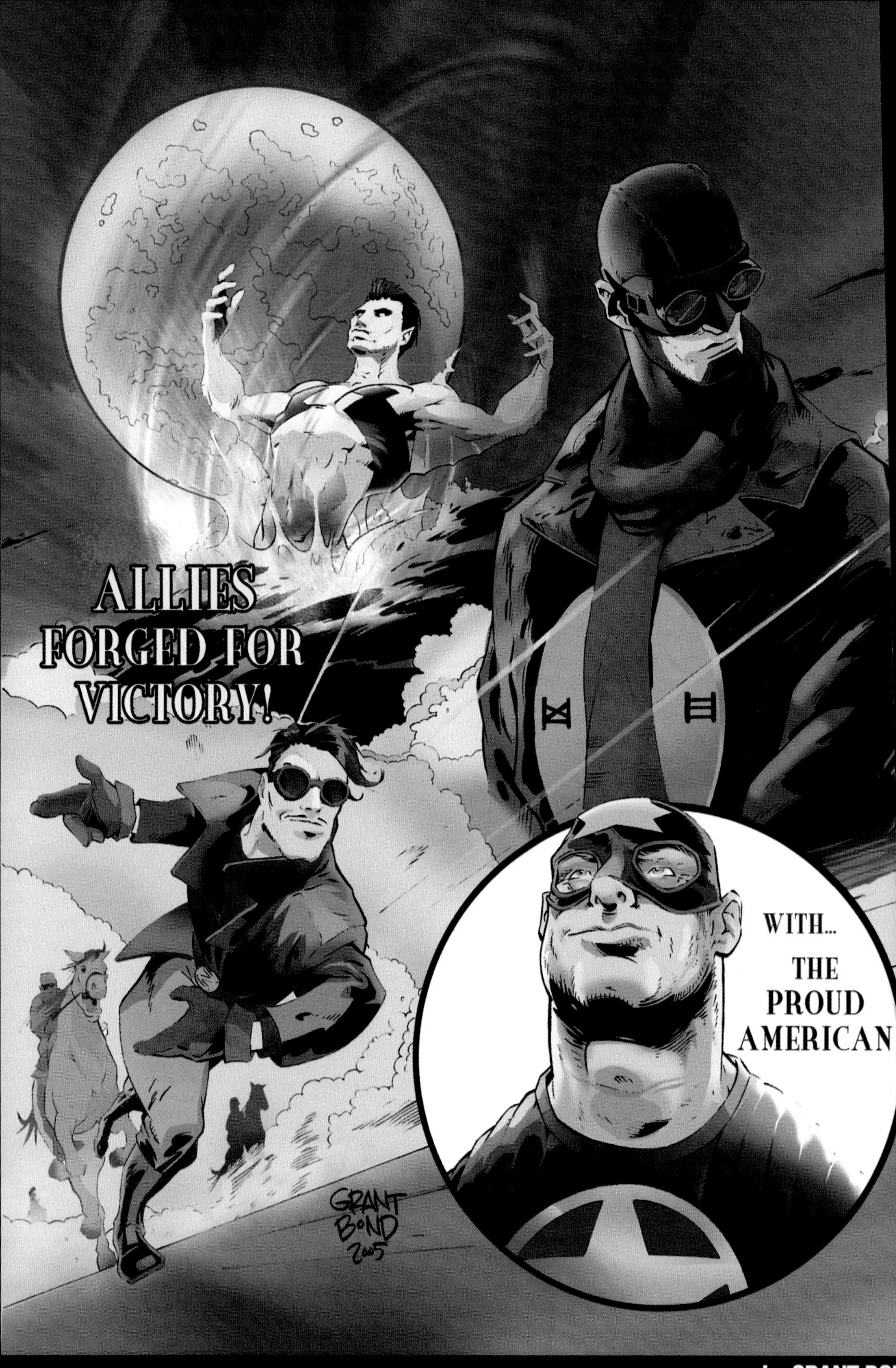
ALLIES
FORGED FOR
VICTORY!
WITH...
THE
PROUD
AMERICAN
GRANT
BOND
2005

by GRANT BON

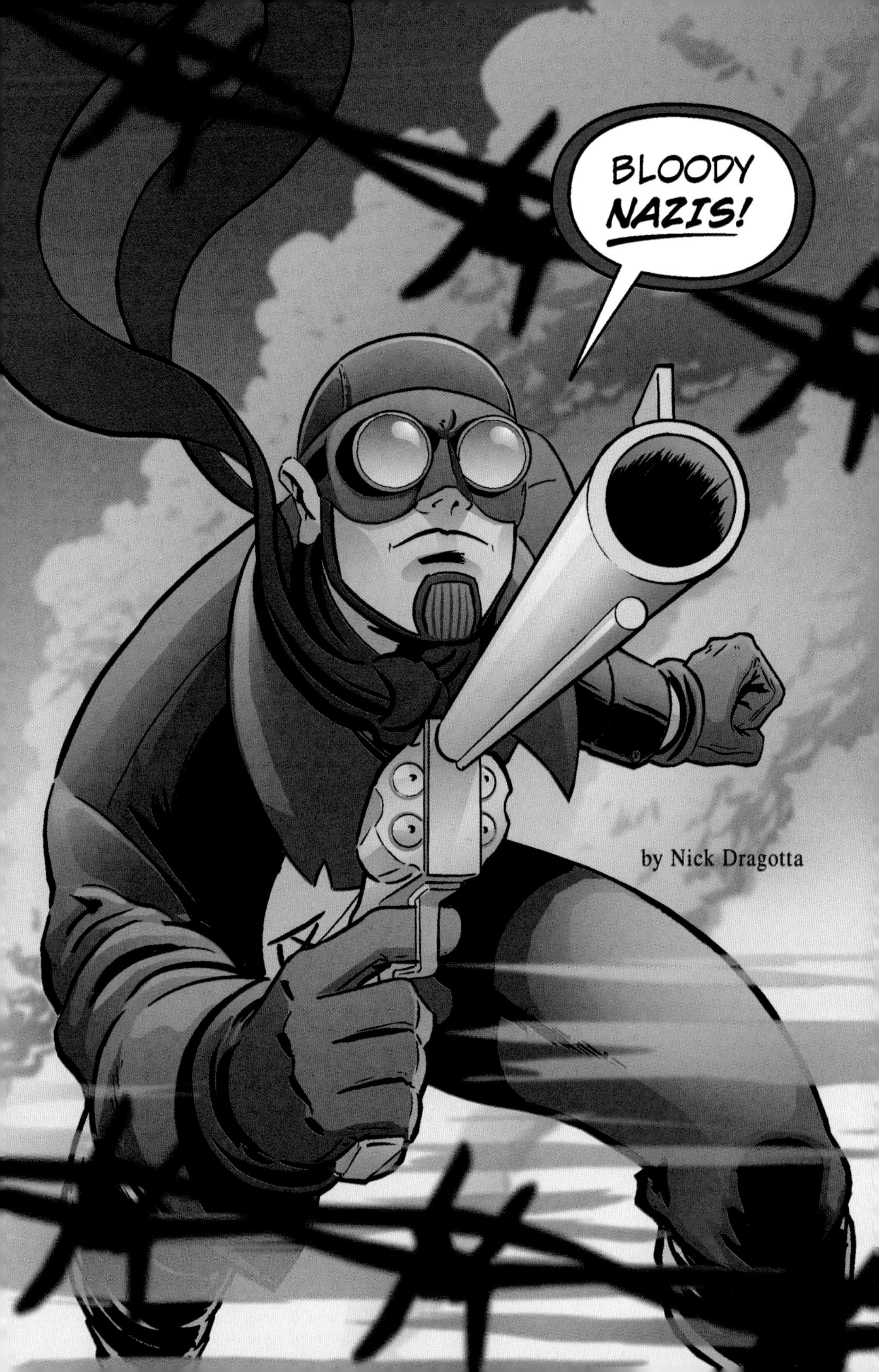
BLOODY NAZIS!

by Nick Dragotta

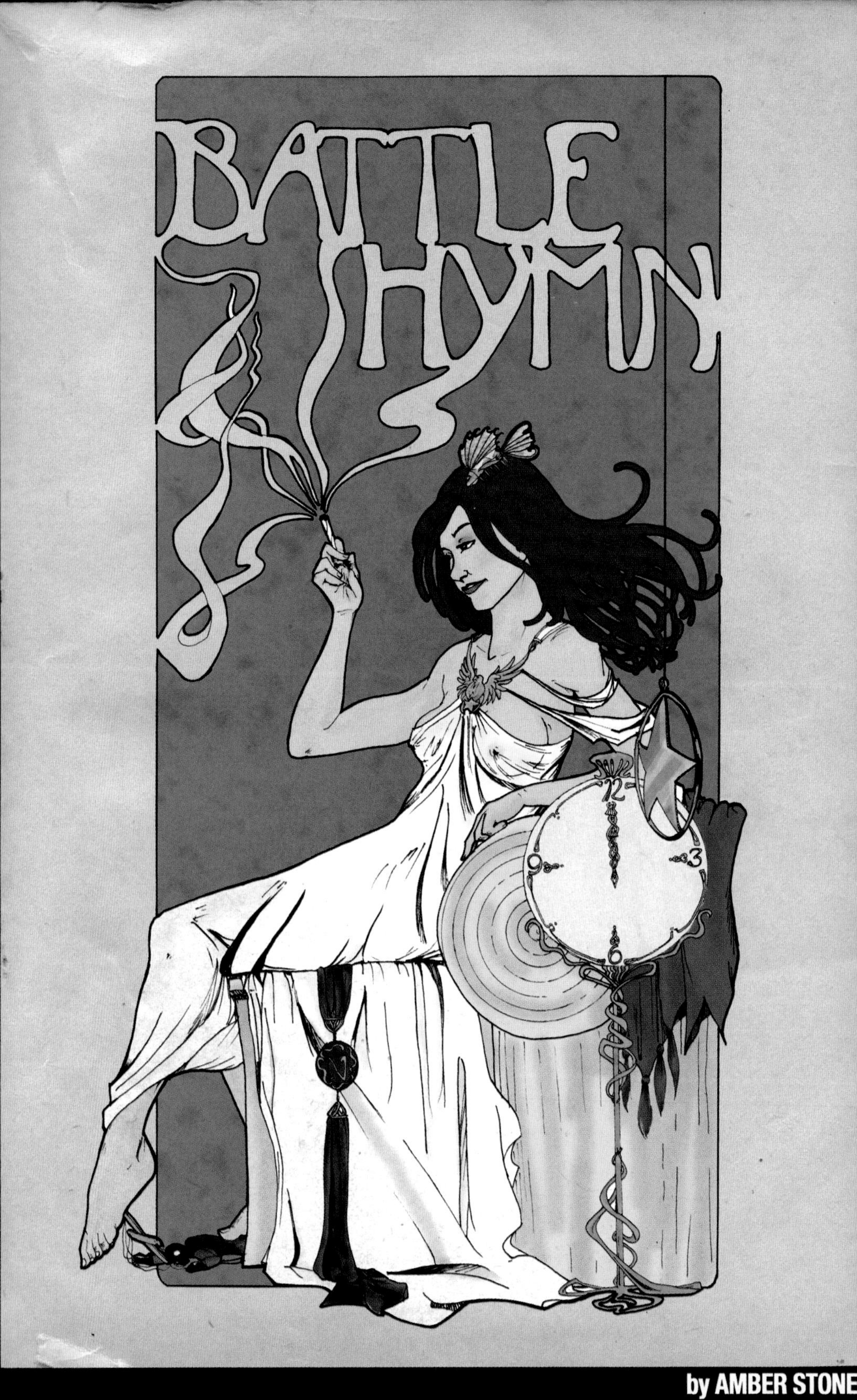
BATTLE HYMN

by AMBER STONE

by Dave Bryant

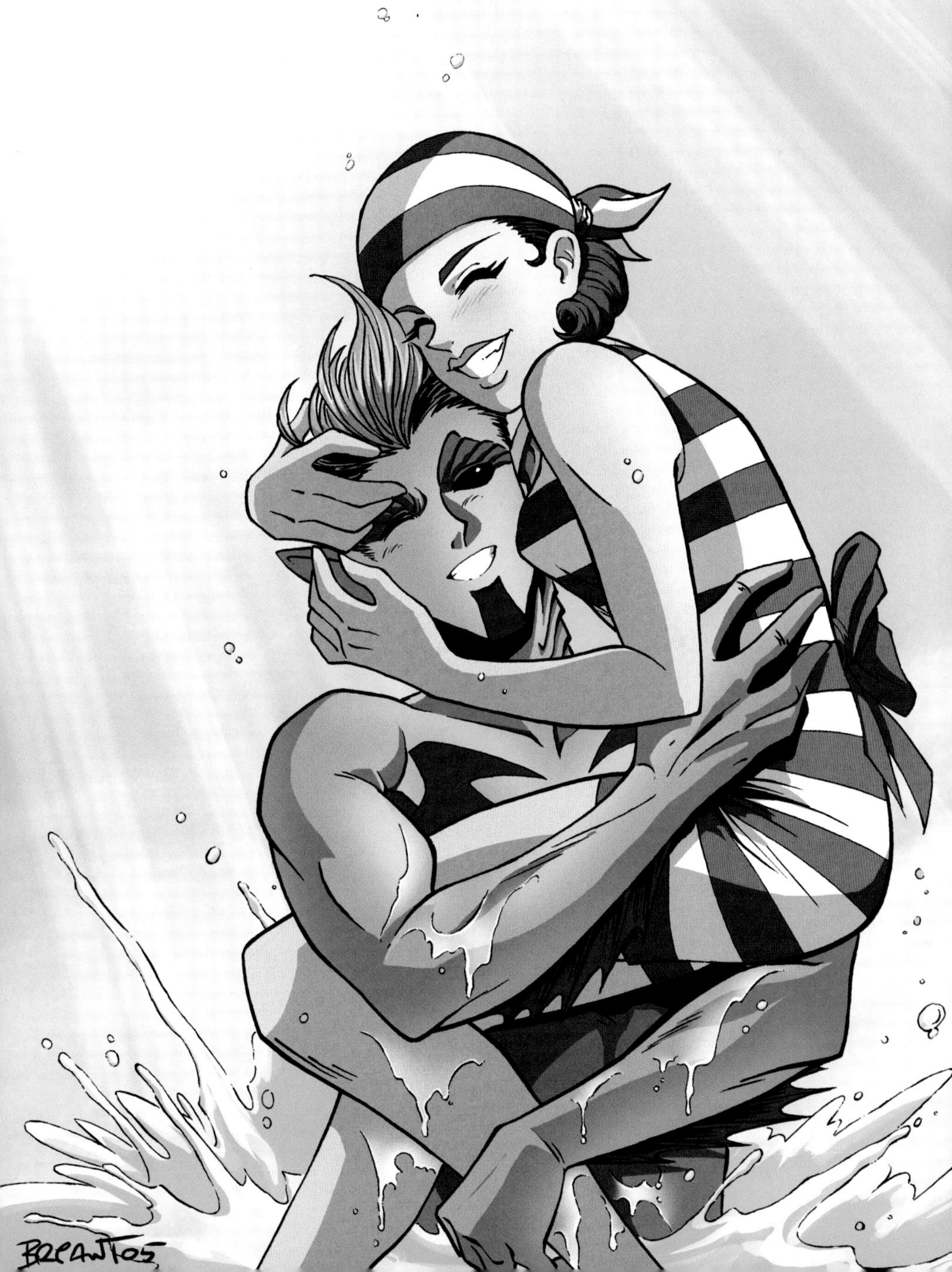

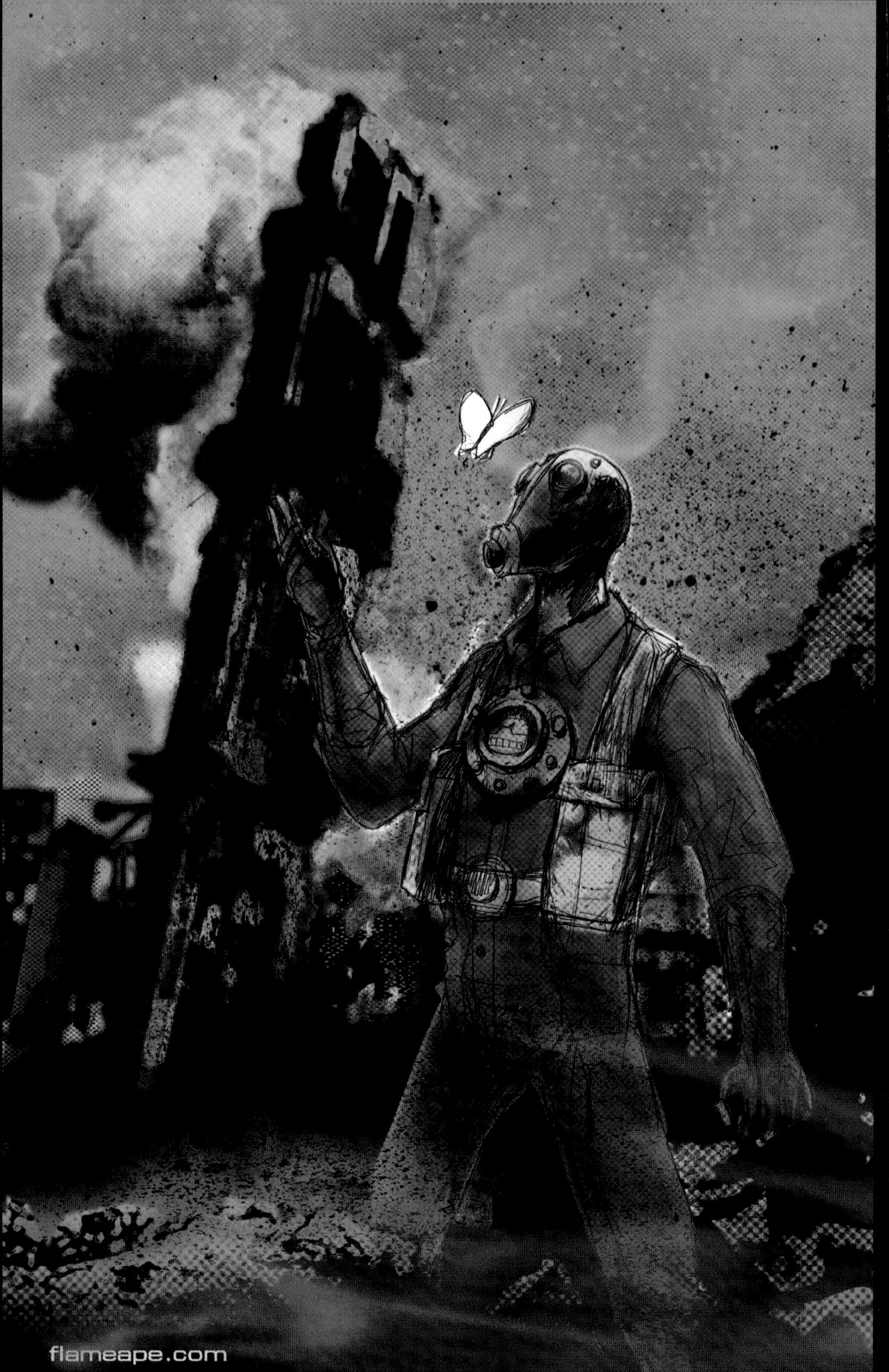
flameape.com

by GREG GIORDANO

by Shawn Crystal

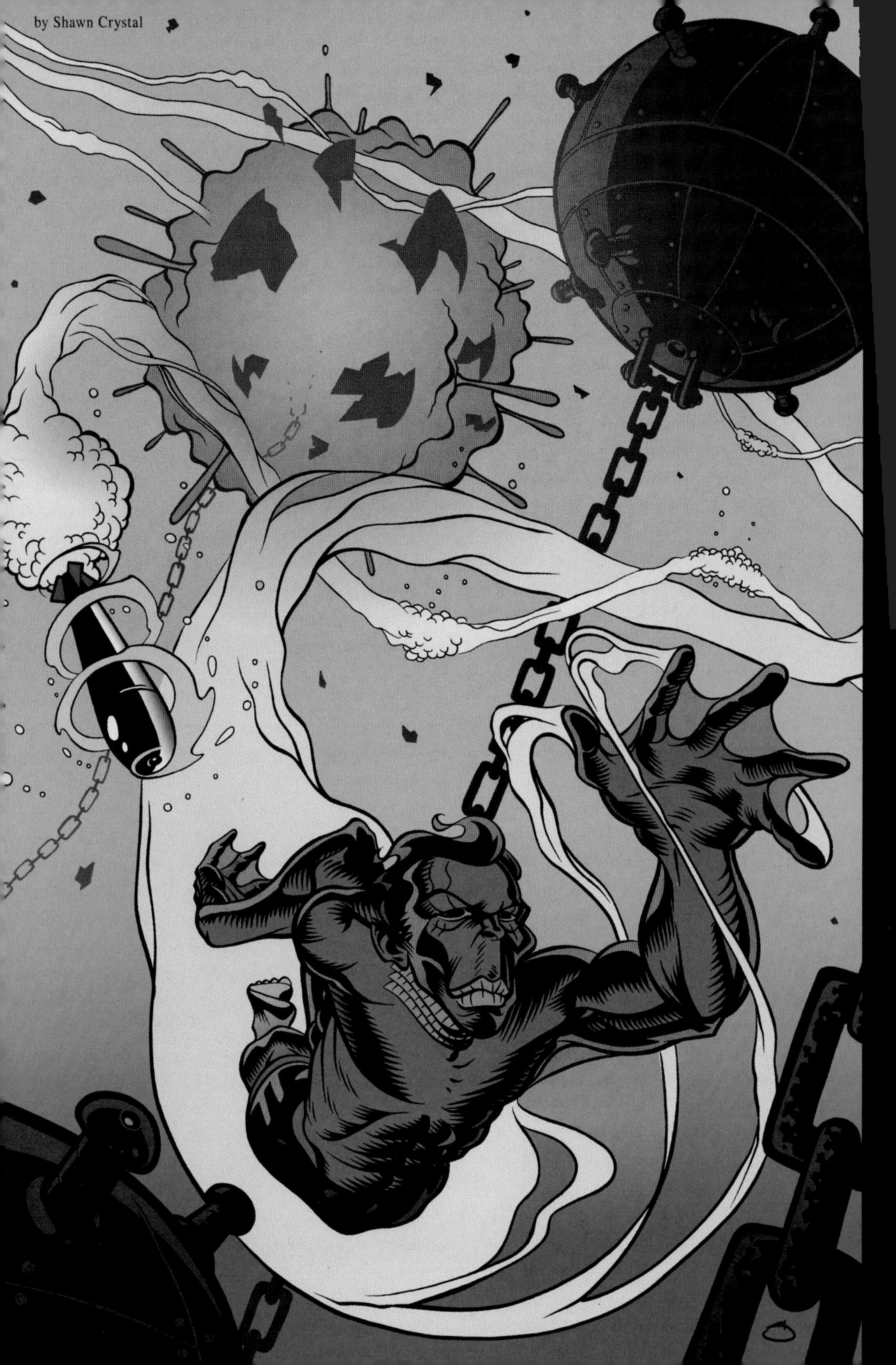

40 OZ. COLLECTED TP
ISBN# 1582403298
$9.95

AGE OF BRONZE
VOL. 1: A THOUSAND SHIPS TP
issues 1-9
ISBN# 1582402000
$19.95
VOL. 2: SACRIFICE HC
issues 10-19
ISBN# 1582403600
$29.95

THE BLACK FOREST GN
ISBN# 1582403503
$9.95

CITY OF SILENCE TP
ISBN# 1582403678
$9.95

CLASSIC 40 OZ.:
TALES FROM THE BROWN BAG TP
ISBN# 1582404380
$14.95

CREASED GN
ISBN# 1582404216
$9.95

DEEP SLEEPER TP
ISBN# 1582404933
$12.95

DIORAMAS, A LOVE STORY GN
ISBN# 1582403597
$12.95

EARTHBOY JACOBUS GN
ISBN# 1582404925
$17.95

FLIGHT, VOL. 1 GN
ISBN# 1582403816
$19.95

FLIGHT, VOL. 2 GN
ISBN# 1582404771
$24.95

FOUR-LETTER WORLDS GN
ISBN# 1582404399
$12.95

GRRL SCOUTS
VOL. 1 TP
ISBN# 1582403163
$12.95
VOL. 2: WORK SUCKS TP
ISBN# 1582403430
$12.95

HAWAIIAN DICK, VOL. 1:
BYRD OF PARADISE TP
ISBN# 1582403171
$14.95

HEAVEN, LLC. GN
ISBN# 1582403511
$12.95

KANE
VOL. 1: GREETINGS FROM NEW
EDEN TP
issues 1-4
ISBN# 1582403406
$11.95
VOL. 2: RABBIT HUNT TP
issues 5-8
ISBN# 1582403554
$12.95
VOL. 3: HISTORIES TP
issues 9-12
ISBN# 1582403821
$12.95
VOL. 4: THIRTY NINTH TP
issues 13-18
ISBN# 1582404682
$16.95

LAZARUS CHURCHYARDTHE FINAL
CUT GN
ISBN# 1582401802
$14.95

LIBERTY MEADOWS
VOL. 1: EDEN LANDSCAPE ED TP
issues 1-9
ISBN# 1582402604
$19.95
VOL. 2: CREATURE COMFORTS HC
issues 10-18
ISBN# 1582403333
$24.95

PARADIGM
ISBN# 1582403198
$13.95

PUTTIN' THE BACKBONE BACK TP
(MR)
ISBN# 158240402X
$9.95

PvP
THE DORK AGES TP
original miniseries 1-6
ISBN# 1582403457
$11.95
VOL.1: PVP AT LARGE TP
issues 1-6
ISBN# 1582403740
$11.95

VOL. 2: PVP RELOADED TP
issues 7-12
ISBN# 158240433X
$11.95

REX MUNDI
VOL. 1: THE GUARDIAN OF THE
TEMPLE TP
issues 0-5
ISBN# 158240268X
$14.95
VOL. 2: THE RIVER UNDERGROUND
TP
issues 6-11
ISBN# 1582404798
$14.95

RONINHOOD OF THE 47 SAMURAI
ISBN# 1582405557
$9.99

RUULE, VOL. 1: GANGLORDS OF
CHINATOWN
ISBN# 1582405662
$19.99

SMALL GODS, VOL. 1: KILLING
GRIN TP
issues 1-4
ISBN# 1582404577
$9.95

TOMMYSAURUS REX GN
ISBN# 1582403953
$11.95

ULTRA: SEVEN DAYS TP
ISBN# 1582404836
$17.95

THE WALKING DEAD
VOL. 1: DAYS GONE BYE TP
issues 1-6
ISBN# 1582403589
$12.95
VOL. 2: MILES BEHIND US TP
issues 7-12
ISBN# 1582404135
$12.95
VOL. 3: SAFETY BEHIND BARS TP
issues 13-18
ISBN# 1582404879
$12.95
VOL. 4: THE HEART'S DESIRE TP
issues 19-24
ISBN# 1582405301
$12.99

THE WICKED WEST GN
ISBN# 1582404143
$9.95